# The Shell Book of
# UNDISCOVERED BRITAIN
# AND IRELAND

# The Shell Book of
# UNDISCOVERED
# BRITAIN
# AND IRELAND

## Anthony Burton

DAVID & CHARLES
Newton Abbot   London

*Photographs*: Copyright owners are credited in the captions.

**British Library Cataloguing in Publication Data**

Burton, Anthony
    The Shell book of undiscovered Britain and Ireland.
    1. Great Britain—Description and travel—1971–
    I. Title
    914.1′04858      DA632

ISBN 0-7153-8746-4

Typeset by Typesetters (Birmingham) Limited,
Smethwick, West Midlands
and printed in Great Britain
by Butler & Tanner Limited, Frome and London
for David & Charles Publishers plc
Brunel House   Newton Abbot   Devon

# Contents

|   | Preface | 6 |
| 1 | Discoveries | 9 |
| 2 | Beside the Seaside | 17 |
| 3 | Island Retreats | 55 |
| 4 | Country Pursuits | 87 |
| 5 | Provincial Pleasures | 127 |
| 6 | How the Other Half Lives | 161 |
| 7 | Underground | 201 |
| 8 | Along the Trail | 227 |
| 9 | Traditional Fare | 257 |
|   | Further Reading | 281 |
|   | Index | 283 |

# Preface

I began my travels around Britain as a schoolboy, walking and climbing the hills in all parts of the country and in all weathers. Marriage and a family changed the pattern of holidays, so that the seaside and gentler country replaced the mountains as the principal attraction. In more recent years, my interests in transport and industrial history have taken me all over these islands and, now that the children have grown up, my wife and I are able to spend more time exploring our own favourite regions and in hunting out new delights. I feel that I know the British Isles reasonably well and have seen a great deal more of them than most people. I have enjoyed the experience of discovering my own country every bit as much as I have enjoyed visiting other, perhaps more exotic, lands. So, what appears on these pages comes out of personal experience. But, as I discovered when I wrote *The Shell Book of Curious Britain*, no matter how much you think you know, there is always a lot more still to be found out. Ever since the book was published, I have been receiving letters from readers, telling me about more curiosities and oddities – and to all of them go my thanks. When it came to writing this book I turned to a good many other people and organisations for help and advice, some of whom not only deserve thanks but deserve a special mention for other reasons as well. I do not wish to burden the reader with the kind of endless list of acknowledgements characteristic of the annual cinematic award presentations. I do thank everyone who helped, but I want to give a special mention to the following because they continue to offer help to everyone.

First on the list come all the national and regional tourist bodies. I used to believe that their only function was to provide glossy brochures and hand out lists of accommodation. They do both, but they do a great deal more as well. Many of the trails listed in Chapter 8, for example, emanate from them, and local offices often have an enormous amount of material on places of interest, and not just the most obvious places either. Next come our three major conservation bodies: the National Trust, covering England, Wales and Northern Ireland; the National Trust for Scotland; and An Taisce for Eire. All have been of great assistance. Again, these are bodies whose activities go well beyond those of their popular image. We tend to think of them principally in terms of stately homes preserved and open to the public, and forget the enormous amount of work they do in countryside conservation. Looking, for example, through the list of properties of the National Trust you find not just the grand houses, the churches and castles, but also gardens and landscaped parks, nature reserves, nature walks, prehistoric sites, industrial buildings and even whole villages. I should like to thank these bodies for the help they gave me and also thank them on behalf of many others for the conservation work they continue to do. They do as much as anyone to ensure that there are still parts of Britain one wants to discover. I have also received help from a number of local authorities and local preservation groups, too numerous to mention.

Finally, a personal thank you to my wife Pip, for keeping me company on my travels over the years, helping research this book and, in particular, for taking on the whole job of picture research.

# 1
# Discoveries

*Looking down over Lyme Bay and Golden Cap Hill* (National Trust: Mike Williams)

When an author produces a book on undiscovered Britain, readers are entitled to know what he means by the word 'undiscovered'. If by undiscovered I wished to suggest that I was about to reveal previously unknown delights, places where man had never before set foot, then I should be guilty of grossly misleading. It is doubtful if there is anywhere on the planet to which the word could be so rigorously applied – doubtful indeed if there has been any such place for many hundreds and possibly even thousands of years. Even the great ages of exploration were not times when man first set foot in an area; merely times when people from this part of the world arrived at distant shores. As an African once said: 'A white man says he has discovered somewhere when a black man has shown him where it is.' So there will not, I am afraid, be any astonishing revelations – no valleys reached through hidden entrances, no secret glens nor long-lost cities. But then if you look up the word 'discovery' in the dictionary, you find that this was not quite the meaning of the word in the first place. It literally means to dis-cover, to remove the cover, to bring into the light those things which had previously been in the dark. That is very much the sense in which I am using the word here.

'This year', the holiday brochures announce, 'visitors are dis-covering the Costa somewhere.' They do not mean that visitors are stumbling upon the costa by accident, but that it used to be an area with little popular appeal, until circumstances changed. This book is about places which have mostly not been discovered in this popular sense – which few people visit, either because they are somewhat off the beaten track or because their appeal is not immediately obvious. It might all be a little clearer if we turn from this rather abstract discussion to a particular example, laying aside the dictionary and picking up the guidebook.

Browsing through a travel guide the other day, I came across an entry for Stanton St Gabriel in Dorset, which began: 'It has almost nothing for the traveller.' That is the sort of phrase that comes as music to my ears, for it offers a double promise. I could not believe that any place with a name so mellifluous as Stanton St Gabriel could really be of no interest, but I had every hope that if enough guidebooks repeated the message of its dullness then it might be free of crowds. And how does the reality match up to expectations? There is certainly not a great deal to the place, at first sight little more than a handsome farm set comfortably down under the lee of Golden Cap Hill – what enticing names this part of the world can boast. But that is by no means the end of the story. Close by the farm are the forlorn, romantic ruins of the thirteenth-century St Gabriel's Chapel, its ivied walls slowly crumbling back towards the earth. From the graveyard you can look out across the cliffs that ring Lyme Bay. This is fossil country. The Green Ammonite beds exposed on the cliff still reveal the long disused shells, the spaces left by former inhabitants of these geometric ammonite houses having been filled by green calcite. It is a place of quiet pleasure, a spot that amply repays time spent on exploration. It may not be what everyone is looking for on a trip to the coast, but it is certainly not the drably tedious spot you might expect from the guidebook description.

I must confess I hesitated before setting out to write this book, for undiscovered places can all too easily become spoiled when publicised. Many might feel that Jerome K. Jerome had the best notion when he sneaked away from a singularly damp trip on the Thames and headed back for London and 'a capital little out-of-the-way restaurant in the neighbourhood of —, where you can get one of the best-cooked and cheapest little French dinners or suppers that I know of . . . and which I am not going to be idiot enough to advertise'. Many of us feel similar understandable reluctance to advertise our own favourite out-of-the-way haunts. Indeed, if this book was no more than a list of unsung delights it would be self-defeating. Many places are described but, more importantly, I have tried to show how readers can set about making discoveries of their own. A recommended spot may prove to be quite delightful, but it can never be anywhere near as attractive as the spot one finds for oneself.

It could be argued that, in this day and age, there is a limit to the number of 'unspoiled' beauty spots and intriguing corners of Britain still waiting to be explored; and there is a good deal of truth in the argument. But the delights of discovery are not confined to remote and forgotten areas. There are discoveries to be made all around us, provided we know how to look for them and recognise them when we see them. Perhaps it is putting it a little strongly, but you might say that there are no dull parts of Britain – only dull people who cannot recognise the interesting. I have certainly been as guilty as any in drawing hasty conclusions. I once wrote that Nuneaton was unrelievedly boring and I was, quite rightly, taken to task by an old

Nuneatonian, if that is the word, who claimed I had not taken time to look at the place. And the criticism was quite justified. I had arrived and found the shops shut, the pubs shut and a phone box that did not work – and had written the whole town off. Now I must confess that I held on to this view for a very long time. What happened to change my mind? For the answer to that question you will have to wait until the end of the book.

Part of the problem of finding the offbeat, the unusual, the intriguing – and even the beautiful – lies in the speed with which we move around the country. Encased in our metal boxes, we zoom along the road seeing little but the tail lights of the car in front. Motorways are the worst possible environment for providing anything other than a quick route and mind-numbing monotony. Yet only a small detour might be needed to furnish something of great interest. How many of the thousands who stop off every day at the Watford Gap service station on the M1 know that they are right beside the Grand Union Canal, which at this very point is rushing up the hillside in a series of mighty leaps known as the Watford Staircase, a splendid set of interconnected locks? How much more pleasant it is to sit and watch the slow movement of boats up and down the locks than it is to sit in a cafeteria munching sandwiches. My own journeys frequently take me along the M40 between Oxford and London, which even at its worst can never match the tedium of the M1. Sometimes, however, just for the pure pleasure of it I turn off on to the old A40 road. In autumn especially, one section is a pure delight, the length of road that winds westwards down the Chilterns from Stokenchurch. It passes through woodland; not the dull conifer plantations beloved of the modern forester, but the old mixed woodland of oak, beech and birch, which blaze over the hillside in reds and golds, growing ever brighter as the days get shorter and darker. Such a drive is unalloyed pleasure compared with the rush of motorway traffic. Some might argue that my route takes longer. So it does. But what are these critics doing with the time they save that is more rewarding than my leisurely amble through the bright woods of autumn?

What is true of motorways is true of much else that will be described in these pages. This is not a book for people in a hurry. Few instant delights are on offer here. You do not find a carpark at

*A canal lock staircase lifting the Leicester Canal up the hillside beside the Watford Gap service station* (Derek Pratt)

*Everyone's idea of the perfect away from it all scene: a distant view of Cader Idris* (British Tourist Authority)

the edge of the perfect, unspoiled beach. The quiet pleasures of a small provincial town are not always set out in properly labelled order, open all year, admission 50p. Those who would look for the out-of-the-way, the unusual and the uncrowded must learn a little patience. They must also, in many cases, be prepared to learn to do without a car and trust to their legs. And nowhere is this more true than in the first subject we shall be looking at: the seaside. It is amazing the difference a little walking can make. My family and I used regularly to holiday in Cornwall, and regularly we found ourselves on the beach at Polzeath, not a spot notably short of summer visitors. First sight can be discouraging: a crowded carpark, deckchairs between the cars and children playing ball among the Fords. Yet each year we found that little more than a few minutes' walk was needed to take us clear of the crowds into a peaceful cove where you could spread out and really enjoy sand and sea. The same is true of many 'crowded' spots. But now we shall be turning our attention to other seaside areas which have their own special, and often surprising, delights to offer, particularly where the crowds have yet to appear.

# 2
# Beside the Seaside

*The cliffs of Slieve League poking up into the clouds* (Kenneth McNally)

Oh, I do like to be beside the seaside,
Oh, I do like to be beside the sea.
Oh, I do like to stroll along the prom, prom, prom
Where the brass band plays, tiddley-om-pom-pom!

The old music-hall song represents one aspect of the seaside holiday – the world of McGill postcards, concert parties on the pier and trips around the bay. Today that has become the world of amusement arcades, the big dipper and a deckchair on any part of the beach that still has room to take one. And there is nothing in the world wrong with all that. No one in their right mind would choose to holiday in a Blackpool bereft of crowds. That's what you go for: the noise and fun, the Illuminations and the massive boarding-house breakfast (the dietician's despair). Resorts such as Blackpool glory in their own loud enjoyment, and if some want to label it vulgar then no one in Blackpool is going to lose any sleep over that. Those who revel in the joys of Blackpool need no book to tell them where to go, but many others go looking for quite different pleasures. They long for the deserted beach, peace, and nothing in the way of entertainment beyond what they bring to the place themselves – and that does not include a portable radio. The sad thing is that so many have the dream but fail to realise it. If 800 families all choose the same tiny cove as their haven of tranquillity, 800 families are going to be disappointed. So what, if anything, can be done?

The answer to this problem depends very much on what the individual is looking for on a visit to the coast, for there are very many different reasons for making one's way down to the sea. Some have as their main objective the acquisition of a splendidly golden tan. This is a comparatively modern notion, and has a close connection with changing social conditions. Until quite recently, suntan was associated with work in the fields, so that a pale skin was a sign of superiority. The young ladies of a Jane Austen novel would take the most elaborate precautions to keep the sun off their delicate features. Today, we mostly work indoors so that the sporting of a fine brown skin is an indication that we are sufficiently well off to afford to hunt out the sun. It is a most odd phenomenon. Sitting on a beach in Goa, an Indian friend mused over the lobster-coloured Europeans, many of whom looked down on him for the colour of his skin, but were suffering a good deal of discomfort in order to try and match it. Very curious, he thought.

For some, the principal attraction of the sea is swimming. Sea-bathers and sun-bathers do have one thing in common: they are, on the whole, creatures of the summer. A few hardy souls break the ice on the sea's edge to take a New Year dip, and some will lie in wind-free corners, heads tilted towards the lowering rays of the winter sun. They are, however, a minority. For less robust bathers who wish to escape the crowds but still enjoy the summer, life can present its problems – but the problems are far from insurmountable. The first aid I always turn to is the 1:50,000 Ordnance Survey map. If the red dotted line, indicating a footpath, that joins the nearest point on the road to a likely looking stretch of coast, is long enough, then the chances are that comparatively few people will make the effort to walk from the car. The map, of course, provides far more information than that. Paths down to beaches are not the only ones to be marked: others include long-distance coastal paths, for those who are looking for something more energetic than simply lying in the sun. There is also the strange wobbly Gothic writing reserved for sites of antiquity which might prove to be worth a detour. Indeed the maps are themselves a great source of pleasure, yielding all kinds of fascinating prospects. But even if the map provides no more than one footpath to one quiet cove, then it will have repaid the purchase price.

Those who do not wish to, or indeed cannot, trek for miles in search of solitude can take the other option of travelling out of season. Cornwall in May, for example, can be a revelation: wide beaches where no Man Friday has left a footprint, sunken lanes where the banks glow with wild flowers and not a traffic jam in sight. But for many neither the long trek nor the out-of-season holiday are realistic options. Are there no places left around our coast that can offer something different; is there nowhere remote from the holiday crowds? Happily there are many rewarding areas to visit and places to be seen. For the rest of this chapter we shall be going off on a coastal tour of the British Isles, looking at just a few of the less obvious attractions on offer.

As this is going to be a circuit it makes very little difference just where we start, so let us begin in the south-east of England at a place which hundreds of thousands visit every year but very few ever get to see: Dover. Now Dover might seem to be a place which is so much on the beaten track that it could be instantly dismissed from a book such as this. Certainly the drivers crawling down the A2 desperately worrying over whether they will be in time for the ferry might well have cause to curse Dover rather than praise it. Through the town they dash for the Channel crossing, and back they come at equal speed some time later, eager to be home. Yet the place has so much more to offer, and not just the famous white cliffs. In Dover Castle, it can boast perhaps the finest castle in all England, and though the great Norman stronghold has been much altered over the centuries its essential robust character remains untouched. The great tower stands 100ft (30m) high, with walls up to twenty feet thick, and that in turn is surrounded by two rings of stout walls to provide yet more protection. The castle has only recently lost its role as a fortress, for it was garrisoned right up until the end of World War II. Within its walls one may see the military mind at work, as each generation of strategists adapted the ancient stronghold to meet changing demands. Walls were altered to meet the new threat of the age of gunpowder and cannon; labyrinths of underground passages were hacked through the chalk and, at the time of the Napoleonic Wars, special precautions were taken to ensure that the soldiers received a regular grain supply. Down the road they built the huge six-storey Crabble Mill, a water-mill with five separate millstones, now restored to full working order. Dover Castle is well known for its grandeur, well publicised and much visited. Roman Dover, however, is another matter.

Today we tend to think of Dover as a port certainly, but one exclusively serving the needs of what are known in the trade as ro-ros, roll-on roll-off ferries. The town seems to have arrived at the same time as the motor car and to exist purely to serve it and its larger brethren. Yet Dover was one of the Cinque Ports; and what a curious institution these were, these ports with a whole range of special privileges. They were more than just free ports in the sense of being free of taxes – they were almost entirely free of regulations of any kind. Thus encouraged, the men of the ports set out with great enthusiasm to engage in such popular pastimes of the day as piracy and plunder. There was, however, a price to pay, for in times of war they were also required to provide ships and men for the king's navy, though this was actually an arrangement that suited both sides very well, since the king got a navy on the cheap and the wars provided ample opportunities for private enterprise. Little remains to remind us of those times, but if we travel back in time still further we find Dover under an older name, Dubris, the Roman headquarters of the British fleet, the Classis Britannica. Quite the most impressive monument of those days is the Pharos, the lighthouse that now stands within the grounds of Dover Castle – a stone tower of a solidity that was not to reappear in any other lighthouse for many centuries. Of the original fort nothing now remains, but a Roman house can still be seen by the few ruined walls of a later Roman fortification. It stands in New Street, and is notable for its rather splendid painted walls.

Finding Roman fortifications and a Roman lighthouse within the castle perimeter might lead the curious to wonder whether just as the Normans built on a Roman site, so too the Romans might have made use of an earlier stronghold. And if that same sense of curiosity then sends the theorist back to the remains of that great castle on the cliffs, then the theorist will find this idea verified. Wander around the castle mound and you will find that what at first sight might appear to be a natural landscape is in fact made up of the great earth ramparts and ditches of an Iron Age fortress. And all this in Dover which we scurry through so often without a second glance. It is as well to realise that the unusual is often closer than we think, if only we have the curiosity to hunt it out.

You do not have to travel very far westward along the south coast from Dover before you come to one of the most surprising stretches of coastline in south-east England, the Romney marshes, though often here it is the area just behind the coast that provides the major interest. The shoreline itself tends to be striped by a seemingly endless ribbon of bungalows and chalets. It is an area that appears to have been constantly on the move in a quite literal physical sense, sometimes slowly shifting, sometimes changing with dramatic suddenness. Shingle has piled up to push the coastline further out into the sea, while in the more distant past gales suddenly moved great piles of the stuff to alter the course of rivers and leave once busy ports literally high and dry, bereft of their access to the sea. We find little towns such as Old Romney boasting mighty churches out of all proportion to the present size of the communities that they serve, and there is an even more dramatic example in the church serving the hamlet of Ivychurch. This is a strange area of flat lands and drainage dykes, much loved by bird watchers who come here for tranquillity. It was not always so. This was one of the great centres of smuggling, for vessels had little difficulty in hiding out among the myriad small creeks and inlets. The smuggler has a somewhat romantic image, but the official who wrote of them at the end of the eighteenth century as 'a standing army of desperadoes, who must pay themselves, and can subsist by no other means but public rapine and plunder' was probably nearer the mark. When under threat, the smugglers could raise an unofficial army of as many as 500 armed men in a few hours. Not that the official army was always an implacable enemy. It was not unknown for the army to confiscate contraband and then sell it back to the smugglers. The peace of the marshes is of very recent origin.

Those who want to see something of the marshes with very little effort to themselves might care to try the Romney, Hythe & Dymchurch Light Railway. It was the brainchild of two racing motorists, Capt J. E. P. Howey and Count Louis Zborowski, though the latter was to be killed in a racing accident before the line was completed. It was begun in 1925 to a diminutive 15in gauge and opened in 1927 with a later extension to Dungeness, so that now the little railway runs for over 14 miles between the marshes and the sea. The locomotives are perfect miniature versions of their grander brethren of the main line in the age of steam, and although it might seem to be every child's favourite old train set grown up this is no toy but a proper railway doing a real job of work. Nor is it, like many

*A real steam railway beside the seaside brought down to miniature: the Romney, Hythe & Dymchurch Railway* (Romney, Hythe & Dymchurch Railway)

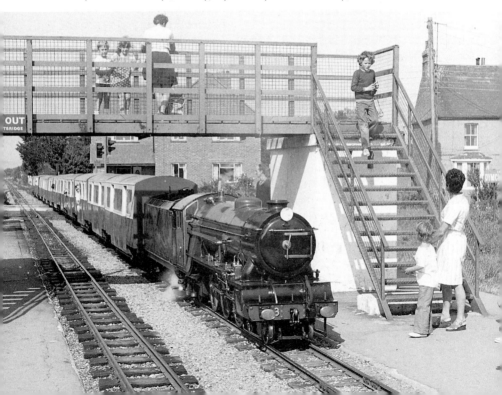

other steam railways, the resurrected and restored remains of an older line, for the little Romney, Hythe & Dymchurch has never given up work – and two of the locomotives are chuffing along just as they did when the line was new. It is a treat for steam buffs and great fun for kids, who get special pleasure out of a railway reduced almost down to their own scale. Ultimately the line delivers you to one of the loneliest spots on the south coast, Dungeness. The mighty power stations could seem an appalling intrusion into this empty land, yet for me they seem only a part of the general air of wild desolation, part of that atmosphere of strangeness that characterises the Romney marshes.

If you find that you have a taste for the little seaside railway you might also care to try the Fairbourne on the Welsh coast or the Ravenglass & Eskdale, more familiarly known as the 'Ratty', which joins the Cumbrian coast to the Lakeland fells. And if your interest runs rather more to historic importance than to scenic splendours or the romance of steam, then why not take a look at the first electric railway in Britain – Volk's Electric Railway on the front at Brighton. Many of the old cars date back, with a bit of patchwork here and there, almost to the opening in 1883.

Those who welcome strangeness, who seek out places of unique character, could do far worse than continue on their journey westward to the Isle of Portland. It has not in fact officially been an island since 1839, when it was joined to the mainland, though even today its island status is occasionally resumed as winter gales whip across the causeway, isolating Portland again. The physical joining of island and mainland may be somewhat tenuous, but the years of being joined to the rest of Britain have at least resulted in a certain improvement in the social behaviour of the Portlanders. They are no longer known as the 'Slingers', since they have stopped slinging rocks at each and every stranger. Other things, however, have not changed. Portland remains a chunk of land with a character all its own. This character derives in good measure from the physical nature of the land itself – from Portland stone, that superb white building stone that has graced generations of buildings from St Paul's Cathedral to the BBC's Broadcasting House in aptly named Portland Place, London. The whole island is dotted with quarries, and dotted with the grotesque monuments of quarrying – the great, squared blocks of stone piled into strange shapes along the cliff-tops.

Portland is like a giant cheese that has been steadily nibbled away by fastidious mice who have left seemingly choice morsels

behind them. To see it at its best, the visitor must leave the spot where the tourists gather – Portland Bill – and wander the cliffs to the east of the island. Perhaps the best starting point is Easton, where there is a small but altogether delightful museum, and from there you can make your way to Church Ope. Here you take the path between the grandly named Pennsylvania Castle, a mock fortress built in 1799 on royal land bequeathed to John Penn by his friend George III, and Rufus Castle, a rather more genuine edifice. It is an area full of interest, with the excavated remains of Portland's first church and a crazy landscape of shattered stone blocks, some resulting from quarrying, some dating from the construction of the railway which carved a passage beneath the cliffs. This is a wilderness indeed of dark holes where ravens nest, secret corners so different from the wide horizons of the sea and the turbulent waters of the famous Portland Race, a wild-foamed tidal rip. There is nothing quite like it anywhere else in Britain. The appeal has not diminished over the years and Portland stone continues to hold a special appeal for builder and carver. The 1980s saw an attempt to establish a sculpture park on Portland. It was not a success, but left behind one quite magnificent monument – a vertical circle of stone, achieved entirely without the benefit of mortar, intended as a grand entrance to the park. The park has gone but the entrance remains, close by the top of the hill that leads up from Fortuneswell.

A book could be written on Portland and its fascination seems endless. Equally intriguing is the great mound of shingle that runs westward away from Portland, Chesil Beach. It is not an obviously attractive feature of the landscape. The huge pile of stones stretching for miles is not conducive to walking, which tends to become a matter of one step up, two steps down. Swimming off the beach is inadvisable except for the very strongest, for there is a vicious undertow: you need do no more than listen to the greedy sucking of the tide to be convinced on that point. Chesil Beach is, however, unique. The sea-smoothed pebbles provide an infinity of shapes to hold and fondle, as satisfying in their way as sculptures by Moore or Hepworth. The brackish waters held back behind the bank at the mainland end provide a home for multitudes of sea-birds and wild fowl. The western end near Abbotsbury is well known for its swans and is much visited. A fine area it is too, but those who want to capture the true atmosphere of the place might prefer to turn

*An extraordinary example of dry-stone walling elevated to the status of art on Portland*
(Anthony Burton)

25

away from the popular Abbotsbury Swannery towards the more peaceful charm of the West Fleet, near Langton Herring; and those who want reminders of just how vicious this coastline can be might prefer to visit East Fleet, where gales swept away almost all of the old church, leaving just the chancel standing. This is the world of Meade Faulkner's romantic novel, *Moonfleet*, where the reality can be as dramatic as the fiction. Nor can Abbotsbury itself, for all its tourist attractions, be quite discounted, for, apart from its fine buildings, it can also stand as a monument to good old-fashioned quirkiness. Here they have a May Day celebration, but there is no point turning up on 1 May expecting to see it, for when the new Gregorian calendar was introduced into Britain in 1752, the locals refused to accept the change. Here the first day of May is celebrated on the date we think of as 13 May, when local children parade with their garlands of flowers which will later be taken out and thrown upon the waters of the sea.

The south-west corner of England is perhaps the most popular seaside holiday area in the whole of Britain, and it is not difficult to see why. The climate is good and the scenery often superb – both of them so good, in fact, that one can only wish that one had been able to come here a hundred years ago when the region was almost totally unknown. Looe was then a fishing village, earning a living from the vast shoals of pilchards that could be found off the Cornish coast, not from the vast shoals of tourists ferried in by the bus-load. Land's End was then just the end of the land, not a souvenir centre where visitors come less to see than to be seen by the camera lens, posing beside the signpost pointing the way home. Yet there is still much to enjoy even if it sometimes seems to require something of an effort to find it. There are still many places which have never quite established themselves as major attractions. I have written in the past, for example, about the Monkey Sanctuary near Looe, but I see no reason not to sing its praises again. This is emphatically not a zoo – it is a home for monkeys who are more or less free to come and go as they please and, being sensible creatures, choose to stay where they can find food and comfort. Such bars as there are keep the idiot humans from molesting the monkeys. It is a place of delights, where monkey and human co-exist, not as equals, for different species can never achieve exact equality, but as species each of which has its own rights and privileges which the other must respect.

There are many aspects of Cornwall waiting to be explored. The Cornwall of mine and engine-house has become better known of late, largely thanks to television, but the dramatic location of engine-houses on the cliffs, such as those of Botallack near Land's End or St Agnes Head, still stops us in our tracks with astonishment at the endeavours and achievement of our forebears. There are, too, places where working Cornwall can be observed, places such as Delabole, the biggest man-made hole in Britain, a vast quarry where they started digging slate some six centuries ago. Not everyone, perhaps, wants to stare down at large holes in the ground, but few can resist the abandoned settlements of the past. Cornwall has its share. There is the romantic cove that was once home to the fishermen of Portquin. It is overlooked by the Gothic folly, Doyden Castle, on Doyden Point which, like much of the surrounding coast, is in the care of the National Trust. This is Cornwall at its best, a land of tall cliffs, deep combes and tiny, almost secretive, coves. Look at the Ordnance Survey map for this area, centred around Port Isaac Bay. You will see that the road moves inland at Port Isaac and then returns, albeit briefly, at Port William. Somewhat tentative tracks point down towards the sea but stop short of the cliffs, and where they end the footpaths take over. The map holds out a promise of freedom from crowds, and the promise is fulfilled.

The coast of north Cornwall and Devon can boast some of the finest beaches in the world. When the children were still young, we decided that it was time to be more adventurous, to shake off our insularity and make for foreign shores. Off we went across the Channel, drove some 1,500 miles and presented them with their new beach. They viewed it with some disdain and firmly declared that it was not as good as Cornwall. I am inclined to agree. I enjoy foreign travel, but I still back those beaches of the West Country against most. But the charm of this coast is not limited to that narrow strip of sand between the Atlantic rollers and the granite cliffs. We shall be looking at some aspects of the inland countryside in a later chapter, but there are places of interest just by the coast, including many reminders that this is a very ancient land. There are the mysterious standing stones, including the quoits – strange structures like overgrown three-legged stools, whose massive slabs rest on vertical stones. There are also stone rings and at Carn Glooze (or Gluze) on Cape Cornwall, a mile to the west of St Just, is a Bronze Age barrow. This ancient burial mound is a complex structure said once to have been the entrance to the underworld. A strange place indeed, and it would not require any great effort of the imagination to see this as a roadway down to the land of the dead; which is not a

*The seaside past re-created at the Woodspring Museum, Weston-super-Mare* (Woodspring Museum, Weston-super-Mare)

thought everyone would wish to contemplate on a holiday excursion.

Travelling back eastwards, one finds the coast taking on a quite different character as the seaway narrows down to the Bristol Channel. It has its moments of splendour around Lynton, which is reached by a narrow road that clogs solid with traffic in summer, but is quite splendid out of season. But, as you journey east, so the land flattens out until by the time you reach Weston-super-Mare, you find one of those extraordinary English seaside resorts which the sea seems seldom to reach. Some claim that it is downright dishonest to call the place 'super Mare' at all since the Mare is such an infrequent visitor. It is, however, well worth a visit if only to see its very fine museum, housed in, of all things, the old gas works maintenance shop. Here there is a re-creation of the seaside as it was, an evocation of arrivals by the wonders of steam train to a world of donkey carts, bathing machines and pierrots – a world most of us recognise, even if we have never, in fact, seen the reality. Beyond is Clevedon with its exceptionally fine house and splendid garden, sadly now beset by the perpetual noise of motorway traffic, and beyond that is the industrial world of Avonmouth and the Severn Bridge to take us across into Wales.

Wales begins once you cross the bridge and the vast majority of motorists either dash straight on down the M4 towards Cardiff, or turn north for the seductive pleasures of the Wye Valley. Very, very few ever turn south to the flat lands known as the Caldicot Levels. This is an area of drained marshland, crossed by narrow, twisting lanes as remote from the bustle of the world as you can hope to find. There are enticing names here, such as Goldcliff, but you will find neither cliffs nor gold, just a land that peters out into the mud and sand of the Severn estuary. What are the attractions of such a region? None that can be easily expressed. The appeal is to those who welcome solitude and are prepared to take their chance on finding just that conjunction of wide waters and wider skies that can turn an apparently featureless view into a majestic procession of clouds that appear above in endless array and are echoed below in sepia reflections on the estuary. It is a landscape that demands patience and vigilance if its pleasures are to be revealed. The Romans, however, found it much to their liking, though as their interest tended more to the strategic than the scenic, they are not the most reliable guides to the beauties of nature. Yet here they built a market town, Caerwent, the defensive walls of which still stand in many places. Nearby, towards Newport, they had their

*The Roman amphitheatre at Caerleon* (Wales Tourist Board)

garrison on Caerleon with a theatre to keep the troops happy, a sort of early ENSA and the first Roman amphitheatre in Britain.

The coast of South Wales is, in large measure, an aggressively industrial coastline. It developed in part from its proximity to the rich valleys to the north and also from the mineral wealth of Cornwall and Devon across the Bristol Channel. It is only recently that we have come to realise that this industrial world can have its own appeal. I am not suggesting that everyone ought to take their seaside holiday at Cardiff Docks; but I would say that those who go there will find a good deal that will fascinate and intrigue. A new generation of industrial museums has been developed along this coast, notably those of Cardiff and Swansea, as fine as any in Britain, while other incidental pleasures include Barry Island, the last repository of many a discarded steam locomotive. Tank engines and main-line expresses nuzzle each other in quiet, rusting decay, like so many old work horses put out to grass. Yet round their necks they carry tags indicating that this old horse is due to go to this preserved line, while that elderly specimen is ready for rejuvenation and service at another. A graveyard it may be, but it is one where the trump of resurrection is often heard.

Industrialisation may be said to end, quite conclusively, when one reaches the Gower, but although there are still no major resorts on the peninsula it has become a popular holiday area. Even so, like Cornwall, it is a region where it is still possible to escape the crowds and find solitude. It is unlike Cornwall in every other way, for where the English south-west is a land of hardy granite, here we find limestone, often carved by natural forces into grotesque shapes and eaten away into caves and grottoes. It is an explorer's paradise, as enticing for the small child who wants to try out the cave echoes at full lung-power as it is for the experienced potholer exploring the underworld. It is, at least, a more varied landscape than that provided by Carmarthen Bay. The British landscape is one of almost infinite variety, and no individual can expect to respond with equal enthusiasm to all its aspects. Carmarthen Bay boasts one of the finest strips of sandy beach in Britain – cars have raced over it, the military fire shells over it, but those who attempt to walk off it in order to swim in the sea can finish up dropping from exhaustion, having walked, it seems, for miles, into water that is still scarcely knee-deep. Pembrokeshire, around the corner, is something quite different.

Some go to Pembroke for the beaches, which are certainly magnificent. Atlantic rollers thunder on to the shore and waves plume upwards, shattering the light, as they break on the rocks. But I would commend Pembrokeshire above all for its magnificent cliff scenery and that means that it is an all-weather, all-season place. There is at least as much pleasure to be gained from striding the cliffs in a February gale with the sea whipping around the base as there is to be had from basking on those same rocks on a balmy June afternoon. Pembroke itself is a quiet town, but dominated by a quite magnificent castle – and castles are very much a feature of this corner of Wales. Carew Castle is another fine pile, and as good a spot as any for a day's outing, for here is not just the castle dating back to Norman times, set square and solid on a fine coastline, but also one of the rarer varieties of water-mill. Carew Tide Mill is, in many respects, a conventional mill, where millstones are turned by the power of the water-wheel. It differs from others, however, in that the water is sea water, impounded at high tide and released at low tide to serve the mill. The miller's life must have followed an odd pattern, as his working days were determined by the steady movement of the tide rather than the more conventional measurements of the clock.

Almost all the rest of the Welsh coast is, it sometimes seems, encompassed by the one phrase – Cardigan Bay. It is an oddly empty coastline. Aberystwyth sits in the middle, basking in a busy popularity, but elsewhere it seems largely forgotten. There are resorts which were obviously intended for greater things, but failed to meet their expected ends. Tywyn has an air of almost desolate melancholy, and wandering among the few holidaymakers who come here one can almost see the little bubbles coming out of their heads with the question inside: 'Why did we come?' The only ones who seem to know exactly why they came are the railway enthusiasts who throng to the altogether splendid Talyllyn narrow-gauge railway for a steam excursion into the hills. Celtic gloom seems to pervade much of this coast, and it is not easy to see why it should be so, and no doubt there are many who feel elation as soon as they get here. It is a land of slowly shifting dunes spiked with marram grass over which blows a west wind with a perennially moist breath. At least it has the advantage over the north Welsh coast, which is dominated by the big, popular resorts – Llandudno and Colwyn Bay, Prestatyn and Rhyl. But you can never quite dismiss any corner of Britain as predictable. What is the greatest ancient monument in Britain measured purely and simply in terms of size? Many would soon arrive at the correct answer: Silbury Hill. And the second largest? A little head-scratching perhaps? The answer is Gop Cairn, a massive man-made hill, similar to Silbury and just as mysterious, for no one knows why our distant ancestors chose to heap up these great piles of earth to stand 40ft above the surrounding landscape – and that is only a measure of what remains. Gop Cairn may well once have been far bigger. You can find it on the hill just north of Trelawnyd on the A5151. Go there and let your imagination have full rein, for your own fancies are as likely to be as right as those of anyone else.

The wide estuary of the Dee separates Wales from England, and beyond that is the Mersey, leaving one large lump of land in between, the Wirral. This is really rather a curious corner, for while

*Something for all ages: the Talyllyn Railway* (Anthony Burton)

one side of the peninsula is represented by heavily industrialised Birkenhead and Ellesmere Port, the other side is a land of rather grand houses, looking out over the mud-flats of the estuary. You might say that on one side men went to work to create wealth, which was then spent by those who lived on the other. But the western side of Wirral certainly has the more obvious attractions, with immense views across the sea to the mountains of Wales and a shoreline rich in bird-life. The other side can at least boast Ellesmere Port, once one of the major canal towns of Britain. It grew up around the junction of the Shropshire Union Canal and the Mersey, with more trade coming in later with the construction of the Manchester Ship Canal. The great days of trade have ended on the canals but here, at least, the memories are still alive for Ellesmere Port is now home to the Boat Museum, a superb collection of vessels that once worked the inland waterways of Britain. Here you can travel by horse-drawn narrow boat and watch steam engines at work, but most importantly you can get a notion of the major role once played by the canals in the development of Britain.

*A collection of canal boats at the Ellesmere Port Boat Museum* (The Boat Museum, Ellesmere Port)

We might perhaps seem to be moving away from our original seaside theme, but then this is a part of the coast where the working port sits alongside the seaside resort. Liverpool is soon followed by Southport, Blackpool and Morecambe Bay. Not much out of the ordinary here you might think, but the following snippet of information may be of interest. Did you know that there used to be a coach connection between Blackpool and the Leeds & Liverpool Canal, which meant that the citizens of Wigan could go on special excursions starting at famous Wigan Pier? And the area does offer one unique experience, the walk across Morecambe Bay. This is emphatically not an activity you should try on your own, but it is possible in the company of a recognised guide who knows the sands and the tides. Those who make it to the northern side will find a coast marked by an old, long-decayed industrial life which gives the region a sadly romantic air. Near Millom, for example, you will find the crumbled remains of the old Hodbarrow iron mines, an area that was all but drowned out as the mining subsidence let the sea in. It was only kept at bay by the construction of a massive sea wall. This is the most melancholy site on the whole coast. Once men toiled here, producing as much as 350,000 tons of ore a year: now all is silent. The death of the trade spelt the end of the old ports as well. Maryport had its heyday in the time when sail ruled the seas, and a newly developed museum is hoping to re-create something of the atmosphere of those days. For some of us, the atmosphere has never quite gone. There are no holiday crowds here to scare away the ghosts of old seafarers. It is rather as if one had stumbled across an old Cornish fishing village which no other tourist had ever discovered. Maryport is a spot to savour.

Across the Solway Firth lies Dumfries and Galloway. Dorothy L. Sayers set one of her Lord Peter Wimsey novels here, *Five Red Herrings*. It begins: 'If one lives in Galloway, one either fishes or paints,' and if this is no longer true, one might perhaps agree with her other assertion, that those who both fish and paint have the best of the region. 'For the weather that is too bright for the trout deluges his hills and his sea with floods of radiant colour; the rain that interrupts picture-making puts water into the rivers and lochs and sends him hopefully forth with rod and creel.' She also adds the very sound advice that cold, dull days can best be spent in cosy bars with the comfort of a dram or two of the malt. If this all makes the place sound like somewhere for quiet, contemplative pleasures, then that is about right. The inland scenery is Highland but not the very grand Highland of the Cairngorms or the Grampians; the coastline is pleasing rather than dramatic. But it is also an area full of delightful little surprises. I once lived in a house which the Victorian builder had christened with the name 'St Ninian', and it was up here that I discovered that this good gentleman had had far too much sense to stay for ever cooped up in the centre of London. At Whithorn, almost at the top of Burrow Head, you will find a narrow road leading to Kidsdale, from where a mile's walk will lead you to the shore and St Ninian's Cave. It was reputedly his retreat, and certainly there are early Christian crosses carved in the cave wall.

If St Ninian's Cave whets your appetite for antiquities you can wander further round the coast to the west to find the oddly named Wren's Egg, a circle of standing stones with little obvious connection with small birds. Perhaps your interests run in other directions. If you take a delight in incongruous connections, then try Gatehouse of Fleet, a picturesque little town – one of those that Miss Sayers populated with painters – which you might think of as just another seaside resort. Yet this was one of Scotland's earliest industrial centres, a cotton town in fact, and you can still see the ruins of one of the mills beside the river. Gatehouse was supposed to be Scotland's answer to Blackburn, when Birtwhistle's came here in the 1780s, but somehow it never quite happened. Not interested in early industry? Then how about tropical plants? Now the one thing everyone thinks they know about Scotland is that the climate leaves much to be desired. Here is an area which puts the lie to that story. Down near the tip of the Mull of Galloway you will find the Logan Botanic Gardens, where palms and tree ferns flourish in almost tropical luxuriance. Logan also boasts an extraordinary sea-water fish-pond. It is a 30ft (9m) deep tidal pool in the rocks, originally constructed to hold fish for Logan House. The fish are still there, and very tame and friendly: this must be one of the few places where you can feed cod by hand. Perhaps enough has been said already to show that this is a remarkably interesting and very beautiful corner of Scotland. Readers can be left to their own devices to find the numerous castles and the rest of the standing stones, not to mention a second cave for a second saint.

The west coast of Scotland offers very different scenery. It is a coast sheltered by islands which seem from the map to be very much what they in fact are, fragments broken from a shattered coast. The southern part is Scotland's holiday coast, complete with busy resorts and holiday camps. This is the coast most readily accessible from

*Loch Torridon on the west coast of Scotland* (Scottish Tourist Board)

Glasgow, so its popularity is not surprising. Glaswegians traditionally used transport other than the train and later the motor car to
get to the coast. They went 'doon the water', taking the paddle-
steamers out along the Clyde. All but one have departed, but the one
survivor is a splendid vessel, the PS *Waverley*, last sea-going paddle-
steamer in the world. Some who travel in her – and the author tends
to be included in their number – seldom see any scenery at all, for
they find themselves unable to leave the sight of the majestic triple
expansion steam engine and its complex of rhythmic movements.
This section of coast with its sea lochs striking far inland is perhaps
best explored by water. I have spent many happy days doing just
that in a converted Clyde puffer, which as its name suggests is a
small steamer of a class that was once the main trading vessel of the

*Going 'doon the water' on the paddle steamer* Waverley (Waverley Excursions Ltd)

Clyde region. It was immortalised in the tales of Para Handy and something of that spirit lives on in the *VIC 32*. It is a vessel in which the holidaymaker can join in the life of the ship, steering, working on deck or stoking in the engine-room – or simply sit back and watch the scenery drift by. How fine that scenery is as you steam up the narrow lochs between enclosing mountains. From the head of Loch Long you can leave ship to climb the anvil-shaped Cobbler mountain, or you can travel up Loch Goil and find almost perfect solitude with few buildings in view, apart from picturesque ruins such as Carrick Castle. Neighbouring Holy Loch, however, boasts more sinister residents in the predatory shapes of nuclear submarines.

Travelling northwards the coastline retains its ragged edge, while the scenery becomes ever more dramatic. It would not be unfair to say that the further north you travel, the grander it becomes. Much of this coastline consists of rocky inlets which, if they are not ideally suited for bathers, are perfect musselling grounds. Few things taste better than mussels gathered by the bucketful and cooked the same day with wine and garlic. The coast does, however, provide a problem for those who wish to explore on wheels rather than on foot. Whole areas are totally devoid of roads, but if you wish to visit this west coast region may I suggest an alternative method of travel? Take the train from Glasgow to Mallaig. There is no more scenically splendid journey anywhere in Britain. It takes you across the wastes of Rannoch Moor and saves the best for last; the journey from Fort William to the coast. Here, to pile delight upon delight, you can again travel – as I did when I first came along this line many years ago – behind a steam locomotive.

Those who do not know the north-west of Scotland are in for surprises, delightful or not depending on your point of view. If you travel by car, for example, following the minor roads between Ullapool and Lochinver you will find it an extraordinary switchback in comparison with which the average fairground roller-coaster is only mildly sensational. There are times when you find the car bonnet pointing skywards as though the next stop might be Mars or Venus. And the scenery is incomparable, with vast shapely mountains such as Suilven and Stac Pollaidh rising straight up

*The old Clyde Puffer* VIC 32 *beside the ruins of Carrick Castle* (Anthony Burton)

from the plain. The coastline is equally splendid with shining white beaches that would be no disgrace to any desert island. Those prepared to leave the car behind and take to their two legs can find a solitude that they might never have believed still existed in the modern world. Recently my wife and I holidayed in this far north-western corner. We drove through Kinlochbervie and then left the car to tramp across the old peat road over the moors to Sandwood Bay. We reached the top of the sand dunes to look down on the great sweep of the bay where our only company was the raucous gulls and a solitary seal whose shiny black snout poked through the surf. There is a whole corner of the country here untouched by public roads and culminating in the great cliffs of Cape Wrath. To reach these you can take the ferry across the Kyle of Durness from just outside the Cape Wrath Hotel and then a private minibus service takes you out to the Cape itself. It is well worth the effort.

This is an area which probably offers greater attractions to those prepared to go out and look for them, though there are a number of spectacular and quite accessible sites such as Smoo Cave, the great hole in the cliffs near Durness. But even if you do no more than motor round the northern end of Scotland there is still something of an air of excitement about the journey, if only because of the rarity of finding an A road which is single track throughout most of its length. It leads on to John o' Groats, one of the better known place names in Scotland, but which turns out to be something of a disappointment. I find it a dull little place with none of the wild grandeur of Cape Wrath. The east coast can, indeed, seem a little tame to someone crossing over from the west, for this is an altogether gentler and calmer landscape. There are still some grand flourishes however such as Duncansby Head, where the sandstone cliffs are scarred by the deep gullies hacked out by the sea and from where you can look out at the three pinnacles of the Duncansby Stacks rising from the water. Even more exciting is the 200ft (60m) deep cleft known as the Bullers of Buchan. Boswell described it as 'a monstrous cauldron', while Dr Johnson was so impressed with the sense of foreboding aroused in him by the high cliffs that he declared that, 'If I had any malice against a walking spirit, instead of laying him in the Red-sea, I would condemn him to reside in the Buller of Buchan.' With such a recommendation what can you do but go and see for yourself?

*James Boswell's 'monstrous cauldron', the Bullers of Buchan* (Aberdeen Journals Ltd)

If the Bullers of Buchan put you in the mood for a little more dizzying splendour, then I can strongly recommend one of the most extraordinary fortresses in Britain, Dunnottar Castle, isolated on a headland 200ft (60m) above the sea, its outer walls staring down straight over the high cliffs. It is no surprise to find that many centuries went by and many sieges were attempted, but the stronghold remained intact. Allied to giddy heights, the castle can also boast gloomy depths, in the form of the Whigs' Vault, the dungeon where 167 Covenanters were held and from which only ten ever escaped. This is a place to appeal to the lovers of the macabre as much as to the admirers of fine scenery.

By this point in our circuit one's nerves are probably sufficiently steady to face any precipice and be ready for one of the most extraordinary sights on the whole of Scotland's east coast – the Whaligoe Steps. They snake down the cliff, 338 slabs of Caithness stone, placed there by the men of the herring fleet. Down they went each morning, and up they came at night hauling the day's catch up with them. They are a testament to the remarkable endurance of the men who went to fish for the 'silver darlings' – the herring of the North Sea. This is very much the fishing coast, with a number of very fine harbours such as Buckie.

If this coast is not as wild as its opposite number to the west, it does offer civilised pleasures by way of compensation. Harrowhill Wick is the home of the famous Caithness Glass. Visitors can see craftsmen forming the individual pieces, blowing the hot glass in a way that has scarcely changed for centuries. Perhaps the region's greatest claim to fame lies in its golf courses – but as all golfers the world over know of them and non-golfers care nothing about them, no more need be said on that subject. But to return to the subject of fishing, I can wholeheartedly commend the villages of the ancient kingdom of Fife. At Anstruther you will find an excellent little museum of the fishing industry and preserved craft in the harbour, including the sailing 'fifie' and its motorised close relation the 'zulu', which acquired its very unScottish name by being designed while the Zulu war was at its height.

Across the Firth of Forth, Scotland presents its more urbane face to the world, with a very mixed country of coalmines and rich agricultural land, a tamer land altogether it seems than that to the north. Things have not always been so quiet. General Cope met the Highlanders at Prestonpans in 1745, where the Scots showed a very unsporting spirit by attacking the English while they were still having breakfast. But the battle has another odd distinction in being the only one in Britain ever to have been fought across a railway. The line of the Tranent to Cockenzie tramway, an early form of railway on which waggons were pulled by horses not locomotives, can still be seen running from the harbour to the battle monument. Cope set his guns behind the low railway embankment.

The coast southward from here and down into Northumbria can best be characterised by its two outstanding features – castles and dunes. Some of the castles are extremely well known, with Bamburgh heading most popularity polls. But there are others just as fine, in settings just as grand. Tantallon Castle in Lothian, for example, stands on a rocky promontory protected on three sides by hundred-foot-high cliffs and to the landward by massive walls, towers and a moat. In the fourteenth and fifteenth centuries, the Douglas family lived here with their private army of up to 2,000 men. The castle has withstood numerous sieges and survived the batterings of east coast gales, hence the local expression 'ding doon Tantallon', which translated means 'knocking down Tantallon' and is used of anything which is thought to be totally impossible. Moving south into England, the two themes of castles and dunes unite in what must be among the most gloriously unspoiled stretches of coastline in the country. It starts somewhat un-promisingly at Beadnell at the northern end of Beadnell Bay, a spot much beset by caravans, but if you follow the golden rule of walking away from such an area as rapidly as possible and head off to the south you come to an area of high dunes flanking superb beaches on to which the North Sea rolls, spectacularly if somewhat coldly. From here on, right round into Embleton Bay, the coast is conserved by the National Trust. It ends at the point with Dunstanburgh Castle. The guidebooks tend to be somewhat dismissive of this old fortress, which is certainly in a somewhat ruinous condition. Yet I much prefer it to the more domesticated restoration of Bamburgh, and children love it. It is a vast site; 11 acres are enclosed within the castle walls, so there is no shortage of space, no lack of towers to explore nor walls to climb. It is a spot where imagination can run free.

The nature of the coastline changes very markedly as you reach the industrial areas of Tyne and Tees, soon to be followed by the more popular holiday area of the Yorkshire coast. Even here you can beat the crowds by taking to your feet. There is a fine coastal path that runs from Whitby to Scarborough, or if you really want

43

*Robin Hood's Bay seen from the old Scarborough to Whitby railway* (Anthony Burton)

something different, then you can walk the track of the old Whitby to Scarborough Railway. Whichever you choose you can be sure of finding peace in the wild country between the moors and the sea. Those who are really looking to escape the crowds should keep on going south to that extraordinary spit of land that runs out into the Humber estuary, Spurn Head. Here your company is likely to be limited to birds. Once, however, you might have seen a very strange sight, for there was a railway here and it was not unknown for waggons to be sailed along it – quite literally sailed with a mast and simple square sail. You might still be lucky enough to see traditional sail from Spurn Head, especially during the summer weekends. The old Humber keel *Comrade* comes out this way, looking very like a ship from the Middle Ages, with her central mast carrying a great square sail and topsail. Sometimes she will have company, her sister ship *Amy Howson*, a Humber sloop; the same blunt-bowed hull but a different sail arrangement. The keel is traditionally sailed from the Yorkshire side of the river, the sloop favoured on the Lincolnshire bank. Today the bureaucrats have turned their backs on centuries of history and – dislodging the old county boundaries – have created Humberside, but old loyalties and old rivalries survive the workings of Whitehall.

If the sort of lonely emptiness of Spurn Head appeals, then I can recommend the area around the Wash. Take any of the minor roads that lead out towards the coast between the Welland and the Great Ouse and you will arrive at a land of marshes divided from the flat fields by a high embankment. There are some areas you visit for the sea view, some for the countryside close by the coast, but this is the place for skies. To see it at its very best come on a day when the tall cumulus clouds are sailing like a squadron of men-of-war across a blue sky. It is an unforgettable sight, part of a world of contrasts. At your feet is a regular chequer-board of fields and drainage ditches, while to the other side of the sea wall are the squirming water-courses of the meadows and up above the constantly changing pattern as the white armada sails on. It is here perhaps that this special atmosphere is felt at its strongest, but something of it persists all along the East Anglian coast.

The general rule for East Anglia would appear to be that the further south you go, the less people you are likely to meet. Suffolk tends, on the whole, to have fewer visitors than Norfolk yet there are certainly some splendid places to visit. Southwold is an elegant town of Georgian buildings, the houses by the sea-front being especially inviting. It also boasts an excellent brewery, Adnams, supplier of fine ales. Better still for atmosphere is Walberswick just to the south, where the Blyth meets the sea. It has a somewhat un-English air about it, rather Dutch in fact, and there is certainly a Dutch look to the gabled houses. It is principally a place of boats, and not just the ubiquitous fibreglass of the Broads. There are fishing boats and boats built of wood, all lined up along the Blyth, and if you walk up the river bank you will find the footbridge which once carried the lines of the Southwold Light Railway, and that in turn will bring you to the Harbour Inn. Once you could have crossed by a ferry, run by a local family. I met a descendant of the ferrymen who had a wealth of tales. My favourite story was about the day the circus came, wanting everything taken across, including the elephants. Now ferries are not normally built to take elephants, but they managed well enough until it came to mother and calf. There was no room for them both, so they decided to put the calf on board and have mother swim behind, attached to the ferry. When everything was ready the motor on the winch was started – and nothing moved. Mother refused to budge and the engine was no match for a stubborn lady elephant. It took a very long time to persuade her to take to the water. This is just the sort of place you expect to find good stories, and you can also find excellent food. The café in the village is rather special, for it can boast a superb collection of paintings of local ships and the sea, some modern and some quite old.

Those who come to Walberswick should head a few miles up the river to visit Blythburgh – it just about counts as being coastal for the tides reach this high up the river. It is a village with a splendour out of all proportion to its size. When ships were smaller it was a port; there was an Augustinian priory here and several grand houses are still to be seen. Finest of all the buildings is the church, and even in a county blessed with many fine churches it is quite outstanding. Fine roofs are a feature of East Anglian churches. There are beautifully carved and painted examples at Mildenhall, March and Neston, but Blythburgh stands comparison with the best. Wide-winged angels stare down at you from on high. They suffered badly in the Civil War when Cromwellian troops used them for target practice, but they have now been restored to full glory. Heavenly bodies up above, earthly sins down below, that is the rule here: pew ends are carved with representations of the deadly sins. I am especially fond of 'drunkenness', who is having a very bad time of it, for not only is he sitting in the stocks but his expression suggests a monumental hangover.

These few miles of coast are full of interest, for just to the south is Dunwich, a village that has been fighting a losing battle with the sea for centuries. Somewhere out beneath the waves are the Roman town and the medieval town. Bits of Dunwich keep slipping away. The graveyard on the cliffs is down to its last tomb, the rest having tumbled and vanished. The little museum down by the beach has a model to show you what once was but is no more. Nowhere along this shifting coastline has anywhere suffered as Dunwich has suffered, though in terms of lost prosperity, Orford to the south runs it a good second. Once it was an important harbour, but the shingle built up to form the great barrier of Orford Ness. Walk down the main street and you can still see the indentation which marks the harbour where ships once rode at their moorings. The castle keep rears above the town, and a very fine castle it is too, with superb views from the top. It looks down on a very attractive pub and what appears to be the local chip shop, which in a way it is. But how many chippies do you know that serve oysters on the shell and smoked eel? It is only recently that I have come to know this coast, but I fell in love with it at once. It has a unique character, a wistful air of having to make do with past glories, as the vast and glorious churches look out over sadly diminished villages to the swaying reeds of the marshes and the ever-changing shore.

Below Felixstowe the coastline seems to break up, the long steady sweep of East Anglia giving way to inlets, bays and estuaries and a complex of river mouths. This is an area I know best from the sea. This is the coast where the Thames sailing barges traded and where they still gather each year to race in a season of barge matches. They are the last survivors of a once busy world of sailing ships and when they meet they make a scene of outstanding beauty. Anyone who has the chance should try and make one of the match weekends; the barges move all round this corner of south-east England. To see twenty or more tacking to and fro waiting for the start is unforgettable. I have had the good fortune to crew in matches and that, of course, is best of all. There are sailing holidays to be had which include match days, but even to watch from the shore is a splendid experience.

England, Scotland and Wales have much to offer and, as I have tried to show, it is possible even in the height of summer to escape the crowds. But those who want to be absolutely certain of getting away from the throngs should take the ferry across the Irish Sea. There are, it is true, one or two places so well known that you will certainly not be free of crowds. It would need a very energetic giant to push his way through the souvenir sellers to the Giant's Causeway, on the north coast, but elsewhere the coastline promises unrivalled peace. I have wandered on to a beach containing two other people and gone away muttering about the crowds to find somewhere more peaceful. Mind you, one is seldom quite alone on an Irish beach, which you might well be required to share with the occasional donkey or a few contemplative cows. Ireland is a land as varied as the rest of the British Isles, and with more than its share of fascination. If you decide to ignore the attractions of the Giant's Causeway, for example, you need only travel a few miles to the east to find the perfect crescent beach of Whitepark Bay, with the little hamlet of Portbraddan slipped neatly into a cleft in the rocks. Here you will find a tiny thatched church, the smallest in Ireland, little more than 10ft by 6ft (3.7m by 2m to be exact and metric). You might prefer something in the nature of a folly, and there is

*Whitepark Bay, County Antrim* (Northern Ireland Tourist Board)

certainly a sense of incongruity about finding a refugee from the Tivoli in Rome perched on the cliffs at Downhill. The Mussenden Temple comes complete with Latin inscription, conveying the very true sentiment that you are better off up here when there's a gale blowing than you would be out at sea in a ship.

The north-east corner is not, however, the area most people head for on their first visit to Ireland. Most seem to favour the west coast, and a very sensible choice it is too in many ways. This a coast shaped and scarred by the Atlantic Ocean. The scenery is magnificent and it scarcely seems to matter where you go, for each bay seems as fine as the next. You can choose between wide sweeping sands or the drama of the great cliffs. There are cliffs here to match and even surpass those of north-west Scotland. The cliffs of Moher stretch for 5 miles along the coast to the south of Galway Bay. To see them at their best, I often think, you should wait for a really bad day of rain brought in on a high wind from the west, when the dark rocks lower out over the lashing sea. Grander still is Slieve League, 2½ miles west of Carrick in Donegal. At their highest point, the cliffs rise nearly 2,000ft (600m) above the sea, though it is not always when they are at their highest that they appear at their grandest. The higher cliffs slope out at a comparatively gentle angle, but go to Canglass Point and you will see them dropping away dizzily, a thousand foot of sheer, multicoloured rock. Unlike the cliffs of Moher these are for calm, bright days; when the wind screams and howls around these rocks you could all too easily be carried away over the edge. Even on a peaceful day, these precipices are not for the fainthearted.

There is far more to Ireland than just the scenery. It is, to the visitor from the rest of the British Isles, a foreign land. I shall just look at one small part to try and give an idea of what I mean. Down in the far south-west corner you will see the Beara Peninsula finger-pointing out to sea. I stayed here in a little farm close to the sea and the mountains of Knocknagallaun. The nearest village was Allihies, which could be reached by road on a tortuous route which had superb views which everyone – except the fiercely concentrating driver – exclaimed over with delight. The alternative way to reach the village was to do as most of the locals did – walk over the mountain. This I decided to do. Suddenly I appeared to find myself away from Ireland and back in Cornwall, for there on the far side of

(previous page) *The cliffs of Moher* (Kenneth McNally)

the mountain were the unmistakable shapes of mine engine-houses. There was, too, a decidedly large hole leading down into what was clearly a copper mine, so it needed very little detective work to realise that the Cornish had come here to work the ore. After my exploration I walked down into Allihies and headed for a pint of that well-known black beverage with the creamy froth on top. Opening hours are, shall we say, flexible in Ireland, and you will be most unfortunate indeed to arrive in a place and not get a drink. Even if one of the many bars is shut the chances are that the local shop has a bar anyway. This is the only country I know where you can be handed a packet of cornflakes and a pint of Guinness over the same counter. Late in the afternoon I walked back on the road admiring the view which as a driver I had not dared to peep at let alone linger over.

I met the postman delivering the morning mail. Our conversation began something like this:

Postman:  Where are you going off to in such a rush? Are you off to catch a train?

Myself:  No, I am not catching a train.

Postman:  You would not be, because there has never been a train in this part of Ireland, so let's sit down and have a good talk.

So sit down we did, and chatted in the sun. The letters remained undelivered and probably nobody minded very much. Ireland is a country for those who want to stop and stand back from the rush of life. Even for those who would say that this lovely coast can get too crowded or is just like any other part of Britain – though I would deny both charges – there are still means of getting even further away. Ireland is a big island surrounded by a multitude of small islands and island life is never quite the same as mainland life. The islands of Britain deserve, at the very least, a chapter all to themselves.

# 3
# Island
# Retreats

*A beehive cell on Inishmurray*
(Kenneth McNally)

Let us start just where we left off, with the islands of Ireland. As no one has ever accurately defined what is meant by 'island', other than a piece of land entirely surrounded by water, the Irish have taken advantage of this vagueness to include a number of barren, rocky lumps and come up with the splendid news that the country has 365 of them, one for every day of the year. It offers the delightful prospect of an entire year spent moving in sedate and leisurely fashion, savouring the delights of each before travelling on to the next. Alas, things are not quite that simple. Some of the islands in the year's collection prove to be too tiny to justify a morning visit, let alone a day; some require many days of exploration for the visitor to enjoy and appreciate; while some are so beset by the Atlantic waves that one cannot get there at all. So the reader who is beginning to pale at the prospect of 365 repetitive descriptions of the whole lot can take comfort, for what follows is a personal selection of some of the best of them. But do remember that it is only a selection. When you omit over 90 per cent of the items in the catalogue, then you are not describing the full show. I have, however, tried to select as rich a mixture as possible, in order to give the true taste of the whole; but experience suggests that if you are lucky enough to find yourself on the Irish coast, and lucky enough also to be offered a boat trip to any island, then take the offer. There is a special magic in the isolated world, a magic that seems to linger round all islands everywhere. It is surely no accident that the most magical of all Shakespeare's plays, *The Tempest*, has an island setting.

Where to begin? Rathlin, off the north coast not far from the Giant's Causeway, has several things in its favour as a starting point but I would choose it because somehow, the idea of an island suggests a contemplative, leisurely way of life. True, there are islands such as Man which have achieved fame through the antics of gentlemen who hurl themselves around the place on high-speed motor bikes, but they are rarities. A far more popular image is of a place where one is left to one's own devices with a few books and a wind-up gramophone. Islands are ideal for the contemplative, and Rathlin can claim to be home to one of the most famous contemplatives in British history, Robert the Bruce. It was on this island, that he sat in a cave and watched the tireless spider weave its gossamer. The claim does not go entirely undisputed. The Scots, not surprisingly, do not like to think of one of their most famous sons

*Bruce's Cave on Rathlin Island* (Kenneth McNally)

finding his inspiration in another country. But it is true that the Bruce was sent in exile here in 1306, and the crumbling remains of his castle can still be seen above the high cliffs and the geometric-ally carved basalt at the north-east corner of the island.

This is the largest island off the northern Irish coast, yet it is not very large, an L-shaped lump, measuring only 8 miles from one tip of the L to the other, yet what a rich variety of scenery it contains. Church Bay is the centre for human life on the island, but humans represent only a fraction of the whole population. Visit Bull Point, with its Gothic spires of volcanic rock rising high above the sea and you will find sea-birds of all kinds, from everybody's favourite, the puffin, to that most antisocial of creatures, the fulmer, which demonstrates its annoyance by vomiting on the object of its

displeasure. The place is a true ornithologist's delight, and even those unattracted by the notion of puking sea-birds can enjoy the wild splendour of the cliff scenery. The island, however, boasts no hotel – very little accommodation of any kind in fact – so most trips are limited by the timetable of the boats from Ballycastle. It is, nevertheless, well worth a visit – and in case you have any doubts let me add one further attraction to lure you on. Where else would you find an upside-down lighthouse? The Bull light is built on a ledge 100ft below the summit of the 300ft (90m) high cliffs and, uniquely, it has its lamp at the bottom and the living quarters at the top.

Not very far away, beneath the tall cliffs to the west of Ballycastle, sits a large hunk of rock, called Carrick-a-Rede, at first sight just another insignificant blob on the ocean. It boasts one cottage, used in the season by salmon fishermen, and not much else. But it is owned by the National Trust, who provide access to the rock by means of a 60ft (18m) long rope bridge that swings alarmingly above a deep chasm through which the waves dash and roar. It is a perfectly safe, if decidedly exciting, passage: though the bridge is removed in winter and bad weather, when the rock returns to its isolation. Leaping across metaphorically if not physically from one corner of Ireland to the other, there is another rather exciting island crossing to be made. Dursey Island is attached to the Beara Peninsula by a cable car capable, the authorities proclaim, of taking six people or one cow and attendant. As you sway across the sea, you might care to contemplate what a cow might think of it all. The trip alone is worth making even if there was nothing to see on the other side. In fact, ghoulish children (and what child is not attracted to the macabre?) should head straight for the graveyard where through cracks in the old tombs they can catch glimpses of the skeletons.

We have travelled rather more rapidly than intended from north-east to south-west, so let us fill in some of the parts in between. In contrast to two islands attached, if somewhat tenuously, to the mainland, we can turn to one 8 miles out in the Atlantic, off Donegal. Tory Island lies off Bloody Foreland, a name that anyone with an ounce of curiosity in their soul will want to have explained. It derives from no sensational murder nor ferocious massacre but, disappointingly for some, alluringly to others, from the blood-red inlets that part the cliff. Not that blood has never been spilled here:

*An exciting approach to Carrick-a-Rede Island* (Kenneth McNally)

the area suffered greatly in the infamous evictions of the local Irish by rapacious landlords in the nineteenth century. It was here that Maud Gower declared that England was waging war on the Irish and that the Irish should, in turn, be prepared to kill the enemy. Tory too has seen its share of violence, for once it was home to a race of violent plunderers and pirates. All that is in the past and today it is, in many ways, an impoverished spot where ever-dwindling numbers of inhabitants fight for a living from the sea. Poor in cash terms it may be, but there is a richness to life here that those who have stayed cherish. The island is not easy to reach, has no tourist trade and those who come here will find an almost bare land where the sea not the soil provides a livelihood. This is a place where the curragh, the traditional rowed fishing boat, its hull made of oiled cloth stretched on a wooden frame, is still in use. These boats seem to belong as much to history as to the present, and it is this sense of history combined with a wild isolation that makes the place so alluring.

Inishmurray off the coast of Sligo can boast a proud, but ultimately sad, history. The pride lies in the island's importance to the development of Christianity in Ireland. A monastery was established here, with buildings erected within the bounds of a more ancient *cashel* (castle). One glance is enough to show how the beehive cells get their name, for stone beehives are just what they look like. Those who believed in the ascetic life would have found it here, in a domed cell, with a stone bed and the low doorway the only source of light. There was nothing here to distract the contemplative. The sadness came with the gradual worsening of living conditions on the island. The cutting of peat for fuel ate away the thin soil covering until, at last, there was not enough left to sustain healthy crops. Reluctantly, in the 1950s, the last islanders packed and went. Now you can hire a boat to take you there to roam among the old ecclesiastical buildings and the collapsing cottages. It is a fascinating, though scarcely cheerful, place.

Continuing down the west coast we come to Clare Island situated at the mouth of Clew Bay. This is very much alive and can even boast one hotel – a solitary concession to tourism. Those who know something of Irish history will know the island as the home of the O'Malleys. The name may mean nothing to most present inhabitants of the United Kingdom, but in Elizabethan times it was

*O'Malley Castle, Clare Island* (Kenneth McNally)

known well enough. Grace O'Malley (or Granuaile) was a ferocious lady who led a gang of pirates that virtually controlled the waters of western Ireland, extracting payment from every ship. Their land base can still be seen – O'Malley Castle, as gaunt and forbidding as the romantic would wish all castles to be. Sometimes here you feel too that, though the place is now peaceful, little has changed in the basic life pattern of the island – except that now, as in so many remote places, there is a steady dwindling of population. Increased tourism might be an answer, but as always there is the risk that this will only hasten the end of a traditional way of life. It is a dilemma which affects all the small independent communities of the islands. It recurs when you reach the best known group of them all.

The Aran group – Inisheer, Inishmaan and Inishmore – achieved world fame when they were featured in Robert Flaherty's documentary film of 1934, *Man of Aran*. The film is not only still remembered in the islands, but still shown and still argued over. Visitors, too, remember, and search out the spots and the people who featured in the film. Others look further back to the works of the playwright Synge and, though they may still meet many Riders to the Sea, they will perhaps not come across any quite as flamboyant as that other western Ireland character, Christy Mahon, for as Pegeen cries out in the very last line of the play: 'I have lost the only Playboy of the Western World.' Plays and films have given the isles

*The ancient fortress of Dun Aengus on Aran* (Kenneth McNally)

an aura of romance, and if you come here expecting something extraordinary, something rich in lore and history, you will not be disappointed. Tourism has grown and change is coming to Aran, but it is a slow change and has, as yet, had little noticeable effect. Many who come here find the greatest enchantment lies in the great historical monuments such as Dun Aengus, the fortress that has been described as 'the most magnificent barbaric monument in Britain'. It dates back beyond written records and its actual age is uncertain. Its magnificence, however, is beyond question. It sits atop a cliff that rises over 250ft (75m) above the sea and at that side no other defence is needed. To landward the defences are equally formidable – an inner *cashel* with walls of massive construction and an outer ring of jagged upright stones.

Those who wish to contemplate less warlike historical relics can turn to the many reminders of early Christian life on the island. For me, however, the fascination of Aran lies neither in the monuments to saints nor the homes of heroes, unless you count as heroes those dogged generations who have fought with the sea and the thin soil to find a living here. It is a hard, rocky landscape featuring the broken limestone pavements of a type found in County Clare and, somewhat further afield, in County Yorkshire. Perhaps they give me, a Yorkshireman, a comfortable sense of recognition. The island of Inishmore is a network of stone walls – walls bordering roads and narrow tracks, and walls dividing off the fields which, to one used to the green patchwork of the mainland, seem absurdly small. At the heart of these stone webs sit the tiny houses, some still the single-storey thatched dwellings of traditional form. Aran is now accessible by air. The old days when Synge listened to the Gaelic chatter of the kitchen through a crack in the bedroom floorboards have gone – but there is still a whole different world to be explored here, a world quite unlike that of the mainland, let alone that of the rest of the British Isles.

Those who have taken the boat trip out to Inishmurray might well feel that they have already seen the most dramatically beautiful of all the abandoned islands. But they have not seen the Skelligs, stark, jagged rock pinnacles thrust out of the waves, rising at their highest point to over 700ft (210m). You may never set foot here, for the weather often denies visitors a landing place, but if ever you get the chance take it, for there is nothing to compare with this anywhere else among all the islands of Britain and Ireland. From the landing place on Great Skellig, 600 steps formed of large stone

slabs lead you up to a monastery. This is no great foundation, just a tiny oratory and six tinier cells, but its situation on a rocky ledge over 500ft (150m) above the Atlantic is unique. One hopes that the men who suffered the appalling privations of this desolate spot received a reward in heaven, for they had little enough comfort on earth.

The Skelligs are not perhaps to everyone's taste, and those looking for a somewhat calmer island visit, but one with a promise of interesting and even bizarre features, might care to try the most southerly of Irish islands, Clear Island. It is rocky, but not so uncompromisingly craggy as the Skelligs. And the bizarre features? Well, go and look at the standing stones on the south-west cliff. Are they prehistoric monuments, tombstones or what? They are, in fact, deterrents to invasion. At the end of the eighteenth century, when there was a threat from the French, the stones were set up, painted and dressed in uniform to fool the enemy into believing that an army stood ready to repel attack. Two other claims to fame for the island are separated by many centuries: St Ciaran, one of the first Irish saints, was born here in the fourth century, and the Atlantic telegraph cable reached here from America in the nineteenth. We have travelled, island hopping, from the far north to the far south and have left hundreds of islands unmentioned – not a word about self-styled Michael I, Prince of the Saltee Islands, or the island known prosaically as Muck or more mellifluously as Nagloragh or . . . and so the line could be extended. Such islands, preserved by their watery isolation from over-much contact with the rest of the world, offer what an outsider at least must feel is the most Irish of Irish experiences. Life in Ireland in any case often seems to move to a different rhythm from that of other countries, and life on the islands is different again. Perhaps this is true of all islands. They offer experience in a more concentrated form, a distillation of national character. This is certainly true of Ireland and certainly true also of some, if not all of the Scottish islands.

The British Isles end at Muckleflugga (there is a pinprick on the map called Out Stack, but much too small really to qualify as a genuine island). This is the northernmost point of the Shetland Isles and a very long way north it is. It is a long way too from the world of the Celts – Shetlanders are closer kin to Scandinavians, which is not

*The lonely Skelligs far out in the Atlantic* (Kenneth McNally)

*The old monastery on the Skelligs* (Kenneth McNally)

too surprising for they sit as close to Bergen as to Aberdeen. This is a Norse as well as a North world. What images are brought to mind by the word Shetland? Mostly they tend to be rather coy domestic images: little girls à la Thelwell bouncing around Surrey paddocks on tubby ponies; jolly and colourful woolly pullovers. The reality of the islands is very different, for there is nothing of the coy about Shetland. Winds that can reach speeds of over 100 mph rush down from the Arctic, for the Arctic circle is uncomfortably close, closer in fact than London. If the islands have been spared the steady decay that has beset so many of the Irish islands, a price has been paid. Oil has brought the vast terminal of Sullom Voe and the executive jet with its full complement of executives. Oil has brought money to the islands and it has brought change. Perhaps romantically inclined outsiders have no right to comment on the nature of that change, and those who have never had to try and wrestle a living in the old ways have no business criticising the world that is growing up in the Shetlands. This is the new prosperity of the islands. I do not much care for it, but it is really not my affair and there I propose to leave the matter. So let us turn to other aspects of this northern scattering off the end of Britain, and if what pleases me seems to be old fashioned and out of touch with reality then I am quite happy to accept the criticism.

By now the Shetlands might seem hopelessly uninviting; cold, windy and crawling with extras from Dallas, but happily this is only a part of the story. For a start any generalisation must be just that, for the islands cover a large area, 70 miles north to south, 35 miles east to west. That does not include the isolated blob of Fair Isle, midway between Shetland and Orkney. It is not merely isolated, but is the most isolated occupied island in Britain. It is famous both for its knitting patterns and as a favourite stopping-off place for migrating birds. The Shetland islands as a whole boast magnificent cliffs: you can find some of the oldest rocks in the world here. There is a rich wildlife which includes a very large bird population among which you may find species you would not expect to see this far north. There are seals all around the coast, basking on the rocks or watching you through the waves with their big dark eyes. There are otters, spared the attention of hunter and hounds. But what strikes most visitors is the sense of foreignness. There are the long days of the Arctic summer, when the evening glimmer seems to stay endlessly in the sky, and there is too that sense of a land that may belong politically to Britain but has its spiritual home in Scandinavia. At Lerwick, a replica Viking longship rides in the harbour, but you do not need that to create the atmosphere or remind you of the coming of the Norsemen. Scandinavian fishing boats are regular visitors. Norwegian and Icelandic are heard as often in the bars as English and the traditions of the islands are all essentially Norse, culminating in the annual ceremony of Up Helly Aa, when a replica longship is dragged through the streets by men in Viking costume and destroyed by fire. This is no tourist spectacle – not many tourists come to the Shetlands in January – but a genuine, living, local tradition.

Times are changing, and it seems now that if you want to see something of the old life of crofting, you have to go to the Crofting

*The past uncovered: remains of the Neolithic village of Jarlshof, Shetland* (Highlands & Islands Development Board: O. Marzaroli)

Museum at South Voe or the agricultural museum near Tingwall Loch. You can, however, step further back in time, to the settlement of Jarlshof, incongruously close to Sumburgh airport. Man has lived in this area for over 4,000 years, and the most spectacular remains are the stone huts actually built below ground level and comparative newcomers from a mere two and a half thousand years ago. But this is not, perhaps, a place to come to for the sights. It is an area with a unique atmosphere, which it takes time to know. Most of us, alas, only have time to come and sample – to get the merest taste of – the Shetlands.

Orkney is a more accessible group of islands in almost every sense. It is easily reached by boat from the mainland – and a very fine journey it is too – and it has less of that air of foreignness about it. The islands are also totally beguiling. Of all the places in Britain I have ever visited this is perhaps the one to which I most wish to return. Such judgements are, of course, very personal and may reflect nothing more than a set of circumstances which set one particular spot for ever in the mind. My wife and I were staying at the hotel looking out over the harbour at Stromness when two ships came in, not yachts, nor motor vessels, but the fully rigged sailing ships *Cuidad da Inca* and the *Marques*, the latter tragically lost at sea during the 1984 Tall Ships Race. The following day they sailed off the quay. They did not motor out and hoist sail, but manoeuvred under staysails alone, as generations of sailing vessels had done before them. It was an unforgettable sight, and as they left we raced up the streets of the town and out to the point, where we stood and watched until the topsails dropped below the horizon. But even before this unexpected joy, I had already fallen in love with Stromness and the islands.

The capital of Orkney is Kirkwall and if you want to appreciate it to the full then go there as your first stop, for attractive as it is it cannot compare with Stromness. Once you have visited the latter anything else must seem second best. The main street of Stromness wriggles down to the harbour; it is paved right across but used by the few cars that pass through the town. Little alleys on the seaward side pass between houses where walls lean in towards each other, giving the briefest glimpse of jetty, fishing boat and clear green sea. To landward the alleys climb the hillside to secretive courts and more alleys. It is a town full of surprises. The Pier Arts Centre boasts a superb collection of twentieth-century British art, and how splendidly the geometric shapes of Hepworth, Moore and Nicholson reflect the outside world of rock, pebble and the rounded swell of the sea. The little town museum is exactly what a little museum should be, a collection of objects gathered with love. It is a place that tells simply the story of Orkney and the sea, and the long history of the island people. Orkney is, in fact, an historian's and more especially an archaeologist's delight. The sites on the islands show tremendous diversity and include some of the most spectacular to be found anywhere in Britain, and all are, without exception, in superb locations. I do not wish to bore those readers with no interest in ancient history, but Orkney's archaeological sites are so special that they just have to be described.

Which site an individual will find the most exciting is impossible to say. Some prefer those which still have their mysteries. Stone circles seem, often literally, to hold a special magic, and so many stories abound concerning strange powers locked within the ancient circles that even wretched sceptics like the author hold them in a certain awe. I defy anyone to visit the great Ring of Brogar on a day when storm clouds are gathering over the sea and feel totally unmoved by the sight. There is a sense that somehow these massive stones, so carefully and so exactly positioned, have a role to play in an elemental world that we of the twentieth century simply do not, and cannot, understand. There are no end of theories about Brogar, from ley lines of power to landing zones for flying saucers, but none that convince me, and so the mystery remains and the visitor is left free to let the imagination fly wherever it will.

Other sites may seem less strange, but still we may feel that our understanding is at best only partial. Maes Howe, the guidebooks will tell you, is a Neolithic chambered cairn with runic inscriptions, which is all very well but in the end tells you nothing about the people who built it or just why it was constructed. From the outside all you see is a huge grass mound surrounded by a ditch. A hole in the mound leads you through a narrow passage, once closed by a great slab of stone, beyond which the passage continues, its sides formed by slabs of stone nearly 20ft (6m) long. Then it opens out into a stone chamber which originally rose 18ft (5.5m) above the floor level but is now reduced in size. Small chambers lead off the main area. It is a vastly impressive home for the dead, but still holds puzzles that we may never solve. Why such immense labour? Whose bodies were placed here? What rituals and what beliefs does it represent?

Skara Brae takes us away from the strange world of the dead to the very ordinary life of the living, though here we are looking at the world of people who lived three and a half thousand years ago. It is Britain's Pompeii, a settlement stopped dead by natural cata-strophe – not inundated by volcanic ash but by a huge sandstorm, and it was another storm that revealed it to the world again. In 1850 a devastating wind ripped away a sand dune on the west coast of Mainland Orkney. Storm revealed the ancient settlement just as storm had once covered and preserved it. Here is a group of round huts, built up of dry stone walls, the roofs corbelled (shaped into a dome). But it is not the huts themselves that astonish so much as the sense of domestic intimacy. So many ancient sites are either monumental and ultimately mysterious, or so ruinous that only the experts can 'read' them. Here, however, the simple living quarters stand revealed, almost ready for use. There are low doorways, with slits where a stone could be slid across to close the opening, a central hearth, a box-bed made out of stone slabs that could be filled with bracken, tiny cupboards and what is clearly recognisable as a Welsh dresser except that it too is made of stone. Think of a one-roomed flat with all your familiar furniture petrified and you have a house at Skara Brae. I can think of no other ancient site where you feel that you can reach out and touch the lives of the ancient inhabitants as you can here on the shore in Orkney.

Orkney can boast brochs, ancient stone towers, and an almost embarrassingly rich collection of burial chambers and even some modern historical sites which are quite out of the ordinary. The Dounby *click* (Norse) mill is a simple water-mill built on a pattern brought to these islands by the Norsemen and quite unlike the familiar water-mill of mainland Britain. The power comes from a horizontal wheel set directly in the stream, so that as the water hits the blades the vertical shaft turns and with it the millstones mounted above – no gears, no complications, a simple system housed in a minute thatched building isolated beside its moorland stream. And if you tire of history and archaeology – and I have done no more than touch on some of the more important sites – there is always the scenery. You can enjoy the splendid beaches of Sanday, where you can also get some excellent bargains from local knitters, or you can go to the grand cliffs of Hoy and see the famous isolated stack, the

*The Old Man of Hoy* (Highlands & Islands Development Board: Eric Thorburn)

*The extraordinary chapel created out of a Nissen hut at Lamb Holm, Orkney* (Highlands & Islands Development Board: Eric Thorburn)

Old Man of Hoy, still a challenge to the very best rock climbers. And if all the sightseeing and walking and climbing is getting a little excessive, then you can always head back to town for a glass of Highland Park, a deliciously smooth malt whisky distilled at Kirkwall. Then if you like what you taste you can pop round and watch it being made. There is one last site which I find irresistible. On the island of Lamb Holm you will find a Nissen hut, part of what was once a camp for Italian prisoners of war. But this hut is unique: Nissen hut it may be on the outside but inside it is a chapel that would not be out of place in Florence or Venice. Every inch of the interior has been decorated to simulate mosaic, tile and stone. It is, in its way, a masterpiece, not for the quality of the painting so much as for the wonderful ingenuity of the transformation. To misquote a well-known authority: 'When a man is tired of Orkney he is tired of life.'

Moving out around the Scottish coast to the west, you come to the Hebrides, Outer and Inner – and they have to be taken separately for the two groups of islands have quite different characteristics. Look up what most people have written about the Outer Hebrides, the Western Isles, in recent years and you will find the accounts touched by a feeling of bemused despair. The islands are beautiful, wonderful, splendid scenery, but – and the 'but' always appears – there is a sense of stagnation, of communities waiting for something to happen and hoping for someone else to make it happen. Litter often seems to reach epidemic proportions, threatening to submerge whole regions of the islands. It is an area that you visit and say to yourself: this could be so wonderful, why is it not? Those who come here have to work hard to find places where they can sense the old majesty of the land. Callanish is one such place, a stone circle set high on an empty moor, more impressive it seems to me than even Stonehenge, if only because it is not so well known, not so endlessly visited, photographed and filmed. But the very lack of obvious charm in the Outer Hebrides is, paradoxically, their greatest asset for those who want to lose themselves in the countryside. There are areas such as parts of North Harris, almost untouched by roads,

*Stornoway harbour, Isle of Lewis* (Highlands & Islands Development Board)

*The Cuillins of Skye* (Highlands & Islands Development Board: George Young)

with tracts of moorland, lake and hill where the tourist never comes. There are deer in the forest, fish in the lochs and a sprinkling of crofts where you might well find the famous Harris tweed being woven. It is not a comfortable land, not a place that gives up its prizes easily. It is emphatically not for those who wish to tour in comfort. It is really rather splendid.

The Inner Hebrides are far better known and in summer islands such as Skye positively teem with visitors, while Iona seems likely to sink back into the sea under the weight of visitors. I was lucky enough to begin my acquaintance with Skye some thirty years ago, spending many happy weeks sleeping out at a price of 1s (5p) a night for a place in a barn and spending my days climbing in the Cuillin Hills. Then there were only a fraction of the visitors that there are now, but even with the crowds Skye cannot be written off. There are still places of quite spectacular beauty which few people visit and if you get there in late spring you will have two great advantages: there will be few people, and you will have got there before the Skye midge, a devastating insect that cheerfully accepts all insect-repellent creams as a tasty hors-d'oeuvre before sitting down to its favourite meal of mainland visitors.

Having reached Skye where do you go for the flavour of the island? For many, the Cuillins will always be the major attraction, a great ridge of rock rising over 3,000ft (900m) above the sea, and consisting of the rough gabbro which is a climber's delight. But there is no easy access. A very minor road runs down from Carbost to Glen Brittle and from there feet take over. These are not hills for the inexperienced. The traverse of the ridge can only be undertaken by properly equipped climbers, for these are not just hills in the accepted British sense but mountains that need to be treated with respect. Failure to do so is lunacy, and having once helped to carry a body down from those hills, I cannot overemphasise the point. But, having said that, there is an immense amount of pleasure to be gained by those who come properly prepared and properly equipped. You need not tackle such horrendous sounding obstacles as the Inaccessible Pinnacle or the Crack of Doom to enjoy these hills, for even a gentle walk on the lower slopes up to the foot of the crags brings its rewards.

Those who are looking for a rock spectacular without the problem of tackling the Cuillins can take the road north from Portree past the fine isolated pinnacle of the Old Man of Storr to the Quairaing, a grotesque landslip, a jumble of shattered rocks and ragged needles lacing the sky. Perhaps the best way to penetrate to the mountainous heart of the island is to take the boat trip from Elgol to Loch Coruisk, a dark, glacial rock-girt sheet of eternally grey water. It is the most Romantic of Romantic landscapes, and the Rs are capitalised for this is a world that seems to belong to a period in painting and literature rather than to present-day reality.

You may wish to pursue a totally different line and encapsulate a different mood of romanticism. In that case head off to the hamlet of Stein on the shores of Loch Bay. It was meant to become a major fishing port, but never made it, and now remains as a wistful, forlorn dream of the days of glory that never came. But if the idea of travelling to your romantic ideal by dodging the tourist crowds seems unattractive then perhaps you should forget Skye altogether. There are plenty of islands along Scotland's west coast.

The major island to the south is Mull, with an atmosphere even damper than that of the notoriously misty isle of Skye – though I have to say that in a total of nearly three months on Skye spread over several trips nine days out of ten have been fine. Statistics,

*Waterfall near Burg, Mull*
(National Trust for Scotland)

*The Little Theatre, Mull*
(Mull Little Theatre)

however, show that if you are visiting Mull and have no room in your luggage for both sunhat and sou-wester, leave the sunhat behind. Mull is a surprising island to come to after Skye, with a quite different character, the hills softer and gentler, the land smoothing out at the edges, not collapsing into harsh crags and spires. Tobermory seems to be not only the most important town, but the one which epitomises the rather urbane character of the island: a cosy protected harbour, lined with attractive colour-washed houses and backed by trees. The island has castles and antiquities galore, but its greatest glory is its coastline. Here you have some of the best beaches in Scotland, and that is saying a great deal. If the first does not take your fancy, and the second has too many people on it, just keep on going until you find the one that is perfect for you. All the best islands keep one little surprise up their sleeve. High on the moorland near Dervaig is Mull Little Theatre: seating capacity thirty-six; total company for administration, direction, stage management and performance, two. No surprise then to find that it features in the *Guinness Book of Records*. It is an extraordinary enterprise that deserves all the success it achieves.

Theatre is not perhaps the main attraction for those who visit the Western Isles, and many who visit Islay have no doubt at all about what they are there to see: some of the finest, and certainly the most distinctive, malt whiskies in Scotland. They are so distinctive that they are also among the most controversial, for the peaty flavour is one that you love or hate. As a devotee of the Islay malts I can only say try for yourself, but *please* do not pollute the lovely liquor with hideous additives. I was once sampling, savouring and, as is the way in this part of the world, discussing the merits of the different varieties from the local distilleries with the hotel barmaid: a young lady with a profound respect for the malt, when we were joined by a gentleman who interestedly joined in the discussion, asked to be pointed in the direction of my personal tipple, ordered same and then proceeded to top up his glass with ginger ale. The barmaid stared in horror and in tones of dark bitterness exclaimed, 'My God, if I'd known you were going to do that I'd have given you——,' and here the laws of libel being what they are, the reader must fill in the gap with the name of whatever proprietary blend seems least pleasing. So be warned.

Distillery tours are available, but the teetotaller need not despair, for there is far more to enjoy here than just the malts. Bowmore, for example, is not just famous for the truly superb whisky that bears its name – and I would contend that there are few finer – but can also boast an odd, circular church. The explanation for its strangely unecclesiastical shape is that it was built, as in legend are so many round buildings, in order to make certain that there were no corners in which the devil might lurk. Islay has another great advantage. If the visitor becomes bored by its confines, then it is a simple matter to take a boat across the narrow channel that divides it from Jura. In 1984, the island received a good deal of publicity, simply because George Orwell wrote most of the novel of that name there. Nothing of that bleak, fictional world touches Jura, which is lonely, largely unpopulated apart from herds of deer, and has a beauty that can seem faintly melancholy. What do you do on Jura? Well, some shoot the deer, but the arsenal is quiet between February and the middle of August. Others may do as they please, for there is nothing in the conventional sense to *do* here at all: simply peace to enjoy.

The smaller islands, too, have their charms. Eigg typifies the idiosyncratic nature of these scattered dots on the western sea. It comes complete with its own, almost feudal, ruler and one of the oddest beaches in the country. The Singing Sands do genuinely sing, if not very harmoniously. The crystalline sand screeches underfoot and in high winds utters banshee-like moans. Rhum is equally curious and boasts a sort of miniature Parthenon, a Greek temple built over the mausoleum of Sir George Bullough, a former proprietor of the island. Small-island hopping is a pleasure in the Inner Hebrides, but to get back to the major islands we have to move on south.

Arran has two distinct personalities: holiday-resort Arran and wild Arran. Which you see depends on where you start. Holiday Arran is in the east, looking out towards the Clyde and Glasgow, approached via Brodick. Western Arran seems a world away and you can reach it through Lochranza. A few years ago I steamed here on the short sea trip from Tarbert, which we left in brilliant sunshine. By the time we reached Arran the clouds were piling up and the wind was stirring, but we decided to continue on under sail. The dinghy was winched overboard and off we set, but we were soon tacking furiously yet making little headway against the rising wind. We decided to abandon the project. By the time we returned the sea was rising, the wind howling and the rain lashing down. Arran can seem comfortably protected, land-locked almost, and that western coast can seem almost tame after Skye, but that afternoon I certainly saw the island's other face and its other mood. Needless to add after that perhaps, that it is the western end that I find the more appealing. Here you can find another of those caves that Robert the Bruce is said to have shared with the busy spider but, more importantly, here you will also find the old island communities of crofters and the old island way of life.

Arran is but one of the islands dotting the Firth of Clyde, and few would argue that it is the most attractive. Bute and the Cumbraes are slightly faded now, their days of glory passed. Once there was a steady procession of steamers coming 'doon the water'; now that only the *Waverley* remains the islands are gently sliding back into oblivion. The tourists have turned away from them and they add a last wistful note to this brief look at the west coast of Scotland. There are islands on the east coast but none to match those of the west, so we can move on to the islands off the coasts of England and Wales. These can seem a little dull after the romantic splendours of Ireland and Scotland, but that is only true if you approach them with the same expectations. The contrast can be extreme, but all these islands have such different characters and characteristics that really no comparisons are possible. This is irritating to authors who like to produce smoothly flowing narratives, but makes no difference in practice since we do not rush away from Arran shouting, 'let's nip over to the Isle of Wight'.

At first the contrast is not so great as it will appear later, for if you move down the coast to the Isle of Man you find a spot that has certain superficial resemblances to Arran. It, too, has a schizoid personality, divided between the comparatively wild countryside and the popular resorts. The contrast between the two, however, is far more marked than on Arran. Here they have casinos, night clubs, discos and bars and a great many other things designed to feed on tourist gold. The island would have no place in this book if there was no more to it than that, but happily that is not the case. For a start, it is an industrial archaeologist's dream, with extensive remains of mining, and not just the famous Laxey Wheel, the 72ft (22m) diameter water-wheel which worked the pumps to drain the mines beneath Snaefell. Man also has large tracts of open country, with secretive glens and open fells. It does remain the case, however, that it is hard work to get away from the rest of humanity here, and this tends to be true of many of the English and Welsh islands.

Anglesey might seem to be similar to Man, when one joins the stream of cars that rush across the Menai Straits heading to and from Holyhead. The resorts are popular and populous and yet what a wealth of fascinating material the island keeps hidden away. It is unique, and I use that much overdone and misused word deliberately. Firstly it is an island of ancient settlement, and of Celtic settlement that continued on into the Roman occupation. You find the earliest remains on Holyhead mountain, where an Iron Age community built their huts for peaceful living and a fort for less tranquil times. They used to be known as 'Irish huts', though there is absolutely no evidence that anyone from Ireland ever lived there. On the opposite side of the island is Din Lligwy, an even bigger settlement where Celtic chieftains held sway during the Roman period. Add to that some extraordinarily well-preserved ancient burial sites and a fine Roman fort and you have as impressive a collection of antiquities as those of Orkney. But for me the main interest is in remains of a much later date. 'Ecology' is one of the key words of our time; it was unknown, and if known would have been unheeded, in the eighteenth century. That was when it was discovered that Parys Mountain was just one giant chunk of copper ore. The entrepreneurs moved in. Men were set to work hacking and blasting, burrowing down and through the hill. The grass, the trees and the shrubs all vanished. Even the soil vanished. None of it ever returned. Today the mountain is a giant, grotesque Gruyère cheese, riddled with holes and totally sterile. It is a hideous lesson, yet strangely impressive with its own moments of beauty. Look at the settling tanks at the foot of the mountain and you will see the water stained with rainbow colours. The ore itself was shipped out of Amlwch, once a major port. But once the mountain had been eaten away, once the last scrap of copper-rich material had been gnawed off its rocky bones, the trade died. The skeleton remains as a reminder of a briefly prosperous but uncaring time.

Wales is not overendowed with islands, and Anglesey with its mainland connections by rail and road seems only just to qualify. With Bardsey, however, stuck off the coast from Aberdaron at the far northern tip of Cardigan Bay, there can be no doubt. This was once a holy island, a place of pilgrimage. The devout of the Middle Ages had only to cross the sea three times to Bardsey to notch up a score in the heavenly account book equivalent to a pilgrimage to Rome. Not much of the sanctity of the past remains in very tangible form: just part of the Augustinian abbey and some Celtic crosses. But tranquillity can still be found here, disturbed only by the noisy passage of migrating birds. Sadly, they are too often lured by the

*An ornithologists' paradise, the Island of Lundy* (Landmark Trust: Derek Sach)

island's lighthouse into which they fly at night. Their fate is no worse than that of the puffins of Puffin Island off Anglesey. In the eighteenth century these were delicacies eaten pickled, and in more recent times their ranks have been heavily reduced by rats, wisely leaving sinking ships and finding a home on the island.

Those who want to see the engaging little puffins, and literally hundreds of other species, would do better to head further south to Lundy, set between Wales and England at the mouth of the Bristol Channel. Owned by the National Trust and run by the Landmark Trust, Lundy has a few day visitors who sometimes seem to be wondering what they are doing there. Those who do know come for two reasons, to climb the cliffs or study the birds, and they go away well satisfied with the place. If you are neither climber nor ornithologist then you are liable to feel slightly out of place here.

A more popular area is the Scilly Isles, to which you can be whirred by helicopter. The Scillies are a group that excite very mixed feelings among visitors. So many go expecting a sort of subtropical paradise, a desert and deserted island off the tip of

Cornwall, and find, too often, a tourist spot much like many others. Visitors to St Mary's find fishermen who fish for tourists rather than the scaly denizens of the deep. There is one genuine tropical island, Tresco, but deserted it is not, for it too can easily become crowded. I first went there when the children were tiny and spent my time pushing a pram up and down the cliffs in search of peace and quiet, and found it hard to come by. Experience now provides the answer: get away to the smaller islands; search out the astonishing clear waters of deserted bays. The brochures tell you that the islands are warmed by the Gulf Stream, in which case I have been singularly unlucky in my choice of seasons for I found it distinctly on the chilly side. But do not be deterred; try St Martin's or St Agnes or, best of all, Samson, uninhabited and unspoiled. Here are glittering white sands where you really can dream your tropical dream. There is, however, one other aspect of the Scillies that is never far away – wrecks. These are treacherous waters in which many fine ships have foundered. You see their bleached ribs and broken backs everywhere, and at Valhalla on Tresco is a collection of bold and brassy ladies who were once the figureheads of fine ships. Wrecks, and wreckers, are an integral part of Scilly history. And finally, just to combine history and curiosity value, visit Gugh, an island boasting both ancient monoliths and the world's smallest post office.

The Channel Islands: tax exiles, duty-free booze and a touch of the French without the nuisance of a foreign language – that is one way to characterise them. It is, of course, unfair, but there is enough truth in it to make one wary of going anywhere near Jersey in the summer and to treat Guernsey with a certain caution as well. You can get away from the crowds on either island, but why make the effort when there are other islands where you are spared the problem? Alderney, Sark and Herm offer very special pleasures, each quite different from the others. If the image of Jersey is of soft living, then Alderney occupies the opposite end of the spectrum. Where other islands are lush and soft, it is harsh and rocky, ringed by grimly vast Victorian forts. It is not to everyone's taste, has no instant delights on offer. It carries also the reminders of its recent, unhappy history, when the entire population left the island rather than submit to Nazi rule. The islanders' place was taken by wretched slave labourers who were set to work adding yet more fortifications to an already heavily defended island. It should be a dour place, but is not. The island is, in fact, remarkably cheery and friendly, with a reputation, well earned, for boozy conviviality. And if you wish to sample the latter at its most extreme turn up on the first Sunday in May, Milk-a-Punch day, when all the pubs on the island dollop out lethal concoctions of milk and rum free to all comers. This is a place for those who appreciate an island of character rather than obvious charm, a friendly place yet one where you can go your own way in peace.

Sark, which is really two islands, Great and Little Sark, is a place of more immediate attraction than Alderney and very much odder. The island's social organisation can best be described as feudal, though none of the islanders seem to want to change it. They share, in fact, a reluctance to join the modern world at all, and have banned the motor car altogether. True it is a small island, 3 miles by 1½, though its ragged edges give it a coastline of some 40 miles; it is small enough anyway for visitors to explore it on foot, by hired bicycle or in a horse-drawn cart. Do not be misled by its size into believing that a day is all you need here. It is an island of beautiful

*La Grande Greve from La Coupee, Sark* (British Tourist Authority)

beaches, and rare plants, butterflies and birds. It is a place to slow down, a place with its own peculiarities. Access to the island from the minute harbour at Creux is by tunnels cut through the rock in the sixteenth century. But the real peculiarities, to outsiders' eyes, are the laws, administered by the island's own court and enforced by it: police from other islands may only land by permission. At the top of the whole system is 'Le Seigneur', not just a nominal but an actual lord of the island. Rights attach to the title, including the slightly bizarre privilege of being the only islander permitted to own a bitch: which must make the Seigneur's residence a popular calling place for all the dogs of the island.

Herm, halfway between Guernsey and Sark, is even smaller than the latter. It is not, alas, a place where many can linger, for most visitors are shooed away at the end of the day. It seems rather a shame, for it is a wonderful island for the naturalist with lush vegetation, and it is a Mecca for the collector of seashells. Shell Beach is not just full of them, but it is made of them, layer upon layer, bank upon bank. Or you may visit Jethou, and combine memories of comedy and tragedy. Here Compton Mackenzie lived, author of such splendid works as *Whisky Galore*; and here, too, in an earlier age, lived the Guernsey hangman, and here his gibbet stood. Take your pick.

We are getting near the end of our island survey, and I shall be returning to one of them, the Isle of Wight, in Chapter 8, so I shall leave it aside until then. Brownsea Island, in Poole Harbour, is an odd little place with an interesting history. Baden-Powell came here in 1907 with a group of boys to show them the secrets of camping out in the countryside. The experiment seemed so successful that he decided to encourage other boys, and so began the Boy Scout movement. More recently the island has been taken over by the National Trust as a nature reserve, with woods and beaches open to the public, and heronry, lakes and marshes as a bird sanctuary. Here you can watch the heron in comfort, but the real treat for ornithologists lies off the north-east coast of England, at the Farne Islands. Huge colonies of birds nest here, screeching and soaring above the grey seals that have also settled in on these lonely rocks. You come here by boat from Seahouses and it is from your bobbing, rocking vessel that you watch. Humans are very much an insignificant minority in this crowded world of creatures to whom the sea is a natural home. You can land on Inner Farne, but the abiding memory is of a small boat on a big sea and of a non-human world with which, for a short while, we have been privileged to make an acquaintance.

This chapter began with the islands of Ireland, many of which have early Christian associations, and it ends with a famous place of pilgrimage. Lindisfarne is joined to the Northumbrian coast at low tide by a causeway, and is cut off again at high tide. Most visitors come on trips and stay the few hours between tides, to see the ruined priory and the castle. Certainly no visitor should miss seeing either, but they do not represent the whole island story. To see it at its best why not stop over? The crowds disappear to avoid being marooned, and you may stroll the solitary sands and the dunes, or explore the old ruins at your leisure. Perhaps that is the message for all island visitors. Never hurry. Allow time for the special island atmosphere to seep through, that atmosphere that distinguishes each island from all others.

# 4
# Country
# Pursuits

*A beautiful canal currently being restored: the Kennet & Avon at Bath* (Anthony Burton)

Britain's greatest appeal lies in diversity. Within a small area you will find just about every conceivable type of geological formation, a fact which becomes instantly obvious if you look at a coloured geological map. The British Isles appear as a brilliant rainbow image, great bands of colour sweeping across the land. You need know nothing at all about geology to appreciate the scenery, but it is the underlying geology that determines what you see in the first place. Man has tinkered and fiddled about on the surface, and the marks of his work are everywhere on view, but the foundations were all laid down millions rather than thousands of years ago. Mostly when we talk about going to the country to look at the scenery it is the 'untouched' scenery we are thinking of, the 'natural' landscape. It is, in reality, very rare to find any spot quite untouched by man; but fortunately past ages have worked with the grain of the country, not against it. In stony land, houses, barns and walls have been built of stone; in rich clay country, that clay has been burnt for brick. It is, or was, a country on a human scale. Much of this is now changed. Under the pressures of modern farming technology, the landscape of small fields is breaking down. Other pressures too are being felt: as roads are improved so the cars crowd in on the lonely places. Local materials are giving way to the drab uniformity of the mass-produced. I do not wish to over-romanticise the past nor contribute my share to the museumisation of Britain. The picturesque, thatched cottage was often an insanitary, leaking hovel; the old pattern of farming was largely one of unremitting drudgery. Nevertheless, it is the diversity of regions allied to a pattern of local building in local materials that gives the countryside of the British Isles a unique appeal. It is not incompatible with improvement and efficiency – and praise be it is still with us.

As any beginning to such a survey of the countryside is likely to be largely arbitrary, I shall start with the place that is foremost in my own mind. It was while writing this book that I took a wintry holiday in the Tamar Valley on the Cornish bank of the river that divides it from Devon. This was an area that seemed to epitomise the virtues that I look for in the country. It had character, seclusion and a fascinating, and sometimes surprising, range of things to see. This is a region which, in the last century, was found to be rich in copper ore and man inevitably set to work to tap these riches. Everywhere you will see the ruins of the old engine-houses, the

*The River Tamar and railway viaduct at Calstock* (Anthony Burton)

visible reminders of the mining past. And not always ruins: go to Calstock, follow the road by the river out under the railway viaduct, keep going up the track through the steeply wooded Danescombe Valley and you will come to Danescombe Mine. Converted by the Landmark Trust, it is now let as a holiday home and it was from here that I went walking and explored the area.

The great advantage of such a place is that there is so much so close at hand. Just walking back to Calstock, you keep finding things to excite the interest. Next to the mine itself is a dark, dripping passageway leading into the hillside, blocked off just a little way in but you can slosh along a few feet for a glimpse of the gloomy interior of the mine. Coming back to the track you meet a little group of cottages, one named Mispickel – not a coy version of an occupant's name but a name for an arsenic-bearing ore,. arsenopyrites. Interesting features abound. Down on the road you can see extensive quays and an odd bridge which seems to carry nothing and go nowhere. What can it be? You need to get a bit further away to arrive at an answer, for then you can see a steep track leading on a very straight diagonal up the hill. The straightness is the clue. This is a railway incline, up and down which trucks were hauled by cable. That might suggest a little excursion, and if you get out the map you can trace the line up to the remains of Incline Station on the East Cornwall Mineral Railway next to the old mine buildings at the top of the hill.

Walk on for a while by the river and you come to Calstock viaduct. People often look and say: 'Great engineers those Victorians; they don't build like that today.' They are out by a reign. Look a little closer at the viaduct: it is not made of stone but of concrete blocks, 11,148 of them to be precise, and it was built not in the last century but in 1907. And if you really want to show off to your companions, try this question: what is the connection between Calstock viaduct and the pre-Raphaelites? Answer: the engineer was Fred Holman Stephens, given his middle name by his art-critic father, who was a great friend of painter Holman Hunt. When you look a little closer at the bridge, you can see large concrete blocks alongside the viaduct piers. A false start perhaps? No, these are the supports for a second line of rails which ran along beside the viaduct to a point above the quay where a steam-powered lift took waggons down to barges on the river.

All this industrial detail may not be to your liking, in which case you can turn to Calstock itself, a delightful little village clambering up the hillside. And here is a non-industrial mystery. Where is the parish church? That is right up on the top of the hill over ½ mile away because that is where the village started. It was the mines and the river traffic that combined to move the settlement down the hill. The church is a great spot for graveyard wanderers. Look for the beautifully carved slate headstones, including one poignant one to a fourteen-year-old lad killed in the mine. If you want more sight-seeing, then wander off downstream from the Danescombe Valley, walking through the woods to Cotehele House. This is a fairly well-known National Trust property and, in my view, one of their finest. In winter it is closed to visitors, disappointing in one way, but there are compensations. The stately homes can seem such museum-like places that it is impossible to believe anyone ever lived there, though Cotehele House is a lot less museumy than most. But in winter, while the occupants live their own lives, members of the public can walk the grounds and feel more like privileged visitors to someone's garden than cash-paying tourists.

The grounds are very fine and there is a little mystery here as well: an odd, circular, domed stone building with a tiny entrance. I thought at first it might be an ice-house, but stoop, go inside, and when your eyes grow accustomed to the gloom you find that it is a dovecot. You can walk on through the woods to Cotehele Quay, a beautifully preserved riverside site with a maritime museum and the restored sailing barge *Shamrock*. It is a fine vessel, but before you begin to yearn for the days when you could have sailed her to trade on the river, it is as well to remember that her principal cargo was manure. Nearby, also restored by the National Trust, is Cotehele Mill and the road leads on through the woods alongside a busy little stream. Few cars come to disturb you and if those few seem too many you can turn on to footpaths. It really matters little where you go, down the deep lanes through the gentle hills, but if thirst and hunger overcome you, then there is always the hope of finding a good, attractive pub for lunch. Looking up the locals in the drinker's bible, *The Good Beer Guide*, I found this irresistible entry for the Carpenters Arms at Metherell: '14th century traditional free house off the beaten track.' It surpassed expectations. A fine old building, Bass straight from the barrel and real home-cooked food. Add to that friendly locals – the only place where I have ever been offered a pinch of *apricot* snuff – and it all seems rather more than you have a right to expect from life.

I have dwelt so long on this one area not because it is exceptional, but because it is *not* exceptional. It is not an area full of spectacular locations, but a quiet corner of quiet beauties, where sun shining through golden reeds on the river bank can produce an unforgettable image. It is a spot which throws up a whole series of questions that it is fun trying to answer – and it really does not matter if you never do arrive at a solution. The pleasure comes in the wandering and the tranquillity, and this place confirmed again what I have so often felt: it is not always the places you are expecting to find that provide the deepest satisfactions.

In the rest of this chapter, I shall be discussing some specific places and specific areas, but I have made no attempt to produce a comprehensive list: one lifetime is much too short to see everything and explore all the forgotten places of the country. The secret lies in not being too ambitious. There is more to be gained in really getting to know one small place than there is in dashing around trying to see a dozen.

The West Country has more than its share of quiet lanes to explore, but those looking for something on a grander scale tend to turn towards the moors. Bodmin Moor receives rather less attention than Dartmoor, but is not necessarily less interesting, for like its neighbour to the east it offers a combination of fine, upland scenery and reminders of an ancient world. The most popular spots are the Cheesewring, weathered rocks that look like a stack of overgrown fossilised cheeses, and Dozmary Pool, a marshy dark lake which would perhaps never have attracted any attention but for Arthurian legend. This, it is claimed, is the pool into which the sword Excalibur was thrown at Arthur's death and from which it will re-emerge when the king at last returns. But those who want the true flavour of Bodmin Moor should set off for its high places, for Rough Tor and Brown Willy, in the centre of the dark moor. It is not an arduous walk, but as with all upland walks those who set off should be aware that a walk on the moors is not without its dangers, albeit avoidable dangers. The jolly afternoon stroll in the sun can become a numbing misery when the weather changes: proper clothing and proper equipment are essentials. What is true of Bodmin Moor is true in even greater measure of Dartmoor.

Dartmoor offers superb country for the experienced walker, and can also offer real pleasures to the dilatory ambler. Certain parts are immensely popular, especially those near road and parking space. Yet even the most popular places are limited to a very tiny part of the moor, and there is much that remains all but untouched. Let me give just one example from the eastern edge of the moor.

Haytor rocks are deservedly popular, one of those great upheavals of granite which children can scramble over for hours. That same granite was also once a popular building stone, and to take it away from the moor the enterprising quarrymen built a unique stone railway. I do not mean a railway to carry stone but a railway built of stone: stone rails, stone loops, even stone points. This is the Haytor Granite Tramway, which can still be seen snaking across the moor to the north of the tor. It is an extraordinary phenomenon. If Stone Age man had ever built railways then this is what they would have looked like. Yet the Haytor Tramway is not that old, just a nineteenth-century railway, built in a land where iron was dear and stone cheap, designed to make it easier for horses to haul truckloads of granite across the moor.

The West Country moors each have their own devotees. There are some who much prefer the smoother, rounded hills and valleys of Exmoor to the harsh stoniness of Bodmin and Dartmoor. Some moors, however, are altogether different. Not moors in that sense at

*The extraordinary Haytor Granite Tramway on Dartmoor* (Anthony Burton)

*Burrow Mump: the hill once guarded King Alfred's Somerset stronghold* (Anthony Burton)

all but areas of wetland, set low between the hills. Such areas can be found in Sedgemoor, Somerton Moor and the other stretches of land that go to make up the Somerset Levels. This is a region which seems to be an émigré, crept across from the Fens and marshes of East Anglia. It is an area for the lonely, those who take their pleasures in walking a wide land under wide skies, looking for little more than the casual interplay of light between earth and air, the magical, if accidental moment when the elements seem to combine and dissolve at a distant horizon. This is a region of slow cattle, of lush meadow-land ruled by drainage ditches, where the willow is still a crop of some importance. Here they grow the tree for wood for cricket bats and still gather the young shoots for basket-making. It is also a land of history. Before the drainage schemes began, man was limited to the island rising above the flooded marshes. It was here that King Alfred came to hide and rally his forces for the fight against the Danes. There is a reminder of those times at Burrow

94

Bridge on the River Parrett. A small but startling hill shoots up from the flatness; this was once the stronghold that guarded the path to Alfred's headquarters. Not many people come here and not all who come find it to their liking, but some succumb to its special atmosphere.

The Somerset Levels derive their nature from the surrounding hills which drain down into them, so that going to the area you experience great contrasts between the flat, wetlands and the surrounding hills. The Mendips to the north are popular in places: Cheddar Gorge, for example, has no shortage of visitors. Yet other parts remain almost unknown. The Mendips is a strange area which also looks as if it has strayed down from another part of England, in this case from the north, for it is a landscape of moorland and hill, laced by dry limestone walls that look very Pennine. It does however, have its own characteristics that mark it as West Country. The thatched cottages that are common in the area are certainly more southern than north country. The Romans came here to mine for lead and later generations followed them. Walk the hills around Charterhouse and you can see signs in plenty: you can pick up shiny black lumps of lead slag, and you also stand a good chance of seeing the occasional adder.

Over in Dorset you have one of the most impressive of all the strongholds built before the Romans came – Maiden Castle, 2 miles south of Dorchester. There has been a fortress here for almost 5,000 years, but do not think of it as a castle like a Norman motte-and-bailey. The immense earth ramparts enclose two hills spreading over 45 acres of ground. It is a place where you can marvel at the scale of the ancient works, and where you can easily envisage the drama that was once enacted here. The Romans arrived in about AD44 and the British were ready with their slings and literally thousands of stones collected from Chesil Beach. The attackers had artillery and well-armed, well-disciplined troops. The outcome was always certain. Archaeologists have seen the evidence of that end. They have opened the graves where the British buried their dead with a mug of beer and a hunk of meat to see them on their way to the next world.

The south-east of England can seem to a northerner to have too many places and too many people for comfort. Even the Downs seem permanently busy. No one can respond with equal enthusiasm to all types of scenery, and this corner always seems to me to be just a shade too comfortable, with its tile-hung cottages glowing bright in the sun, its rich pasture and arable land and the well-ordered neatness of villages long since given over to the prosperous commuter. I like the woods best, the ancient forest of the Weald, the area where once the forges rang out to produce the great array of iron swords, spears and arrows for the soldiers of the Middle Ages. The memory resides in shaded ponds in the woods – Hammer pond, Forge pond, names that tell you of old uses. Here men dammed the streams to hold back the water that would eventually be released to the water-wheels that powered the great hammers. Yet these are, at best, faint echoes in a world that is often too urbane for my taste, but which, I have to admit, gives immense satisfaction to others.

There are so many places in England to visit, so many varied scenes to enjoy, places where you really feel you can lose yourself not just in the landscape, but in the past as well. If I seem to enthuse unduly over East Anglia, it is because for me it has been a comparatively recent discovery. I always felt that the hills were my stamping ground, not the flat lands of Norfolk, Suffolk and Cambridgeshire. I was prepared to tolerate the Broads in the days

*The two churches at Swaffham Prior* (British Tourist Authority)

when people moved over the water in civilised fashion under sail, untroubled by the summer clamour of fleets of motor cruisers, but that was about all. When eventually I did begin to explore the region, I found old prejudices slipping off like discarded snake skins. The first surprise was the churches, briefly mentioned in Chapter 2, churches which often appear amazingly grand but to have carelessly mislaid the important communities they were intended to serve. They are, in fact, memories of a more prosperous past, when the region was the centre of Britain's wool trade. Look at the glorious rich stonework of Long Melford's church, for example, or the splendours of Lavenham. The oddest place in the whole region, however, must be Swaffham Prior in Cambridgeshire, which can boast two fine churches in the village – not widely separated, not stuck away in opposite corners, but side by side sat in the middle of the one churchyard. One's curiosity is inevitably aroused. There were, it seems, two lords of two manors. Each of them built a church and the locals went to one or the other depending on where their allegiance lay. Whether this is an example of splendid piety or petty rivalry is now all conjecture. You can spend an age wandering around East Anglia doing little more than marvel at the splendour of the churches, but there is a lot more to see as well.

The Breckland is unique, Britain's equivalent of the Dust Bowls of America. Once it was fertile land but successive generations stripped it of its cover of trees; the east winds blew and the thin soil blew with them. Ultimate disaster struck somewhere around the end of the thirteenth century when a sandstorm hit the area, burying fields and obliterating settlements. Farming was ended, but the area was not altogether useless. The sand may have been disastrous for the human but it was perfect for rabbits, and the big landlords promptly claimed ownership of the rabbit warrens just as they had of the older fields. Warreners were appointed to keep hoi polloi away from the game. This was not an occupation that was very popular with the surrounding villagers, and the warreners' houses were like little castles. You can still see the warrener's lodge that was set up by the Prior of Thetford. But the Breckland is changing, for forestry has taken over much of the land. The sand is still there underfoot but the old sense of desolation has largely gone. It is an area where you can wander from woodland to heath and back to woodland again. And you can also, thanks to the work of archaeologists, catch a glimpse of life before the great sands came. At West Stow the old Anglo-Saxon village was carefully excavated

and then re-created using traditional materials and traditional methods.

The Breckland is essentially an arid, almost desert region, dotted with tiny meres; a good deal of East Anglia is quite the opposite, wetland, the land of fen and broad. The Broads need no extra publicity from me but the Fens are a different matter. At their heart lies Ely cathedral, the great tower of which dominates the whole landscape. Once Ely was an island, but drainage has altogether changed much of the area so that little true fenland remains. One area has been preserved, Wicken Fen and the surrounding land, now in the ownership of the National Trust. It is a bird sanctuary, and the majority of visitors come to watch the wildlife; but non-ornithologists also find this a strange, slightly mysterious place of still water, reed and sedge. There is a reminder, too, of what happened to the wetlands, in the form of a small windmill, typical of so many that once powered pumps in the area. But to get the true feel of the region it is probably better to see it from the water than from the land.

The popularity of Britain's inland waterways for holidays has grown enormously in recent years, and the amount of advertising in the national press might suggest that all are crammed with boats. Some are. If you wish to get away from the crowds I would not recommend, say, the Thames below Oxford or the Llangollen Canal in high summer. This is not the case with the East Anglian waterways with the exception of the Broads. The Great Ouse, the Cam, the lovely wandering Nene, are all surprisingly little known, while the navigable drainage canals of the Middle Level are all but deserted. These are the main streams but there are even more remote tributaries to explore which offer equal delights. And there is so much to enjoy in the area, from its own version of Cup Final Day, when the village of Ashton is home to the National Conker Championships, to the wildness of Pope's Corner, and one of the best puns I know on a pub sign, of the Fish and Duck Inn.

Other canals around Britain still offer comparative seclusion, even in the crowded Midlands, and as with the Fens it is tempting to say that here is the best way of exploring the region. Walking in agricultural areas is often a frustrating experience. Footpaths shown on the Ordnance Survey map fail to appear on the ground,

(opposite) *A gamekeeper's fortress, Warren Lodge in the Breckland* (Crown copyright, reproduced by permission of the Controller of HMSO); *the reconstructed Anglo-Saxon village of West Stow* (West Stow Anglo-Saxon Village Trust)

*A lonely Fenland junction where Bevils Leam and Whittlesey Dyke meet* (Derek Pratt)

having been ploughed up by overenthusiastic farmers. There are also untouched areas of the Midlands but these are few and, it often seems, getting fewer. The Midlands can, however, boast one of the most remarkable small regions of wetland in the whole country, Otmoor to the north-east of Oxford. Seen first from the hill at Beckley it appears as a chequer-board of ditches and boundaries, a resemblance noted by an Oxford don in the last century and one which gave him the notion for a book with chessboard characters. That author was Lewis Carroll. It has changed since then but not so dramatically as to lose its individuality, and it remains unique for its wealth of flowers and butterflies. Come here in summer and you will find an incredibly rich landscape with a profusion of orchids that would put the most exotic florist's shop to shame. The moor has been under attack – both from the local water authority who wish to drain it, and from the Department of Transport who wanted to build a motorway over it. Both have been soundly resisted and defeated, a victory for once for those who see the need to keep at least some of our countryside open and wild. Though, given the obduracy of bureaucrats and politicians, one can never be certain of having achieved final victory.

Otmoors are somewhat scarce, so let us return to the canal theme. Canals offer routes through the depths of the countryside for boaters – and routes for walkers, for the towpaths are open to all. Take the

Ashby Canal, for example, which runs lock-free from a junction with the Coventry Canal to Snarestone, for much of its way wriggling and winding like a river or stream rather than an artificial waterway. You can stop off at Shackerstone and take the steam train to Market Bosworth, a pleasant town with one particular feature to appeal to the beer fraternity. If you wish to test the expert knowledge of a beerophile, try this question: in 1982 I went for a drink in a Hoskins pub; where was I? The answer is the Red Lion at Market Bosworth, then the brewery's only house. Those with an interest in the past – or in a mood to declaim soliloquies whilst adopting grotesque poses – might prefer to visit nearby Bosworth Field where Richard III failed to get a horse at any price. And when the waterway comes to an end, you can still continue on foot following the towpath along the unnavigable canal (see page 254).

An equally splendid and remote route can be found on the Chesterfield Canal, while a great favourite of mine is the Caldon, which starts in Etruria at the heart of the Potteries and then wanders off into ever more lonely countryside as it edges up to the Staffordshire moors. Similar stories can be repeated about other canals in other parts of Britain – for example the Brecon & Abergavenny which runs through the Brecon Beacons National Park or the recently restored Ripon Canal in Yorkshire. There is no space to list them all here – and I do not wish to be accused of riding my own hobby horse for too long, as I have been more or less besotted by canal travel for well over twenty years. Those who want to try out the waterways should look at one of the specialist books on the subject. If you want a simple test of how crowded a particular route is likely to be just check on the hire firms in the area and the number of boats on offer.

To return briefly to the Caldon Canal, it is an interesting route in many ways quite apart from the splendid scenery it can offer. You can stop off at Cheddleton where a pair of old water-mills have been restored, not grinding grain for flour but flint for use in the pottery industry. It ends in the basin at Froghall. And here you have a number of options. You can set off and explore the moorland of Staffordshire. People tend to ask you to repeat that phrase, thinking that they must have misheard. The moors of Staffordshire? Surely the county is potteries and Black Country not moorland. But the moors are there, far less frequented than the neighbouring Peak District of Derbyshire and all the better for that. A second alternative is to continue the exploration of the lovely Churnet

*The Derbyshire hills with the deep V of a railway cutting on the horizon, now used as a footpath* (Anthony Burton)

Valley which the canal had been following until it came to this abrupt halt. Or you can pursue the other system that has taken over from the canal, the tramway or early railway on which trucks were hauled by horses. The old line can be followed as a footpath above the massive lime kilns. It heads off to the quarries of Cauldon Low which gave the canal its name. In fact, you can use this as an introduction to an alternative method of exploring the countryside, by disused railway. Just to the north of Cauldon Low, on the main A523 road, is the village of Waterhouses, which was once the terminus of the Leek & Manifold Valley Light Railway. The railway itself is long gone, but the trackbed remains, resurfaced and available for use by walkers and cyclists. You do not even need to possess a bike to ride along it, for there is a bicycle hire centre here,

just one of a number in the area, all designed to help the visitor make the most of the old railway.

Not everyone is attracted to the idea of walking or cycling old railways, envisaging no doubt long, dull straight lines confining the traveller. This is not the case here. True, railways have by their very nature to keep a more or less even route, but in order to do so the engineers have often been forced to extreme measures: valleys are crossed on embankments and viaducts which give bird's-eye views of the countryside; hills are pierced by tunnels and cuttings which, if not giving worm's-eye views, do limit the traveller to inspecting the immediate environment. Of all the railway walks on offer throughout Britain, this region offers one of the finest selections and certainly the route up the valleys of the Rivers Hamps and Manifold stands comparison with the best. The start is gentle enough, but soon the valley narrows, the limestone crags loom above the path, grandest of all being the hills around Wetton with the spectacular Thor's Cave, a yawning mouth near the summit, and if you climb the hill to inspect the cave – and it is well worth the trouble – and carry on over the top to the next valley, you will find another railway walk, the Tissington Trail. The character of this line is quite different, that of a comparatively modern railway, shouldering aside the natural obstacles of hill and dale. This one takes you to the heart of the Derbyshire Peak District, a land where hills and valleys are tied together by a network of dry stone walls of limestone that glistens palely in the sun. This trail in turn links in with another, based on the old Cromford & High Peak Railway.

In recent years I have walked many old railways but few that can compare with this Derbyshire line. It was built before the age of the steam locomotive, though it lasted well enough to survive into the later era. This was a time when railways went up hills the short way, climbing steep slopes with the trucks hauled by cable. This line has a series of these inclines carrying it up from the Cromford Canal down in the Derwent Valley to the high land of the Peak. One of the original steam engines used for this work is preserved at Middleton Top Engine house, a splendid sight not to be missed by anyone using the trail. But even those who take no delight in steam will find the route itself superb, for once the engineers had got their line to the high ground they could only keep it there by snaking a complex route through the hills. Walk it or cycle it, the High Peak trail provides a superb introduction to the scenery of Derbyshire. As with canals, there is only space to list a few railway walks among many spread throughout the country. There are seaside lines, country lines and urban lines; lines where a whole range of original features have been preserved, such as the station complex at Tintern Parva in Gwent, and others where something of a detective instinct is required if any traces of railway use are to be identified.

Our excursion on to the railways has brought us north into the Pennine hills. The north of England has always been, for me, essentially hill country. Certainly there are flat bits; the Vale of York can scarcely raise a pimple on the horizon, but such areas were always regarded by those of us raised among the hills as foreign to the essential nature of the region. Yet, even here, distinctions were made between the essentially rural areas and those besmirched by the muck of industry. Not surprisingly, it is the former which have received the most attention and which in recent years have been given a massive dose of TV publicity to the extent that the Dales have become known as 'Herriot country' after the vet turned author.

But the Dales have not had it all their own way: there has also been a movement towards re-examining the old cotton-spinning valleys of Lancashire and the woollen districts of Yorkshire. For a long time tourists have been visiting Haworth and exclaiming over its picturesque charm, having been lured there because of the Brontë connection or possibly even the rail connection, for the town is served by the Worth Valley Steam Railway. What is only just being realised is that there are many more villages with the same visual, if not literary and railway, appeal. What is that special appeal?

It seems to me to be twofold. It starts with the buildings themselves and the materials they are built from, for these are places of stone and not just any stone but that same black gritstone that can be seen thrusting through the hilltops. There is nothing soft here, for the Pennines can be a harsh area, especially in winter, when the buildings seem to huddle together for warmth, but that same sense of closeness means that you get little gaps and alleys, chinks in the strong defences, constantly changing viewpoints. The other appeal to me is that this is still essentially a working world, even if the depression of the 1980s has hit hard. This was the birthplace of the industrial world and there is a pride in past achievement, even if occasionally accompanied by a romantic aura that fits uneasily with the harshness of those times. The reality survives if only because the places themselves are so essentially, so sturdily uncompromising. Even in places such as Hebden Bridge, which now has a host of antique and craft shops, the past has not been submerged. And if you go up the steep hill with its old cobbled packhorse route to Heptonstall, with its unusual hexagonal Wesleyan chapel, you really do enter the old world and no doubt about it. You can travel on back down into the valley to Todmorden, where the prettification has not yet taken hold. But all these places share another characteristic: they sit solid on the landscape and draw their strength from the hardness of the land – and the wild landscape is never far away. You can walk out of a little Lancashire cotton village and find yourself in almost no time at all in a spot as remote as you could wish. Walk east out of Nelson and you find yourself heading towards Wadsworth Moor, walk west and you are faced by the isolated splendour of Pendle Hill.

If I want more traditional dales and moorland scenery then I prefer to head away from the more popular areas, but there are at least one or two things which no one should miss. The North Yorkshire Moors, especially in the area around Goathland, are

*Wade's Causeway, the Roman military road on the moors above Goathland* (Derek G. Widdicombe)

deservedly popular: but take the road out of the village to the west and then walk up the hill past the youth hostel. On top of the moor you will find Wade's Causeway, an extraordinarily well-preserved Roman road, not one of the famous straight-line highways but a military route. You can see how it is built up on a low embankment and paved with great sandstone blocks. Look especially at the little culverts under the road, beautifully constructed out of stone. It is as impressive in its way as any of the Roman remains of Britain. Looking further north, you find the well-known attractions of Teesdale and how very splendid they are. The great waterfall of High Force is much visited, but equally fine and far less frequented is Cauldron Snout. If even that seems too popular, why not move on again north from Teesdale to one of the best and least appreciated of all the dales, Weardale. It is not too surprising that these river valleys have much in common, for they all drain down from the

Pennine hills. Up on Cross Fell you can walk in no time at all from the source of the Tyne to that of the Tees.

The waters draining down to the west come to the Lake District, one of the first areas to be 'discovered' by the tourists of Britain. They came here in droves in the eighteenth century to hunt out the picturesque. They were followed by the Romantics of the nineteenth century, searching for Wordsworth's daffodils. And we still come today to look for wild beauty and solitude, and too often find traffic jams instead. I shall be looking at one aspect of Lakeland travel in Chapter 8, but for the moment why not turn away from the heartland of the Lake District to the surrounding areas? The Eden Valley stretches down from Carlisle in the north to reach into the more popular tourist regions, but throughout much of its length it encompasses the scenery of moorland and fell without the clamour of the coach party and the guided tour. What you lose in high drama you more than gain in seclusion and peace. For those who would look for ever wider horizons, one could turn to what is perhaps one of the emptiest and loneliest of regions, the Borderland between England and Scotland. This is countryside quite unlike that of the rest of Britain – mountainous certainly, but without that hard edge that marks so much of the upland scene. Here the ground swells and heaves itself into great, rounded masses – a soft, almost indistinct sort of landscape. The border itself is no clearer, and historically it seldom has been clear. The Romans tried to mark off one division, when they built Hadrian's Wall, but the border has never seemed a precise affair. It was a no-man's-land, open to raiders from north and south.

The land itself may not be harsh, but its history has been and that history has left its mark on the region. There may be little hint of a bloody past in the all but deserted Cheviot Hills, but drop down into almost any settlement and a different story soon becomes apparent. The village of Elsdon, for example, on the southern edge of the hills, typifies much of the region. At first sight it is as peaceful a spot as you could wish to find, with pleasing Georgian houses looking out over the village green, beneath the smooth, grassy hills. But· go to the church, a turreted fourteenth-century building of considerable charm, and another side of the story appears. Archaeologists found hundreds of skeletons along the church walls, victims of the Battle of Otterburn of 1388. But it was not the big wars as much as the repeated small raids that really left their mark. If you were important enough and rich enough in those bloody days, then you

turned your house into a fortress. That is just what the rectory of Elsdon is, a stronghold and a refuge against the marauders. There are strongholds of even earlier date to the north in the ancient earthworks of Manside Camp, and even when you feel peace is the order of the day, evidence appears to cast a dark shadow. The road south towards Rothley offers magnificent views and a famous ancient landmark, the Steng Cross – but here too the other, darker side of history can be seen in the decaying eighteenth-century gibbet. Today it all makes a most extraordinary contrast between what is and what was, between one of the most peaceful parts of the land and history shot with blood.

'The border' was first fortified in really massive fashion by the Romans. Hadrian's Wall is so well known and so popular with visitors that the sheer numbers are giving real concern to those responsible for its preservation. It is not, however, the only Roman fortification to divide north and south. The Antonine Wall, further north, was built around AD142, and some have said that the main reason for building it was the need to keep the soldiers busy. There was a good deal of grumbling about being stationed in the lonely, chilly north, and grumbling within Roman armies had an unhappy tendency to lead to mutiny. Better give the chaps something to do, might well have been the commander's response. What they did was build an earthwork defence, a high rampart and a ditch, with forts set every couple of miles. It is not as impressive as Hadrian's Wall, but it does have its own fascination. There is a bathhouse at Bearsden, but perhaps the most exciting spot is Rough Castle, off the B816, 6 miles west of Falkirk. What you find when you reach Rough Castle might lead you to believe that the wall was something more than an early Manpower Services scheme. Mantraps were dug beyond the wall, and were disguised by twigs and brushwood. The pits beneath contained sharpened wooden stakes ready to impale the incautious Scot.

Those who go north into Scotland tend to think in terms of Highland scenery and regard the country between the border and a line drawn from Edinburgh to Glasgow as an area to dash through as quickly as possible. It is true that the region cannot match the more northerly Highlands for grandeur, if you measure hills off by height above sea-level. But those who know the Lowther Hills would argue that they can boast a scenery as fine as any, combining

*Border country, the summit cairn on the Cheviot* (Derek G. Widdicombe)

*The Antonine Wall and the Roman fort of Rough Castle* (Royal Commission on the Ancient & Historical Monuments of Scotland: J. Dewar)

*The Miners' Library at Wanlockhead* (Wanlockhead Museum Trust)

beauty with a fascinating, working past. I have made several visits
to the area around Leadhills and Wanlockhead. It was once, as the
first name might suggest, a lead-mining area, and evidence of that
activity is not difficult to find – and there is ample evidence, too, of
the serious nature of the lead-miners. The Leadhills subscription
library – the Allan Ramsay Library – was founded way back in 1741
and is still there today. Not of itself a remarkable building perhaps,
but it was remarkable to find such an institution at such a place and
at such a time. This is a region full of interest, but never full of
people; a stark, bare landscape. Those looking for a more gentle land
might prefer to move south to what often seems to be Scotland's
afterthought, the region of Dumfries and Galloway. But do not
think for a moment that this is not a very Scottish region, for here
you will find two 'Bruce's Stones', commemorating Robert the
Bruce's victories over the Sassenachs. Nowadays, the locals can
afford to be magnanimous towards the losers, and welcome them to

the Galloway Forest Park, 150,000 acres of forest and loch, home to herds of wild deer. I think of this region as being one of Scotland's best-kept secrets.

Inevitably, however, those who come to Scotland begin to hanker after Highland scenery. Loch Lomond is, as they all tell us, bonny, but it is not a patch on Loch Katrine, where visitors can travel the waters aboard the vintage steamer, *Sir Walter Scott*. Steamers are rare survivors in this day and age, but there is an excellent reason why this one is still with us. The loch is used to supply water for Glasgow and any other form of powered vessel, petrol or diesel, would pollute the water. So steam it must be, and this elegant vessel has been puffing to and fro ever since she went into service in 1900. Beautiful scenery seen from a beautiful craft – what more could you ask? In fact all that many of us ask is to be allowed to go off on our own, on foot, to enjoy the mountains in solitude. This is still possible in many parts of Scotland, but I must again add a note of warning. Those who wish to enjoy the mountains to the full must be properly equipped and aware of what they are taking on. Properly equipped means properly shod, provided with good, genuinely waterproof clothing and having large-scale map and compass – and, of course, the ability to use the last two. This may seem too obvious to need stating to the experienced walker and unduly fussy to the inexperienced. To the former, I can only say that no one starts off with

*The steamer* Sir Walter Scott *on Loch Katrine* (Strathclyde Water Department)

*The Five Sisters of Kintail* (Scottish Tourist Board)

experience, and to the latter, if ever you get caught in the hills by a change of weather for which you are not equipped, just pray very hard that you survive to learn from the experience. Having sounded that sombre note, I have to say that the effort of getting properly equipped is amply repaid. I have been walking the hills since I was a schoolboy and hope to continue for as long as my legs will take me. There are books in plenty for the hill-walker specialist, and it would be out of place here to list all the delights of the mountain regions of Scotland; so I am going to offer just a few suggestions to those who wish to make a first acquaintance with some of the world's finest scenery.

One very useful way of gaining an introduction to the hills is via one of the visitors' centres run by bodies such as the Countryside Commission and the National Trust for Scotland. The latter have two excellent centres near the west coast from which you can take planned walks ranging from a comparatively gentle amble to a

rugged and arduous day's outing. The Torridon Visitors' Centre is an ideal starting place for an exploration of the surrounding hills. There are carparks near the starts of routes and well-defined paths, but these are more than short strolls. You will know you have been on a proper hill walk by the time you get back. The Visitors' Centre at Morvich on the road to Kyle of Lochalsh is a starting point for the exploration of Kintail, an area known for the splendid range of peaks, the Five Sisters. Here, too, you can find one of the most satisfyingly wild and romantic spots in the whole of the Highlands, If you could drive up to the Falls of Glomach you would scarcely see them for visitors, but you can't – you need to walk from the Forestry Commission carpark at Dorusduain, and if you follow the recommended walk, a circular trip via Loch Gaorsaic, you need to allow seven hours for the trip, though you can shorten the walk by just going to the falls and back, no more than three hours' exercise. It is well worth the effort. It is not just that these are among the highest falls in Britain, for size alone means nothing if the setting is wrong. I shall always remember the hopeless sense of anticlimax on seeing Niagara. The falls themselves are splendid, but the surrounding buildings and souvenir stalls removed all sense of being in the presence of a natural phenomenon. It almost seemed as if the falls were artificial, built for the tourist trade. There is no sense of that at Glomach. This is a wild, dark, rocky ravine where you could spend the day with no company but the buzzards and where you might, if lucky, catch a glimpse of a great golden eagle high above you.

You can see scenery of equal grandeur with less exertion on your part, but inevitably you will not experience that special pleasure that comes from solitude. Travel northwards and 12 miles south of Ullapool, off the A835, you will find Corrieshalloch Gorge. This 200ft (60m) deep narrow wooded cleft is a mile long and contains the high falls of Measach. There are walkways through the woods and a spectacular view from a little suspension bridge across the gorge. You are now, in any case, on the very edge of a region where there is no need to go hunting for the wilderness: it is all around you. The north-west corner of Scotland seems scarcely touched by roads; there are just tracts of empty lands, of rivers, lakes and mountains. No need here for a guidebook to point you in the right direction – just go where you will and the splendours will appear. I must, however, make just one suggestion: do try and get at least a glimpse

*The lonely Falls of Glomach* (National Trust for Scotland)

*The Corrieshalloch Gorge* (National Trust for Scotland: Stewart Guthrie)

of the most remarkable mountains in Britain. Go north from Ullapool and see the lonely peak of Suilven and the great cliffs of Quinag, facing out to the west, and best seen in the evening when the setting sun flares them to a startling, brilliant red. For the rest, just choose your area, explore and discover for yourself a genuinely unspoiled area of Britain.

Wales, too, can boast its unspoiled areas, and its ancient border fortifications. Offa's Dyke was built by Offa, King of Mercia, in the eighth century. Having driven the British back into the mountains of Wales, he set about keeping them there by building this great earthwork of bank and ditch, which runs from Prestatyn in the north to Sedbury, near Chepstow, in the south, 149 miles in all. Those who blanch at the notion of following the route of the whole dyke might like to sample some of the more interesting sections. Just north of the Vale of Crucis is a memorial to Offa's enemies. Eliseg's Pillar is a tall, incised stone celebrating the deeds of Eliseg, King of Powys. The other main features of the area are the hill-forts, their ramparts following the natural contours of the land. Dyke and hill-fort meet at Breidden Hill, to the north of Welshpool. In many ways, this border area has a great deal in common with the England–Scotland border. There are the well-known border castles, but there are too areas of almost unknown territory to explore. There are regions such as the Radnor Forest or, even more remote in feeling if not in geography, the area of Shropshire countryside around Snailbeach. This is old lead-mining territory, but the miners have long gone, leaving an eerie landscape behind them. This is the sort of region where all good industrial archaeologists hope to be sent when they die, but seems, in fact, to fascinate all who come here. Nature is slowly recolonising the old workings, but still the landscape seems to belong to a quite different planet.

Wales itself is conventionally divided, like Gaul, into three parts. There is the North, which is mountains, National Park and beautiful; the South, which is miners' choirs, industry and ugly; and the bit in between which no one is sure about. It should by now come as no surprise to the reader to be told that such categories are misleading. The North has a good deal more to offer than simple scenic pleasures. Only those who have never spent time in South Wales could ever think it ugly. And central Wales, far from being nondescript, can seem to encapsulate all that is best in the country.

In many ways I have always felt at home in South Wales, for the essential character is very similar to that of my native West

Yorkshire. You have the same areas of industrialisation in the valleys, with the same scenery of mountain and moorland reaching down to the doorsteps. There are certain very popular areas such as the Brecon Beacons, though even these have never attracted the crowds in the way that, say, Snowdonia has. But my inclinations have always led me to the valleys. Here it is the combination of scenery and history that gives the area a very special appeal and I shall look at that in more detail in Chapter 8 when we start to follow trails. For the moment, as a taster, let me commend a little walk that I followed recently. I set out to trace the track of the Penydarren tramway. This is just one of many transport routes connecting industry to canals and ports in South Wales. It was used by horsedrawn trucks and the iron rails were set on square, stone sleeper blocks, many of which survived as clues to the direction that the old route took. This one has a very special significance for it was here in 1804 that Richard Trevithick set his newly invented steam locomotive on the tracks, hitched up a train of waggons behind it and chuffed away in style. The railway age had begun. You can follow the line from Quaker's Yard, northwards towards Merthyr Tydfil up the beautiful wooded valley of the Taff. As you go you can imagine the little fire-breathing, snorting monster-of-an-engine off on its way to open up a new world. What a shock it must have been to anyone coming upon it by chance on that day, and how odd it seems now to follow this quiet, country pathway and then to think of it as providing the setting for the drama.

North Wales is the best-known region for those who wish to enjoy the delights of mountains and, like the Lake District, requires no extra publicity, though there are aspects of the region that we shall be looking at in a later chapter. Mid Wales offers a very different prospect. It is difficult to categorise it except for a series of negatives. It is not industrialised like the South; it is not as mountainous as the North. There are no great towns; there are not, in fact, many towns of any size at all. It can seem little more than the empty heartland of the country. But you can wander at your leisure over wide tracks. You can watch the hill farmers of the Black Mountains visiting their flocks, often on horseback, riding sturdy Welsh mountain ponies. You can even take a peep into what may be a view of the future in an old slate quarry near Pantperthog. The Centre for Alternative Technology was set up to investigate new ways of using the natural elements, sun, wind and water, to provide heat, to generate power and to keep us in comfort. It looks at our

*An experimental wind turbine at the National Centre for Alternative Technology, Machynlleth* (National Centre for Alternative Technology)

throwaway rubbish as reusable material not just as filth and litter. The alternatives to conventional sources of power may turn out not to work, but most people who go there come away feeling refreshed. There is a sense of man working with the rest of nature, not just endlessly destroying and polluting it. It may all be a dream; but it makes a change from the nightmare.

I was talking to an Irishman recently who said that he regarded most of his country as being undiscovered and I am inclined to agree with him. I have never found any part unduly crowded – even famous Blarney Castle, home of the even more famous stone which you can kiss if you don't mind dangling down from the battlements, was uncrowded in midsummer. Another famous beauty spot is Meeting of the Waters in Wicklow, praised in verse by Thomas Moore and much visited by tourists. Yet you need only travel a very short distance to find other visual delights. Up the hillside you will find an old estate replanted by the Irish Forestry and there you may sit or walk and watch the bus-loads down below at the Meeting, while all around you the rhododendrons and azaleas bloom. And if you prefer even grander, wider vistas, then follow the signpost up a steep and winding road to the Motte Stone, a gigantic boulder which can be climbed by an iron ladder. Once on top you have the whole of Wicklow at your feet and beyond that the sea. Few people seem to have heard of the stone and nor would I have done had it not been for a friendly correspondent from An Taisce.

Ireland is a wonderful country for going in any direction the mood takes you. Roads are blissfully uncrowded so that even driving becomes a pleasure. And if you have ever wondered how it came to be called the Emerald Isle then your first sight of the miraculously lush pastures will answer that one. It is also a country of water, of lakes and islands, and that provides as good a way as any of gaining an introduction to the country. Get on a boat. If the roads of Ireland have about the same volume of traffic as pre-war England, then so too the waterways are notably uncrowded. The Irish are keen to promote their waterways: they hand out badges and free beer to anyone coping with the little-used Barrow Navigation, south-west of Dublin. The less adventurous might prefer Lough Erne, just north of the border, which is really two lakes joined by a short navigable channel. The area covered is immense, equal to all the Lakes and the Broads put together with a couple of Scottish lochs thrown in for

*A double-faced Janus figure on Boa Island* (Kenneth McNally)

120

good measure. It is not, however, just a great expanse of water, for there are 154 islands, some inhabited, others not. On these islands you will find some of the most interesting and most mysterious carved figures you will ever see: there are the two-faced Janus statues of Boa Island, the Celtic carvings of Devenish and the strange figures of unknown origin that stand on White Island. There were early Christian settlements on the islands, while the Devenish round tower is one of the best preserved in the country. You can island-hop or investigate the settlements on the shore and you can cruise beneath the shadow of the great limestone cliffs of Magho.

The most popular waterway of Ireland is the Shannon, which well deserves its popularity. It is no ordinary river, for in many places it opens out into broad loughs, ensuring that if you travel the whole navigable length of over 100 miles you will never get bored. If, however, you are looking for sailing rather than motor cruising, and like to have a lot of room to play with then you will find room enough at Lough Neagh, more of an inland sea than a lake with over 150sq miles of open water. Come here in springtime and you can witness a most extraordinary sight. Go along to the eel fishery at Toome and you can watch the migration of the elvers. These tiny eels have taken three years to cross from their spawning grounds in the Sargasso Sea and they find their way up the River Bann to Lough Neagh; around twenty million of them every spring.

Ireland has always seemed to me to be a place to visit with as few preconceptions, and as little planning, as possible. There is nowhere in the world where there is more to be said in favour of chance encounters. On an early visit we became friendly with a local farmer and joined him and his sons up on their bog, loading peat into the farm cart. The cart was filled and we lay back in the sun enjoying pavement-slab-sized sandwiches. Then the kids clambered on top of the peat, and the horse was set back into the shafts to saunter off back down the empty lanes. It is such incidental pleasures, such unlooked-for delights that make an Irish holiday so very different. But if you do wish to make definite plans, then the ancient history of Ireland might entice you. There is no better starting point than the Valley of the Boyne between Drogheda and Slane. Here you will find Brugh Na Boinne, not just the finest prehistoric site in Ireland but one of the most remarkable to be found in Europe. This is a graveyard of kings, a Stone Age burial site of great complexity

*The River Shannon at Killaloe* (Kenneth McNally)

The mysterious interior of Newgrange at *Brugh Na Boinne* (Commissioners of Public Works, Ireland)

An Ogam stone at Dunloe, County Kerry (Commissioners of Public Works, Ireland)

dating back to the third millennium BC. The first sight may not be immediately encouraging. You turn off the Old Bridge–Slane road on to a country lane and there on high land enclosed by a bend of the river is the ancient graveyard, stretching over a distance of some 2 miles. There are humps and bumps and standing stones, scattered in no immediately obvious order. But this is not a place for surface show; the true fascination lies beneath the huge mounds that dominate the scene. The best-preserved of these mounds is Newgrange, over 40ft (12m) high and nearly 300ft (90m) in diameter. A stone entrance leads down a long, stone-lined passage to the heart of the tumulus where it opens out into a magnificent chamber. A variety of geometric patterns have been carved on the stones that form the chamber. Their significance has long since been lost, though this has not prevented – indeed has encouraged – speculation. It is said that some of the more complex patterns are 'staring stones': if you follow the convoluted lines with your eyes you release energy which is supposed to be able to affect distant objects and aid telepathy. I remain a sceptic.

There is no shortage of antiquities to discover: there are literally hundreds of Ogam stones, for example – standing stones incised at the corner with lines which represent a simple alphabet. Deciphered, the Ogam writing becomes recognisable as the Irish language. There is so much to see but those who hunt for the Irish past must always end up at one spot. It is not spectacular, little more than a few earthworks on a low hill, but the hill is the hill of Tara near Ceanannas Mór in County Meath, which is the ancient crowning place of the Celtic kings of Ireland. It was chosen because it was already an ancient, and it seemed to them, a holy site from days long past. It is a place to pause and muse over a long history. And pausing and thinking, or even just pausing, are a central part of the experience of Ireland.

# 5
# Provincial Pleasures

*The magnificent interior of the Crown Liquor Saloon, Belfast* (National Trust for Ireland: Anderson & McMeekin Photography)

The word 'provincial' has come to have something of a pejorative meaning. 'How very provincial,' people say, implying a lack of sophistication, a hick-town mentality. Yet most of us live in the provinces, and even those who make their homes in the capitals do occasionally creep out for forays into the hinterland. Somehow, though, the feeling lingers that provincial means second-best, a country cousin, straw behind the ears. This may be nonsense but it colours our view of the provinces. For me enlightenment came in 1976 on the Shropshire Union Canal which I was travelling as part of a thousand-mile watery trip round England. I found myself actually looking at the Provinces: not just at countryside (it has always been acceptable to admire the open country), but at the ordinary towns, small and large, met along the way. It was a revelation. I found a wealth of interest which was totally un-expected. I wrote at the time: 'This is one of the great secrets of the country, the not-quite-hidden, rich diversity of the unassuming provincial town.' I have not changed my mind since then.

Where do you start to talk about the thousands of towns in these islands? I shall begin with the little town of Brewood which was to prove my own eye-opener. Those who come by canal can quite easily miss the place altogether, for the canal shoots through in a deep cutting and you get a quick glimpse of two churches, one to each side, peering over the rim. I stopped, and very glad I am that I did so. The churches, for a start, provide a fascinating contrast. The older of the pair is one of those English churches which, happily, proliferate throughout the land, and are only passed by because they are so numerous. It is handsome without quite being outstanding, a place of dignity with tall spire and long, well-proportioned nave and chancel. Local bigwigs are commemorated in alabaster and among the memorials is one to Colonel Carters, who bundled Charles II into the famous oak tree and saved him from the Cromwellian troops. Across the water is the Victorian version of church architecture, the Catholic church designed by the arch-apostle of the Gothic revival, Pugin. The town, however, is essentially Georgian; well mannered, restrained and urbane architecture on the whole but with one glorious exception, Speedwell Castle. It is not a castle at all but a decidedly unrestrained town house in the Gothic style

*The Gothic extravaganza of Speedwell Castle, Brewood* (Anthony Burton)

with ogee-arched windows cavorting across the façade. It was named after a racehorse which did indeed speed well, well enough anyhow for the successful gambler to build this house on his winnings. And all this can be found in just one, small, unpretentious provincial town – and it is by no means exceptional.

My own journey on that canal trip took me on northwards into Shropshire and Cheshire and on to two towns whose citizens seem to have shared a common carelessness with fire, for Market Drayton was burned down in the seventeenth century and Nantwich in the sixteenth and if, on the whole, Nantwich got the better of the rebuilding, they are both fine places. Both counties are famed for their timber-framed buildings, the 'black and white' houses, though I for one prefer to see the exposed timbers unblackened. Both towns have a goodly share of such houses, but Nantwich also manages to score a Georgian bull's-eye with some superb terraces reflecting the prosperity of a town founded on a successful salt trade. What both these market towns have, however, is a sense of cohesion, of being all of a piece, seamless creations. They have grown with the years and developed a harmony of proportions that even the crasser developments of our own age have not managed totally to destroy. But those who want to see timber-framing really dominating a townscape should travel a little further south to the county of Herefordshire. This really is one of Britain's best-kept secrets – an area of lovely wooded hills dotted by the rather grand farms and with towns of great architectural richness. Towns such as Ledbury or Weobley, for example, are not great showplaces, not major tourist attractions but, my goodness, they offer pleasures in abundance to anyone prepared to walk and look. And this really is the whole point about towns. Time and again you will find that a town which, if you rush through by car, looks as dull as can be, has its own corners of excellence waiting to be discovered. And the duller the town, the more the excellence shines through the surrounding gloom.

Everyone, I imagine, has an answer they would come up with if asked to name a thoroughly dull town, but, if one excludes new towns which have not had time to develop character and identity, I would guarantee there is something of interest in each of them. In fact, even the new towns have their moments. Look at Milton Keynes, with its geometric ground plan and weird road system like a series of chess moves – advance to K1, back to M3 and so on;

*The one that got left behind: an abandoned locomotive by the old railway line at New Bradwell* (Anthony Burton)

surprises can be found even here. Lurking in the centre is a splendidly preserved piece of Victoriana, the terraces of New Bradwell, first built to house railway workers. And after I visited there I was told that this was also a regular meeting place for a witches' coven. It does make one think; if there are witches in Milton Keynes what might you find elsewhere?

To return to dull towns in general: I conducted a poll among friends. It was not admittedly a large sample, but a clear winner emerged for the title of dullest town – Middlesbrough. The challenge was on. What could I find to say about Middlesbrough that would encourage anyone to deviate so much as a yard from their chosen route? That was no challenge at all. Had they been to see Middlesbrough's two unusual bridges? You can start with the transporter bridge, which looks to me as if it was designed by that awful boy next door who could always make anything he wanted out of his Meccano set and which never even fell down when it was finished. A platform is suspended by cables from a high-level trolley

*Middlesbrough transporter bridge* (Northumbria Tourist Board)

that runs backwards and forwards on a tall framework high above the river. The platform connects up with the roadway. Cars drive on, passengers walk on and off, and it trundles from one side to the other – a system designed to avoid obstructing shipping on the Tees. Newport bridge was designed to solve the same problem and the designer found a different answer. Here the entire bridge, 1,350 tons of steel, is lifted vertically, rising 100ft (30m) in less than a minute to accommodate the river traffic. So much for dull Middlesbrough.

The moral is: never believe anyone who tells you a town is dull. Go out and look, and something, somewhere, will appear to arouse your interest. In many cases, however, you arrive in a town carrying with you certain expectations, and here the secret is to look beyond the obvious. Even those places which are accepted as being among the most popular tourist haunts in the country can offer something different, something very much off the beaten track. Take Bath, for example, famous for its Roman baths, its Georgian terraces and elegant Pulteney Bridge across the Avon. What can you possibly say that has not already been said a thousand times? Where can you recommend that is not already too well known to require comment? Well, many people have not heard of the Camden Works Museum in Julian Road, a place where you can spend as fascinating an afternoon as any in Bath. It is a decidedly odd place. The building in which it is housed was originally a court for real tennis, the game where you use roofs and walls as well as the more conventional ground surface. Not that you get much of a hint of that original use, for almost the entire building has been transformed into a facsimile of the manufacturing company of J. B. Bowler, a family firm begun in 1872. When the works closed everything – absolutely everything – was moved here and rearranged just as it had been. And what did J. B. Bowler do? What did he not do! Here you will find a plumbers' and fitters' store. If you needed a piece for your old gas mantle, Bowler's could supply it. A new brass tap? No problem at all. Nothing was ever discarded. Stock bought in when the firm was started was still there waiting for a customer a century later. And that is just the start. This was also a light-engineering works, and the original machinery is still there in working order. And they were brass-founders, casting a whole range of goods in brass. Most unusually of all, they made aerated waters – fizzy drinks. All the old plant is retained and is still demonstrated. The place is unique and one feels that such diversity will never be seen again. It is a reminder that, for all its elegance, Bath was and is a working city.

*Camden Works Museum: the essence room where syrups for mineral water were made (Museum of Bath at Work: Russell Frears)*

You can also see another old craft being practised in Bath – art it can seem as much as craft – bookbinding. A well-bound book must be one of the most satisfying objects in the world, for the feel and smell of good leather, beautifully tooled, can do so much to enhance even the most ordinary volume. At the Museum of Bookbinding in Manvers Road you can see superb books of the past and the work of the craftsmen of today. It is a welcome reminder that even here in a city noted for its architecture of one period – the Georgian age – past and present can cohabit. Just look at the eighteenth-century octagonal chapel in Milsom Street – a lovely piece of very Bath architecture, yet happily providing a home for that most twentieth-century of arts, that of the photographer.

All too often, we visit villages, towns and cities knowing just what we are looking for, quite certain what to expect. We visit this town for its church, that for its town hall, another for its medieval buildings or its picturesque cottages. We are seeing places as fossils, bits of the past for ever stuck at a particular moment of time. There often seems to be a real danger that the entire country will be thought of as a tourist museum, a sort of Disneyland on a national scale. Of course there are places that cry out for conservation and preservation but the greatest satisfaction comes in discoveries made in the ordinary town going about its business in the twentieth century. And there are discoveries in plenty to be made, even when the surroundings seem at their most unpromising.

The first essential is to try and block off much that the twentieth century has done to so many town centres. The plastic fascia and the plate-glass window no doubt help to sell what is inside, but all too often they spread a drab conformity along a row of shops. The old, the characterful, can easily be lost beneath the modern trappings. But look up to first-floor level and a whole different world can appear. Sometimes it is fairly obvious. Look, for example, at the rich façades above the homogeneity of the shop-fronts in Oxford's Broad Street. At ground level the shops are just shops, even if they include some of the best bookshops in the world. Up above all is diversity – and fun, visual fun.

Perhaps Oxford, of all places, has little need of extra trimming, for it is still full of visual splendours in spite of the worst efforts of the city planners and developers. So, by way of contrast, go up north to Wigan. Exactly the same story can be found here. Look up and you find an almost baroque splendour, a splendour which elsewhere in the town seems to be limited to the inside of the Victorian pubs. And that brings us to another point about towns: do not take them at their face value. Wigan might seem a child of the industrial revolution, but the town got its charter from Henry III and there was not much industrialisation around in his day. There is still an old town lurking down there waiting to be found and appreciated. And there is still a good deal of character in the place. Just try the market hall – not the modern plastic market but the proper market hall with tripe stalls and black pudding on sale. But hurry along there for there are moves afoot to destroy this splendid place. It is incredible to think that anyone should want to knock it down, especially when local authorities have had the good sense to realise that their other most famous spot, the area around Wigan Pier, is worth preserving.

I am not trying to say that all towns are of equal interest, or have an equal share of fine buildings, simply that almost without exception, there is more to a town than appears at first glance. I want to look at four towns, each quite different from the other, to try and see something of the way in which they were shaped and developed, and to point out some of the interesting and unusual features you might find. My first choice is an example of the sort of happy accident that can provide several hours of pleasant, relaxed pottering. On holiday in Norfolk, I wandered into the town of Wymondham, discovered that the local Wymondham Society had produced a pamphlet, 'A Walk Around Old Wymondham', and decided to spend the rest of the day in exploration. One advantage of having the leaflet is that it gives you a perspective on the town, fills in some of the historical detail and tells you why the town grew up there in the first place. You do not absolutely need such information to enjoy a walk through Wymondham, but it does help: and what a shock it is to discover that this peaceful little town had a violent and bloody past.

This is an agricultural area; the rich meadows and pastures of the Tiffey valley surround the town, which was built on what is now a scarcely perceptible platform. The origin was Anglo-Saxon, but William the Conqueror handed out the local manor to a mate, William d'Albini, who founded the priory that was to become Wymondham Abbey, and the town's importance was assured. Abbey and town quarrelled from the first, and kept on quarrelling for three centuries, until eventually the abbey was handed over to the parishioners. That might have been the end of the rows, but at the Dissolution a local bigwig, Sir John Flowerden, took the roof lead; as he was a big enough wig, no one called it theft, at least not in public. When, however, the same gentleman began enclosing and taking into his own hands the old common fields, the locals decided they had had enough. The peasants rose up, led by the Kett brothers, destroying the fences and hedges illegally set up by the landlords. The government, not surprisingly, sided with the landowners and hanged the Ketts. It is worth thinking of that story as you walk around the town. When we talk of the peace and order of the old church buildings and their air of sanctity, we ought also to remember the rows and the quarrels and William Kett's body hanging from the tower. It certainly gives a different perspective to life in the old town. Perhaps the greatest physical change dates from June 1615 when a fire started in a stable and spread to many other buildings. Most of what you see today dates from the rebuilding following the disaster and you can start your tour at one of the most important buildings set up immediately after the fire.

The Market Cross is an octagonal building, open at the ground floor with a room above where the market court once sat. The woodwork is carved with a whole array of objects which could be made from wood – from spinning tops to spoons – a reminder of the town's major industry, woodworking and wood-turning. It is an interesting note of continuity that woodworking has not yet left the area: there is a brush factory built in the nineteenth century, and a more modern co-operative brush factory, the tall chimney of which makes a prominent feature on the Wymondham skyline. But for the moment let us keep to the centre of town. The Market Cross stands, not surprisingly, in the market-place. The market was begun here early in the thirteenth century and lasted until the railway age. Take almost any street away from here and you will find the old traditional timber-framed buildings of the town. You will also find several excellent old pubs. The Cross Keys has splendid seven-teenth-century timbering, and the Feathers has the finest selection of ales for many miles around, but the Green Dragon takes the architectural prize, one of the finest buildings in the town. It is all of a piece, an old exterior matched by an interior which shows the same marks of antiquity. It dates back to the fifteenth century, and if you look at the timbers on the outside you can still see the scorch marks from the seventeenth-century fire: it was a very close thing indeed for the Green Dragon. Lots of good pubs and inns here, and once there were a great many more. Walk down Bridewell Street and next to the Queen's Head is a house which also once served as an inn and which, the owner boasts in Latin over the door, offered both good and cheap service. The inscription can be translated as, 'My servant is not a dormouse, nor the host a leech.'

Bridewell Street consists almost entirely of houses built just after the fire, many showing the typical jetties – the upper storeys leaning out over the narrow road. The street names are good clues to old uses. There was a bridewell – house of correction – here; Fairland Street takes you to the open land where fairs were held; Brewhouse Lane did have a brewery, but alas no more; and they did indeed make chains at Chain Entry. Every street it seems has its story to tell, its quota of interesting buildings. There are some appealing oddities as well. Look at the entrance to the carpark off Market Street. It is another case where lifting your gaze above street level reveals the unexpected detail. Here is a terracotta relief of firemen's helmets and equipment, marking the 1883 head-quarters of the Volunteer Fire Brigade. All this and so much more, and we still have not touched on the main attraction for visitors to Wymondham, the abbey. There are, in fact, two ecclesiastical buildings of interest. Certainly the abbey has its magnificence, and is still in use as the parish church, though you can see from the surroundings just how much was destroyed by John Flowerden and friends. You might also note that the building is approached down Becketswell Road – another hint and, yes, there was a sacred well here and pilgrims came this way to take the waters. There is also a Chapel of St Thomas à Becket back in the town centre though it is many a long year since anyone worshipped there. It has served many uses. Once it was the local grammar school and today it is a most unusual public library.

The Wymondham Walk ticks off thirty-seven places of interest for you to see on your way round the town, and it never even gets round to mentioning that the old Great Eastern Railway station is remarkably impressive and that the Deerham branch boasts a lovely little mock-Jacobean crossing cottage. This is a small town, yet there is so much to see – and this is just one small town out of hundreds which are equally enticing. It also represents just one type of town, the market centre serving an agricultural region. It is the sort of town you are likely just to come across much as I did. My next town has a somewhat different character, and is a place you are perhaps more likely to go past than actually go through.

Newark-on-Trent in Nottinghamshire was always destined to be an important strategic place, for it stands by a crossing point of a major river. The Romans came here, and the Fosse Way runs through the centre. The Normans settled and for generation after generation the town was fortified. Its most important moment in the drama of English history came in the Civil War, when it was a Royalist stronghold. At that time, the entire town was surrounded by stout defensive walls and dominated by the castle overlooking the river. At the war's end, much had been destroyed, but the shell of the castle still stands above the water and a surprisingly large proportion of the old town defences remain. Newark's importance did not die with the ending of the Civil War. It still stood at a major crossing point where the Great North Road met the Trent. In the present century, thousands have seen more of Newark than they wished, for it was a notorious road bottleneck that was often corked. Now a bypass has been built. The thousands still pour up and down

*Newark Castle overlooking the River Trent* (Derek Pratt)

the A1 but they no longer stop at Newark. Peace has fallen over the town, and those who turn out of the stream of traffic find a quiet place to enjoy. I say quiet place, but there seem to me to be two Newarks: one the handsome, picturesque town and the other a world of work. I find them equally enchanting.

I am not going to go into the sort of building-by-building account I gave for Wymondham, but I should like to try and characterise those two worlds. The picturesque world is the more obvious. The ruins of the castle loom over the river, a single oriel window providing a more domestic note to the blankness of defensive walls. From here the defences spread along the river and reach inland to surround the old town, and are among the best preserved Civil War defences to be found in Britain. The other great dominating feature is the parish church, as grand as a cathedral. Yet its appeal is not just in its grandeur, which includes a spire rising over 250ft (75m). It is, like so many of our churches, a hybrid, begun in Norman times and expanded and changed over the centuries. It boasts a mixture of styles. The Early English tower was built in 1230, the octagonal spire added a century later. The south aisle was begun in the Decorated style, but then the plague years brought everything to a halt and when work began again it was completed in the Perpendicular. And so the story goes on, and yet, miraculously, it all holds together. The whole is magnificent and the detail fascinating. Carved wood and stained glass abound but the carved stone figures are my favourite features here. Look at the impish, grimacing faces of the gargoyles set high on the walls by some anonymous carver centuries ago.

Between castle and church stands the elegant town, a largely Georgian creation. They say that the town hall, designed by John Carr in 1773, is the finest in Britain – a claim that would certainly be most strongly challenged by my neighbours in Abingdon, where we can boast a seventeenth-century hall by Christopher Kempster, who had worked for the great Wren. But, looking at the market square as a whole, what a splendid effect has been achieved here. The overall impression may be dignified Georgian, but there are glimpses too of an earlier age. The White Hart is a fifteenth-century inn with rows of terracotta saints decorating the main façade – whether there for a quick one or to encourage imbibers to more sober ways is unrecorded. Inns are, not surprisingly, a major feature of this main-road town, with huge coaching inns such as the Saracen's Head and the Clinton Arms. But there is another side to the town, another connection that has had a strong influence on the lines of development. The market may have depended to a large extent on the town's important road connections, but trade also comes by water along the navigable Trent. This was a thriving inland port. There is not much room for classical posturing here in the busy world of the docks, and from here there is a busy look, too, about the town, which is seen as a jumble of houses clambering up the hill. This is also working Newark, with maltings lining the approach to the lock by the castle. So we have a town of great contrast, each part having its own special appeal.

I suppose the major attraction of a working town is that it seems to have a special sense of purposefulness, has something to do other than just sit there waiting to be admired. Recent years have seen an increased interest in the world of work, but not always the same degree of interest in the life that surrounds the workplace. In Chapter 7 we shall be looking at the Big Pit Museum at Blaenafon in Gwent, but how many of its visitors think anything of the town itself? This is certainly no ancient settlement, but a place that has grown directly out of the industrial revolution, a town built both literally and metaphorically on coal and iron. For it was the presence of those two minerals beneath the soil that brought the English here at the end of the eighteenth century. Coal from the pit went up the road to the furnaces where the ore was smelted. What had been an empty land now crashed with sound, and the hills were alternately lit by flames and submerged beneath smoke. It is quiet again now, but the furnaces remain, as does the town built to serve them, to house the families who were brought here. The great bank of furnaces make an impressive sight, even in ruins, but just look at the houses built round them. They have a story of their own to tell. It is hard to imagine what life must have been like so close to the heat and noise of the foundry, but we know a good deal about it. We know, for example, that one of these plain houses was the truck-shop, where the company sold essentials to the workers at company prices; and we know that other cottages held the men who marched

*Workers' cottages at Blaenafon ironworks, Gwent* (Chris Abram: APR Ltd)

to Westminster to protest against this system. There were battles fought here as bitter as any waged in Civil War Newark. Iron ruled the people's lives – and their deaths. Go to the local churchyard and you can see the cast-iron covers laid over the graves. There was no escaping iron in Blaenafon.

Blaenafon is not a beauty spot, and most who now visit here come to sample the strange world of deep mining and perhaps only stumble on the fascinations of the town by accident. I would like to take a brief look at one other industrial town – another industry, another country – which you only go to because you make a deliberate effort to get there. New Lanark stands at the end of a road that leads down to the Clyde. An industrial town it may be but it stands in a setting of great beauty. Here, as at Blaenafon, the English came to establish industry, this time a cotton-mill powered by the waters of the Clyde. Here, too, a town had to be built to house the new workforce. Everything here is of a piece, mill and town built together, the one dependent on the other. The housing was all tenements, a style that was common in Scotland long before the word 'flat', let alone 'highrise', had entered the vocabulary of the rest of the world. They stand in tiers on the high bank above river and mill. It would have been just another mill town perhaps if it had not been for one manager who came here, Robert Owen. He introduced revolutionary ideas: education, not mill work, for children; shorter hours to increase efficiency; and a co-operative movement to pay for the facilities needed for the whole community. His spirit lingers round the co-operative shop he founded and above all in the New Institution, the school which he regarded as the most important place in the whole community. New Lanark was a bright spot in a dark age and remains miraculously all but complete, and is currently being restored and refurbished. It is also a beautiful spot, for it stands beside the Corra Linn Falls. When you get tired of buildings you can wander off through the riverside woodland.

In these brief sketches I have tried to give an indication of the rich mixture of pleasures to be found in our towns. A few, such as New Lanark, appeared and then neither grew nor altered again. The great majority, however, have developed and changed, continue changing and will go on to change again. A good deal of the appeal of town exploration lies in being able to see that change on the ground, not just as something recorded in documents and maps but visible in street patterns, in buildings old and new. The more you look, the more you find – and the more you see, the more you begin to understand what an amazingly complex object each and every town really is. You can find your own way through all the complexities, but it is often a great help – and often great fun – to turn to those places where explanations are ready-made for you. There is now scarcely an aspect of town life which is not covered by some museum or other, often with great flair and imagination. But before diving into a museum it is a good idea to try and get at least a glimpse of the town as a whole. Just occasionally this can be achieved in a thoroughly entertaining and even surprising way. There are two quite different, but equally fascinating, examples to be found in Scotland.

In Edinburgh, high on the castle hill, you will find the Outlook Tower – an obvious way, you might think, of seeing the city. All you have to do is pay your entrance fee, climb up to the top and admire the view. All of this you can indeed do: but you can also do a great deal more, for this is a Victorian camera obscura. This extraordinary device is based on a principle which has been known for nearly a thousand years. If you allow light to pass through a tiny hole into a darkened room, you will get an inverted image of the outside world on the wall opposite the hole. You can intensify the image using lenses and mirrors, and this is what you have in Edinburgh. The image is projected down on to a table presenting a panorama of the city, not just a photographic image but a moving image reflecting the life going on outside.

The camera obscura was the forerunner of the modern camera, and the photograph has largely replaced its shadowy reflections of reality. Many tourist centres use photographs to introduce visitors to the delights of their town or the surrounding country, but one display is unique. You find it in Perth, where a 360° slide show, complete with sound, is on offer. It is housed in a fine, classically styled building with what appears to be a grand stone dome at the top. All is not what it seems. The dome is not stone, but cast iron and a piece of industrial disguise, for this was originally a water tank, part of the Perth waterworks built in 1832. The master of disguise was the works engineer and architect, Adam Anderson. I can think of no other slide show on offer in a water tank – nor indeed can I think of any other water tank designed by a Professor of Natural Philosophy, for that was indeed the post held by Anderson at St Andrew's University.

You can see towns as they are, you can see pictures and photographs which show towns as they were, but it is only recently,

with the development of open-air museums, that you have been able actually to wander back into the past of towns. One of the first, and still one of the best, is the North of England Open Air Museum at Beamish in Durham. The ambitious aim of this project is to bring back to life a northern community of the turn of the century. To achieve this a whole variety of buildings have been taken down brick by brick, stone by stone, and carefully rebuilt at the museum. A town is coming back to life. You can walk into a cottage and find an old-style kitchen with a fire blazing in the hearth. It is a scene remarkably similar to one I saw many times as a child in this part of the world, and this of course is a good part of the appeal. The past that is being re-created is not so far distant that we feel it is beyond our understanding. The pub, the shops, the band playing on the bandstand, seem almost like old friends. But it is a whole community that is being re-created here. There is a station and steam trains, not the local station but one brought across from Rowley near Consett. (Incidentally, you can go and see where the station once stood, for although the line has gone, the route has been opened up as a public footpath, the Waskerley Way.) Electric trams clank through this new old town – though, as all transport enthusiasts know, the best place to see and ride a tram is the Tramway Museum at Crich in Derbyshire. The world of work is equally well represented. The old colliery scene is very much a local affair, for the steam winding engine has only moved a few hundred yards from a site up the road. Here you step back even further in time with the working replica of *Locomotion*, built for the Stockton & Darlington Railway in 1825. You need at least a day to see everything there is to see at Beamish, and you need to keep going back for it is changing all the time. For example, 1984 saw the addition of the local Co-op shop, and this again is part of the appeal of Beamish: it makes you want to ask questions about the different components. When did the Co-operative movement begin? Where was the first Co-op? The answers can be found in Rochdale and if you wander over there you can have everything explained at the Rochdale Pioneers Co-operative Museum housed in the old shop in Toad Lane. A visit to Beamish helps you to appreciate what a complex organisation a town really is. Our next few calls will be to places enabling us to look at just a few aspects of town life in more detail.

*Perth's Tourist Information Centre housed in a cast-iron water tower (Perthshire Advertiser)*

*An old street scene re-created at the Open Air Museum at Beamish* (North of England Open Air Museum, Beamish)

We take an awful lot for granted these days. We assume for example that if we turn on a tap, water will duly appear. This, however, is a comparatively modern phenomenon, and the idea that everyone should be able to wallow in the luxury of a private tub is a very recent notion. The public bath, however, goes right back to Roman times – though it became notably less popular once the Romans left. The bathhouse turns up in some fairly unlikely places. If you are in London and find yourself near Aldwych station, turn down adjoining Surrey Street and into Strand Lane. At number 5 you can peer in from the footpath at the Roman bathhouse, restored in the seventeenth century. Although it is in the care of the National Trust, you cannot actually go inside, so that it does not compete with the better-known example of Bath itself or Chesters

146

*The original Rochdale Co-op* (Co-operative Union Ltd)

on Hadrian's Wall. But surely the oddest preserved Roman bath is the one to be found at Welwyn in Hertfordshire. This is not a public bath but was originally part of a villa. It is a subterranean affair and now it is preserved in a vault right beneath the roaring traffic of the A1(M).

That we can today enjoy a bath with very little trouble to ourselves is largely due – as are so many things in our towns – to the work of Victorian engineers. They built the waterworks that ensured a regular supply of water, and they built the sewers to carry the waste water, and other waste, away. The water supply involved pumping, and the pumps that were used in the nineteenth century were driven by huge and grand steam engines. The Victorians were proud of their engines and tried to provide them with suitably

147

impressive houses. These can be really quite exotic, as at Ryhope near Sunderland, where the engine-house is built in a Jacobean style, an unlikely accompaniment to a nineteenth-century steam engine. For many, however, it is not the exotic building that forms the main attraction, but the steam giants themselves. The greatest of all the engines is to be seen at the Kew Pumping Station near Kew Bridge in London. It is the biggest steam engine in Britain. Those who have never seen a beam engine are invariably astonished by the size. We think of engines as occupying at most one room. This one is not even the size of a house, more like the size of a small block of flats. To give you an idea of the scale, just think of the piston in a car bobbing up and down in its cylinder. Now think of the piston and cylinder in the big Kew engine. This is a 100in cylinder – that is not the height but the internal diameter, meaning that it is over 8ft (2.4m) across – and the vast piston rises and falls 11ft inside it. To see the engine working much as it did when first installed in 1869 is to see engineering on a heroic scale. And that is only one of the engines they have in steam here, for Kew houses the finest collection of stationary steam engines to be seen anywhere in the world. You can even hire the whole place, as indeed I did when I had a twenty-first book party here, and had the pleasure of introducing friends and colleagues to these lovely engines which nodded and hissed throughout the evening.

Kew is only one of a number of old water-pumping stations that have been preserved. The Herefordshire Waterworks Museum at Broomy Hill, Hereford, beside the River Wye, announces its presence by its ornate, somewhat Italianate water-tower. But the main attraction again is the sight of steam at work, this time with quite different engines. Initiates into the mysteries of steam might care to know that the 1895 vertical triple-expansion engine is the oldest of its type in Britain; non-initiates can get just as much fun watching the wonderful, smooth motion of a splendid machine. They can also enjoy themselves making things work, like pumps and gauges. They can admire the fire-engine, for as an assured source of water this was an obvious home for the horsedrawn fire-fighting equipment for the city. Coal for the boilers was brought in on a narrow-gauge railway which now has a curious armoured loco-motive, not because waterworks were exceptionally violent places, but because such engines were brought over for civilian use after

*The giant beam of the Kew pumping engine* (Clive Penfold for the Kew Bridge Trust)

service in World War I. And all this just to get water from a tap.

Of course your bath water would still be cold without power to heat it, and the only reason we no longer have to heat buckets of water on the fire is that power comes in at the touch of a switch. Again it is something we are inclined to take for granted, even though power stations are among the most prominent features of the modern landscape. I actually like them, and when I once wrote that I thought I was probably the only person who did, I was deluged by letters from other enthusiasts extolling the virtues of their own favourites. The River Trent is the great gathering centre, for the whole river seems dotted with massive, shapely cooling towers, busily forming their own personal clouds in the sky. My choice, however, goes to the one I can just see out of our bathroom window on a clear day, Didcot. I love the curves of the towers balanced against the bold straight lines of the main building. And I am always delighted by the great cooling tower disappearing trick. Have you ever tried counting cooling towers as you drive along? At any one power station each tower is the same shape and size as the next, so, as the viewpoint changes, they can disappear one behind the other.

No one has yet preserved a power station – though there are plans for Battersea – but a smaller generating station has been transformed into the Milne Museum at Tonbridge in Kent. It serves as a reminder that in its infancy the electricity industry, like the water-supply industry, went in for the ornate, for extravagant detail. It is a reminder, too, that all these supplies that we now take for granted were once important, even astonishing, innovations.

We might muse in our tubs, as we soak and scrub, over the supposed relationship between cleanliness and godliness, a dubious connection I have always thought. It seemed even more dubious during a period when I used to go in and take an evening class in one of Her Majesty's more secure penal establishments. It was the clean, smart ones that usually turned out to be the most ungodly. Crime and punishment, as the world of literature endlessly proves, are fascinating subjects. Certainly the average law-abiding citizen finds it interesting, which no doubt explains why the forces of law, order and retribution find their place in the world of museums. A good starting point is Ripon, where the Victorian prison has been converted to tell that particular story. It is an ideal start, because it

*A judge's-eye view of the old courtroom, Walsingham Shirehall Museum* (Norfolk Museums Service: Walsingham Shirehall Museum)

is one of the few museums to deal with the police work that gets the criminal behind bars in the first place.

However, as all are innocent until proved guilty, there is one vital stage to be considered: the trial. The Shirehall Museum at Walsingham in Norfolk is a perfectly preserved example of an eighteenth-century courtroom. It would not perhaps do to dwell too closely on the nature of the justice doled out from here two centuries ago. It can be equally disturbing to contemplate the punishments facing the convicted. You can get a notion of early nineteenth-century prison life from a visit to the old Castle Jail at Jedburgh, but quite the most forbidding establishment I have ever seen is the old gaol at Beaumaris on Anglesey. Before visiting it you should be aware that this was a 'model' prison built in 1829 to the new humanitarian standards set by the Gaol Act of 1823. Its designer was Joseph Hansom, rather better known for the horsedrawn cab which bears his name. At the end of a visit you are left wondering what, if this is the best, the worst gaols must have been like. Here you can see the rough cells, and the rougher punishment cells, where bread and water was the only diet. You can see the workrooms where men carved their initials on the floor, and women had ropes by their workplaces which they pulled in order to rock the cradles where their babies slept on the floor above. You can see the treadmill where the 'hard labour' prisoners marched up and down for hours every day. And, most macabre of all, you can follow the walk from the condemned cell to the scaffold. This is not a visit for the squeamish, but does at least provide a salutary reminder of the standards that were quite acceptable up to a short time ago. I must confess I prefer to look at our local gaol in Abingdon, a handsome building which now serves as a sports centre.

Those who still want more on the subject of crime, or rather crime prevention, might care to contemplate the work of the locksmith. His efforts baulk the criminal or, if those efforts fail, can be employed to restrain the offender. The Lock Museum at Willenhall, in the West Midlands, has locks of every shape and size from the earliest to the most modern. This is one of those odd museums which there is very little point in visiting unless you are really prepared to spend a bit of time. Locks either intrigue you or bore you to distraction, depending on how you feel about the intricacies of mechanism. I find the best of them to be all but miraculous examples of man's ingenuity. The locksmiths were probably the world's first true mechanics, but they were also much more. They

152

were men who could solve puzzles, and, better still, could set puzzles others were unable to solve. The very best locks are as finely balanced and as accurate in their movements as the most expensive clock or watch.

We seem to have strayed a little way from our main theme of towns, but we can get back again now by going to the main street. An essential part of the life of any town is trade, the supply of the necessities and the fripperies of life. Shops have changed in the past and are changing, with extraordinary rapidity, in the present. 'The Shops' used to form the core of every town, but recent years have seen the growth of two phenomena: the shopping precinct, a posh name for a faceless, uniform row of plasticated buildings; and the out-of-town shopping area. Both are dominated by the supermarket. This is a trend that has drifted over the Atlantic from America, where thousands of towns now seem no longer to have any core at all, no real heart. You drive in looking for the centre of the town and never get there. Instead you find yourself out on the other side at the 'shopping mall'. The trend seems, sadly, to be irreversible and we must look forward, if that is the phrase, to a time when real shops are only to be seen in museums. You will have to go somewhere like the Gladstone Court Museum at Biggar in Scotland, where a street

*The restored telephone exchange at Biggar's Gladstone Court Museum* (Biggar Museum Trust)

(previous page) *The unique collection of old ironmongery at Halliwell's House, Selkirk* (Ettrick & Lauderdale District Council Museums Service: Neil Paterson) *and* (above) *The Victorian Pharmacy, York Place, Edinburgh* (Pharmaceutical Society of Great Britain)

has been laid out to show changes from about 1850 to 1920. You can peer in at the grocer's, the china shop, the chemist and the ironmonger, or try the town services of bank, library and telephone exchange.

The Scots seem, in fact, to be particularly good at preserving these aspects of the town past. Selkirk has a unique ironmongery collection in Halliwell's House, part of a row of seventeenth-century cottages. There are pots and pans, tools and instruments, all gathered together by one man, who has spent a quarter of a century putting the collection together. Rather more official is the Victorian Pharmacy at York Place in Edinburgh, organised by the Scottish department of the Pharmaceutical Society of Great Britain. Here you can see the magnificent, if generally useless, bottles of coloured water, plus all the chemicals neatly labelled and stacked away in drawers. Balances, scales and machines for making pills complete the scene, a very evocative re-creation of the days when everything in the pharmacy was measured out on the spot.

Today's shops are dominated by pre-packed goods. Without them the supermarket could scarcely function and the advertising business would be sunk. Once upon a time, long ago, packages were only intended to keep the contents dry and clean. Modern packages still do, but their business is equally to act as a lure to the customer. The package has become a document of social history, and you can see that literally colourful history at the Robert Opie Collection, or 'The Package Revisited', at the Albert Warehouse, Gloucester Docks. I think this is a marvellous place to visit and not just because of the tremendous number and variety of boxes, tins and packets. In fact it would be worth coming here even if the museum did not exist, just to see Gloucester Docks themselves. They are a superb example of nineteenth-century dock architecture – sober, monumental and grand. And while you are visiting do pause to look at the Sailors' Church, for there can surely be few maritime churches so far from the sea.

Towns are places to work and shop, and also places to come for a night out. One traditional way of passing the time is to go for a drop of ale in some parts of Britain, or for a drop of something of a more spirituous nature in others. The brewing of beer and the distilling of spirits are ancient crafts, arts one might say, each with its mystery. You may sample those mysteries, and the end product, at the breweries and distilleries that open their doors to the general public. Stamford, in Lincolnshire, for example, has a complete

*Robert Opie and just a fraction of his collection of packages* (Robert Opie Collection)

Victorian steam-powered brewery which acts as a brewing museum; and Burton upon Trent has the Bass Museum, based on one of the mightiest breweries in the land. This latter brewery operated on such a vast scale that at one time there were 16 miles of private railway within the complex, along which a thousand waggons a day were hauled. Now one locomotive and the old directors' coach remain – and neither goes anywhere. Perhaps the only brewery that can rival this scale is the mighty Guinness of Dublin, and they have their brewery museum in the Old Hop Store in Rainsford Street. Distilleries will be putting in an appearance in Chapter 8; but neither brewery nor distillery is much use, unless the precious liquids reach the throats of the consumers. A few words cannot cover the tremendous diversity of the British drinking establishment, but as we have been looking at evocations of towns of around a century ago, perhaps one building might stand for many. The Victorian pub was a place of polished mahogany, rich tiles, etched glass and shining brass. There was nothing restrained about the town pub, and there is probably no finer example than the Crown Liquor Saloon in Great Victoria Street, Belfast – somewhat improbably owned by the National Trust. This is no museum piece, however, but a proper functioning pub.

The town is a conglomerate of services, uses, shops and amusements, but primarily it is a collection of individual buildings. Demands made on the town may change, but many buildings survive those changes. They may be houses in one generation, shops in another and banks in the present day, yet through it all their essential characters can, with luck, remain intact. We shall now turn to a closer look at the individual buildings which do so much to establish the character of a place.

*The Stamford Brewery Museum* (Stamford Brewery Museum)

# 6
# How the Other Half Lives

*Hill House, Helensburgh, the splendid home produced for W. W. Blackie by Charles Rennie Mackintosh* (National Trust for Scotland: Stewart Guthrie)

Until recently, any tourist who announced an intended visit to an old house was assumed to be referring to, at the very least, a stately home. We were all expected to admire the Great House, with its collection of Chippendale and Sheraton, the paintings by Old Masters (preferably foreign) and the tableware from Meissen. Attitudes have changed. Today we are beginning to realise that it can be just as interesting to examine the way of life of people rather more akin to ourselves. The 'ordinary' house may not be able to exhibit great works of art, but then, truth to tell, neither can many of the stately homes, which have to make do with family portraits by decidedly second-eleven painters: for every Van Eyck there are half a dozen Joe Bloggs. I am sure that I am not alone in feeling an air of detachment when visiting many of these places, offering as they do reflections on a way of life so very different from my own that I might just as well be inspecting the habitat of the greater spotted auk. We ordinary, workaday folk have a past as well, which if less glittering than that of their lordships is not a jot less interesting. This is not to say that the grand house is devoid of interest, simply that for far too long it was deemed to be the only house of interest. The result has been that crowds have flocked to the stately homes and ignored the more humble. In this chapter I hope to redress the balance, concentrating on those preserved houses which show the life of the middle and lower orders of our society.

There are two theoretical ways of viewing a house – as a structure pure and simple, or a container for a particular way of life. In practice, the two are hopelessly intermingled, for the shape of the box and its components affect the way of life within, while the notions of how life should be lived determine the form in which the box is built. It is, nonetheless, an interesting experiment occasionally to take a step back from the house and ask: how is it all put together; how does it work purely and simply as a construction? This is most easily achieved when the house can be taken in isolation, uncluttered by surroundings that have changed and altered over the centuries, and in circumstances in which there are none of the very personal feelings which go with the fixtures, fittings and furnishings of the individual home. A few large-scale, open-air museums have brought together strange mixtures of buildings, uprooted from their original surroundings and placed down in unlikely new relationships. At the Weald & Downland Open Air Museum at

*A flint and brick house of the seventeenth century after restoration by the Weald and Downland Museum* (Weald & Downland Open Air Museum)

Singleton near Chichester you can find a medieval house close by a Victorian school, or a working water-mill near a Tudor market-hall. Each building has been brought here and re-erected because it has a particularly interesting character of its own, not because it necessarily fits into a pre-arranged plan. The buildings are all very much of the area; yet each building contrives to exist in isolation, there to be judged on its merits.

A similar museum offering an equally wide variety of structures drawn from an even wider area is to be found at Holywood, not a place with a Disneyland, but Holywood, County Down. Cultra Manor is the home of the Ulster Folk and Transport Museum, where town and country sit down side by side. It is the country part that I want to concentrate on here. The overriding feeling on approaching the old farmhouses is of a simplicity decreed by poverty. Just look at the Meenagarragh Cottier's House, which is no more than an earth floor, four walls of stone and a roof of thatch. This contains the whole living area, while the 'bedroom' is an outshut – a space provided by

163

extending the roof-line down beyond the walls to provide a space big enough to lie down in, though no one could stand up. Even when you get to the rather grander-looking Cruckaclady farmhouse you find things are not quite what they seem. One end holds the kitchen, but the other end was given to the cattle. There was a family bedroom above the byre, and the cows down below provided the central heating. The nineteenth-century houses are none too grand, but at least the humans had them to themselves. The great virtue of this excellent museum is the care taken not just in the restoration of the houses but in giving them appropriate settings. The feeling given is of arriving at a country cottage which has actually, and miraculously, been moved to this site, yet has carried its own countryside along with it.

The Avoncroft Museum of Buildings at Stoke Heath, near Bromsgrove (Hereford and Worcester), is, as the name suggests, primarily concerned with the rescue of notable buildings from destruction and the display of building methods and techniques. Some of the buildings are very functional – a windmill, a chain shop,

*Cruckaclady farmhouse, a simple structure shared by the farmer and his animals, now at the Ulster Folk and Transport Museum* (Ulster Folk & Transport Museum, Cultra Manor)

a nailer's shed – and it is nonsensical to try and divorce them from the work they were required to house. So nails and chains are hammered out, while the sails of the mill turn and wheat is ground into flour. Modest visitors will be pleased to know, however, that the museum's latest acquisition, an eighteenth-century three-seater earth closet, is only there to be looked at, not used. The domestic buildings are largely left empty and unadorned, so that nothing distracts from the simple invitation to see just how they are put together. Look at the fifteenth-century merchant's house from Bromsgrove, with its wooden frame and its wattle-and-daub walls, created by providing a frame of split hazel twigs and covering that in daub consisting of such unsavoury ingredients as mud, cow dung and boiled mutton fat.

Because it is all there on view without distractions, the plan and form of the house stand clearly revealed. If you go on from here to a town with similar houses you immediately seem to understand just how they too fit into the scheme of things. Sometimes, to return to an earlier theme, a town trail will help you with this understanding process. The really excellent trail for Ledbury, for example, gives you features to look for in the timber-framed houses. The timbers were prepared off site and then, to make sure the right pieces fitted together, they were marked with Roman numerals which can still be seen today. This was an early form of prefabrication. The later, better-known version can be seen back at Avoncroft. Remember the post-war prefab? There are not many left these days, but they did their bit to fill the gaps left by German bombs and now one has an honoured place in the museum. Unlike the other buildings here, it comes complete with fixtures and fittings, since these were an integral part of the prefab design. Avoncroft's buildings cover an historical range from medieval to modern, but man's habitation of these islands covers a far greater period. You can construct a fascinating tour, following the gradual development of the houses of Britain. Here, as an example, is a roughly chronological selection, taking us all over Britain, starting with the settlements of around 1000BC.

If you take the B3212 westward out of Moretonhampstead, in Devon, then turn south after 4½ miles on the minor road that leads past Hameldown Tor and follow this road for 1¼ miles, you will reach a footpath that leads up toward the tor itself. It is good walking country, but you need only walk a few hundred yards up the track before you reach the Bronze Age settlement of Grims-

*A village street of 200BC at Chysauster, Cornwall* (Crown copyright, reproduced by permission of the Controller of HMSO)

pound. You might not recognise it immediately, for all you will see at first glance is the remains of a dry-stone wall, about 9ft (2.7m) thick, enclosing an area of some 4 acres of rough moorland. Inside are twenty-odd stone rings, about 15ft (4.5m) in diameter, which are the remains of huts. This was a fortified village. The people would go out to graze their cattle on the moor, and terraces on the hillside show where they raised their crops. At night they retreated back behind what was then a high stone wall. It requires a real act of imagination to envisage life here 3,000 years ago. There was certainly little luxury here. You can see stones in the centres of the rings where the central roof-poles stood, and remains of simple hearths. That seems to be it: a harsh life in a harsh landscape.

Moving westward into Cornwall, we also move up in time from Bronze Age to Iron Age with the settlement of Chysauster first built around 200BC. To reach it, take the B3311 from Penzance towards St Ives and after 1½ miles take the minor road to the left at Badger's

Cross. Chysauster is a mile down the road. No problem here in recognising what's what, for this is a recognisable village, with eight houses neatly arranged in two rows. Each of the houses is oval, with rooms running off a central courtyard. They may still be crude in modern terms, but the floors are paved, there are proper drains and the absence of a massive perimeter wall suggests that life was a little more placid than at Grimspound. Those who find difficulty in understanding a village when faced with such sparse remains might prefer to visit Cockley Cley, near Swaffham in Norfolk, where an Iceni encampment of just slightly later date than Chysauster has been reconstructed on the original site. It is interesting to compare this with the Saxon village at West Stow, mentioned in Chapter 4 (pages 97–9).

Roman houses are better known – and rather better preserved – than these more ancient settlements, even though the painted walls of the house in Dover (page 21) are among the few that rise more than a few inches above ground level. The principal survivors are the rather splendid pavements to be found in many villas, covering that very sensible Roman solution to the cold and damp of the local climate – the hypocaust or underfloor heating system. Grandest of all the pavements is that at Woodchester in Gloucestershire, but as that is only put on view about once every ten years, it can scarcely be included in a regular tourist itinerary. But at Chedworth, not very far away, between Cirencester and Cheltenham, is a fine villa with superb mosaics – and the man who designed the mosaics went off to Oxfordshire and did another set at North Leigh. Other notable

*Reconstruction of an Iceni village at Cockley Cley* (Sir Peter Roberts, Bart.)

villas can be found at the well-known sites of Bignor and Fish-bourne, both in West Sussex, and on the Isle of Wight, which seems to have been a popular spot with the wealthier Roman residents.

The difficulty about trying to see the ordinary life of the distant past is that the houses of the poorer people were generally insubstantial. They collapsed or were replaced and have left few traces. You can get the notion that Roman Britain was full of people living in elaborately decorated houses of some grandeur. There were, it is true, a fair number of houses like that, but there were a great many more people living in houses that scarcely differed from those of Chysauster. The same problem remains as we advance towards more modern times. You get the idea that people of the Middle Ages lived in castles and then, when times grew more peaceful and settled, moved into fortified houses. Certainly that is the impression given by most of the places that visitors get to see. There are, of course, very good reasons why people like to visit castles – they are massive, impressive and carry an aura of romance. Most such places are too well known to need recommendation here, but I should like to mention a couple, slightly off the beaten track.

Stokesay Castle, built in the thirteenth century, is the best preserved fortified manor house in England. It needed fortifying for it stood on that much disputed land of the border between England and Wales. Like most buildings of such an age, it has been added to and embellished over the years. Its true glory, however, is the great hall with its roof timbers arching across over 30ft above the stone-flagged floor. Over in Wales, Tretower Court and Castle, in the Usk valley show the movement from keep to fortified house very clearly, for both survive. One theory is that when Llewellyn captured the castle in 1260 he made such a dent in it in the process that when the Normans eventually recovered it, they had no choice other than to build a new home. Whatever the reason, it is all very fine and my memories of visits here are especially pleasant. This is an official Ancient Monument and the official guides – at least on visits I have made – have the liveliest line in commentary I have ever heard. It is, one should perhaps add, a very Welsh view of history that is given here.

That other border, between England and Scotland, had at least as much need for fortification as did the Welsh marches. If anyone had been taking a census in the region during the fifteenth century, and if the local inhabitants could have been persuaded to co-operate and answer truthfully, then a large proportion of the population would have had to enter in the column marked 'occupation' the description 'border raider'. Anyone who was going to live in the area needed a stronghold into which he could retreat for safety when the raiders came. The strongholds were known as 'pele' towers, and there were over seventy of them spread through the region at the beginning of the fifteenth century. Preston Tower, near Chathill north of Alnwick, is one of the few, and certainly one of the best preserved, of the survivors. It was built by the governor of Dunstanburgh Castle as a refuge where the local people could go with their cattle in times of trouble. It was certainly built for security not comfort, with grim tunnel-vaulted rooms, more like cells than living quarters – a gloomy place that tells of a dark time.

It is almost a relief after all this talk of war and raids to turn to the more peaceful world of towns and town houses. An old house can seem as rich and varied in its detail as a small town. The Strangers' Hall, Charing Cross – Norwich not London – is a fine, late-medieval house which has been used as a display area to show the changing tastes of domestic life. It is, in many ways, the ideal place to demonstrate the ever shifting patterns of fashion, for the house itself has grown, developed and changed over the centuries. The undercroft is still pure medieval, reflecting a time when shape and form were the essential elements that gave character to the house. This, the oldest part, dates from the early fourteenth century, while the Great Hall was added a hundred years later. Much of the building's personality, however, derives from sixteenth-century improvements – a dubious phrase, at best, for although the comfort of the house was undoubtedly improved, much of its elegant simplicity was lost. The work was put in hand by a rich grocer, who went on to become Mayor of Norwich. Change did not stop with his efforts, though later changes were often of a superficial character.

The early rooms seem totally different from those of more recent date, but, on closer inspection, those changes often seem to relate as much to the furnishings as to the rooms themselves. The Victorian sitting-room, for example, overwhelmingly portrays the extra-ordinarily claustrophobic atmosphere in which our ancestors lived. The room itself has the most generous proportions, but nothing in it is allowed to be still – every surface is decorated, busy with pattern and adornment. Look at the fireplace, ornate enough in itself, but further embellished with gilt-edged mirror, mantelpiece ornaments, tapestry fireguard and gleaming fender. The same holds true throughout the room, where upholstery relies on the richness of plush velvet and the sombrely lowering colours of brocade. The effect is overpoweringly rich. Yes, you say to yourself, I see what they mean – but how could they bear to live with it?

The Dutch Cottage on Canvey Island represents a totally different tradition. The cottage was home to one of the many workers brought over from Holland to help the engineer, Cornelius Vermuyden, in the drainage of the wetlands, particularly the fens of East Anglia. No one who looks around that region today can long remain unaware of the Dutch influence on a whole range of buildings. The influence is even reflected in place names such as New Holland, the area to the south of the Humber. Other regions where they worked are not so well known, but had it not been for the work of those Dutch engineers, Canvey Island might still be largely under water today. Quite apart from this little house which seems to belong to a transplanted piece of Holland, Canvey Island is a very odd region altogether. Great efforts were made to turn it into a resort area to challenge nearby Southend, but the efforts failed. It has its devotees, and I sometimes prefer the rather melancholic air of such places to the brash loudness of success that hammers down over so many coastal areas. But success or failure, Canvey Island would never have been given the choice at all without the work of those Dutch engineers who won the battle with the sea. So this little house is not just of interest in its own right, but serves as a reminder of what the east coast owes to the men from across the North Sea.

The house at number 33 St Andrew's Street, Plymouth, is officially known as the Merchant's House. This is rather in the nature of a euphemism, since the original 'merchant' was William Parker, who might more accurately be described as a privateer. His wealth came from the open seas and distant lands, but nothing of that is reflected in his home. This is a good, solid Tudor house and no nonsense about foreign fripperies and outlandish tastes. It was built at a period when the man of property looked more to comfort than security against intruders. Walls were panelled for warmth, and the panelling was often intricately carved to make a virtue out of necessity. I find these Tudor interiors a trifle glum and oppressive. Details in panelling may be beautifully carved and one can appreciate the delicacy of the work, yet the overall effect quite dominates the interior. I much prefer the other decorative form of

*Preston Tower, Chathill: a place of refuge against the Border raiders* (Northumbria Tourist Board: Photo Centre, D. M. Smith, Alnwick)

the period, the fresco. The plain plaster wall, often painted with remarkably vigorous scenes, seems to bring lightness to a room where oak panelling, however fine, brings a more brooding air. Look at the fifteenth-century Tudor Merchant's House on Quay Hill, Tenby, for example. It is a fine house in its own right, and boasts some truly spectacular Flemish chimneys, but its early frescoes are its greatest glory. Frescoes all too often, however, tend to dwell on somewhat doom-laden subjects. The object of such pictures is pious: if the last thing you see when you close your eyes at night is a reminder of the fires of Hell, then perhaps you will regulate your waking hours to walking in the paths of virtue. I once slept in a bedroom in a house in Devon with such frescoes on the wall, not to mention a resident ghost which appeared to prowl the old creaking house. I cannot honestly say that it made me notably more virtuous.

Not everyone, not even the comparatively wealthy, lived in the sort of splendid house we have just been looking at. As early as the beginning of the seventeenth century, the good citizens of Edinburgh had abandoned the private house in favour of the block of flats or tenements. It was, in fact, here that the word 'tenement' in this sense originated. In medieval times, the tenement was the strip of land attached to a house; this was so in both England and Scotland. But the old town of Edinburgh, clustered round the castle and the rock, suffered a vast expansion of population in the sixteenth and seventeenth centuries. Land became so scarce that the only way to house the extra numbers was to build on the old tenement plots. It was rather like Manhattan in the twentieth century: there was no room to spread out, so you had to build up, sometimes as high as a dozen storeys. The name tenement was transferred from the land itself to the building that now occupied it. One of those who acquired a building on such land was Thomas Gladstone, who took possession in 1617. His building now belongs to the National Trust for Scotland and is known as Gladstone's Land. You will find it in Lawnmarket, a narrow stone building, six storeys high, with cellar. It has been restored and refurnished in period style, with shops and booths at ground level and living quarters up above. If the name tenement suggests a cheap, rather slummy block of flats, then call in here and look, for example, at the living quarters with the magnificent painted ceiling of 1620.

(opposite) *The fifteenth-century Tudor merchant's house at Tenby* (Wales Tourist Board) *and* (overleaf) *Gladstone's Land, Edinburgh showing the original wall and ceiling paintings* (National Trust for Scotland: John W. Wilkie)

*Georgian elegance at Charlotte Square, Edinburgh* (National Trust for Scotland: John W. Wilkie)

There was a limit in Edinburgh to the numbers that could be squeezed into the old town, even if tenements were built on every available plot. The answer was a new town at the bottom of the hill. This other Edinburgh was planned, whereas old Edinburgh had jostled and elbowed for space. This was to be a spacious elegant city and in Charlotte Square you can see that elegance in its finest form, in the work of architect Robert Adam. Number 7 has been

176

refurbished by the National Trust for Scotland in the style that would have found favour with the original occupants. It has been renamed The Georgian House, the use of the definite article suggesting that it might perhaps stand as an example of all that is best in Georgian architecture – an arrogant claim it might seem until you visit here and see what a truly splendid house it is. There are, however, others laying claim to the title.

Bristol remains one of the finest cities in Britain, in spite of the heroic efforts of planners and road-builders to destroy all its character. Bristol defeated them, and remains a city dominated by water. Think of Georgian Bristol and your first thoughts turn to Clifton. I have never been certain of the best way to view it: should one stand on the suspension bridge and look at the magnificent houses or stand by the houses and view Brunel's magnificent bridge? But the Georgian House is not in Clifton at all. It is down in the dockland area, in Great George Street, not far from the floating harbour. This was the home of a sugar merchant, who clearly liked to live close to the source of his wealth, and the house reminds us that a good deal of cash was required to keep such a home going. In this house, much of the emphasis is on the domestic arrangements. One becomes used to the display of the fineries of gracious living but here we are given the kitchen, the laundry and the plunge bath. The owner used to dive into the chilly waters of the bath every morning.

The Georgian House at Bristol has made some concessions to the modern world, but the Argory in County Armagh is unique in still retaining gas lighting – not the old-style town-gas lights, but acetylene lighting using gas provided by the house's own gas plant out in the stables. This is a country mansion rather than a town house, very grand, built in 1820, and if not so refined in detail as the others, it is a handsome enough place which is now seen much as it was at the beginning of this century. The Argory also offers walks through 200 acres of woodland beside the Blackwater River. You might also, if you walk out down the country lanes, chance upon a game which is unique to Armagh and County Cork, road bowls. This is not the sedate game of the green, but a far more exciting affair, in which the players send the iron bowls hurtling at speed down the lanes, and sometimes, to the considerable alarm of spectators, bounding over walls and hedges as well. Those who find that they still hanker after that very special form of graciousness offered by the Georgians should now wander off to see the Mall in Armagh itself, a city which at its best can rival Bath.

*The Argory, a country house in the grand style at Armagh* (National Trust for Ireland: A. & C. Photography)

Restraint and refinement are only a part of the Georgian story, for the taste for something more extravagant was there as well. Where would you look for such a display? The chances are that the name that would not spring most readily to the lips is Neasden, a London suburb which, thanks to the magazine *Private Eye*, has the unenviable distinction of being thought of principally as a joke. But down Neasden Lane you will find a stable block which was converted around 1810 into a rather splendid Gothick cottage. Inside is a local history museum and a set of interiors from different periods in the house's history.

The nineteenth century saw more than just a start to the Gothic revival; it saw vast expansion of industrial towns. Lately this side of

the past has been hopelessly over-romanticised, so that an image has grown up of jolly chats over the garden wall, of jolly little terraced houses full of jolly characters. The reality was frequently a good deal less pleasant. At Lark Hill Place, Salford, Manchester, you get a whiff of reality – though not too literally, which is perhaps as well since the owners of the cottage here would have had to make do with a bucket for sanitation, and share the privy with half a dozen other families. Here you see a typical two-roomed cottage of the Victorian age, home to a whole family, with no drains, no refuse disposal and the only water supply a communal pump. Not much romance about that, and not much to romanticise over in most of the working-class districts.

Earlier we moved from Edinburgh tenement to Edinburgh Georgian, and now we shall move back to the tenements again, but

179

ones of very different character, the tenements of the nineteenth century. Victorian Glasgow was a city full of the new-style tenements and you can see them still around the city edges, mostly built in the very distinctive local red sandstone. Number 145 Buccleuch Street close to the city centre, just to the north of Charing Cross, was built in 1892 and is typical of many such buildings. Recently the National Trust for Scotland acquired a first-floor flat complete with its contents, the homely accumulations of the family that lived there for fifty years. It is a great pleasure to see bodies such as the NTS concerning themselves with such buildings. When it was founded in 1935, the NTS was entrusted with 'the permanent preservation for the benefit of the nation of lands and buildings in Scotland of historic or national interest or natural beauty'. The Trust has amply demonstrated its willingness to care for areas of natural beauty; in acquiring and preserving buildings such as this it is now demonstrating a welcome concern for the social history of the country. To visit this tenement is to partake for a while of an essential part of the developing life of Glasgow. It is especially welcome, for Glasgow has for too long been the city visitors never went to at all if they could possibly help it. Edinburgh is so near, they said, so why bother with mucky, noisy Glasgow? There is no easy answer, for Glasgow is not a place you get to know easily or quickly, but it has a true vitality that it is difficult to find in places more dominated by the need to satisfy tourists. It caters for a tremendous range of interests from the rarefied world of the finest of art objects in the Burrell Collection to the city's own story on display at the People's Palace.

Not so very far away, down the Clyde at Helensburgh, is the Hill House in Upper Colquhoun Street. This is very much a house with Glasgow connections, for it was built for the famous Glasgow publisher, W. W. Blackie, by Glasgow's most famous architect, Charles Rennie Mackintosh. Mackintosh was associated with the art nouveau movement of the turn of the century, but never quite fitted into the European pattern. In this he was rather like another famous outsider, the Spaniard, Gaudi, but where Gaudi was all flamboyance, colour and curlicues, Mackintosh was all gentleness and restraint. They did, however, have one thing in common: they both believed in total design. Gaudi, when designing flats in Barcelona put his touch on everything right down to the teaspoons –

*A typical Victorian tenement in Glasgow preserved just as it was when built in the 1890s*
(National Trust for Scotland)

and even today if you want to move in, you have to take Gaudi in toto or not at all. Hill House shows the same concern for detail. Although it is clearly built within the Scottish tradition, it is equally clearly a Mackintosh building complete with Mackintosh furniture. To step inside is to walk into his world, and those who feel they would like to linger to soak up this unique turn-of-the-century atmosphere can do just that for a flat is available for rental, thanks to that other excellent body, the Landmark Trust. You can pursue the Mackintosh story in more detail by going back to Glasgow to look in on the Mackintosh Society at their headquarters in a former church, Queen's Cross, designed of course by the architect himself. There is a small exhibition, but the church itself is probably the greatest attraction.

Looking around our towns and cities at the individual houses, one cannot help wondering what future generations would choose to preserve from our own age. The most obvious feature of recent years might seem to be the tower block, but size alone makes this an unlikely candidate. Would we in any case wish to see them preserved? My vote would go, looking a little further back, to the '30s semi. Here was a true expression of an age and still represents an ideal to many people. Perhaps somebody might find a candidate in, say, Wembley, where it might also double as a memorial to that chronicler of suburban life, the late John Betjeman. The nearest we can come at the moment is not so much a '30s semi as an aspiration towards it. This is one of my favourites among all the houses, not just for the building itself, but for the strange haunted air of a forgotten and almost vanished community.

On the western edge of Basildon in Essex you will find the remains of what was once known as the Dunton Plotlands. The story starts with the agricultural-depression years at the start of the nineteenth century, when a good deal of farming land was sold off to land speculators. It was then marked out into small plots and sold again to individual buyers. The main years of development came between the two World Wars when London families began building their holiday bungalows here, avenues of trim little houses. This was very much a do-it-yourself project with no help from authorities. Houses were laid out in rows and named First Avenue, Second Avenue and so on, but no one paved the new roads, no one brought in mains services and no one helped with the building either. Families would come down for weekends, sleeping out in tents and getting on with the job. Then, in World War II, Londoners

*Local schoolchildren visiting* The Haven, *a thirties self-built bungalow at Dunton* (Basildon Development Corporation)

began to move out of the bombed city and the holiday homes became permanent homes – but still without amenities. The end of the Plotlands came with the establishment of Basildon New Town. The authorities began buying up the cottages as people moved out, and today most of the plots have gone back to nature. The avenues are grassy tracks, and the carefully tended gardens have run riot. But you can still wander through the area and find the foundations of the little bungalows and the few survivors – and the local authority has provided a Dunton Plotland Trail to help the visitor. One bungalow, The Haven, has been kept as a Plotland Museum. It was built by Frederick Mills in the '30s, and he lived here for over forty years. It is tiny but trim, the perfect suburban villa in miniature; but a suburban villa without a suburb. In place of that there is a little wilderness, where domestic flower-beds riot among the more familar buttercups and dandelions.

The houses we have been looking at have been chosen because they give a taste of the lifestyle of the occupants. Until the age of radio and television, entertainment in the home had to be home-made. Reminders of these more recent innovations can be seen at the Bygones and Broadcasting Collection at Silver Street, Barnstaple (Devon). It is astonishing how quickly the early years of radio seem to have receded into the distant hazes of the past. The old valve radio looks as antique as a Chippendale chair, while the early personalities of the age seem equally distant in time. How remarkable it now appears to contemplate the idea of announcers arrayed in full evening dress for the news, even when no one could see them. But all this touches only a very recent past, archaic though it now appears. Where does one look for a glimpse further back in time? I would suggest looking at the world of children – not because, as harassed parents can be heard to mutter, they dominate the life of the house, but because their world often seems to represent the adult world in miniature.

There are two principal types of museum about childhood: those intended for adults who want to look at a world they have left behind, and those intended primarily for the children themselves. The former far outnumber the latter, and some of them are truly excellent. The toys of yesterday have, however, become the expensive antiques of today, though it is not just cash value that keeps them locked away in glass cases. Many are fragile and irreplaceable. A Victorian doll's house, for example, with its delicately made furniture, can now only be admired from afar. There are excellent museums of childhood, such as those at Bethnal Green and Menai Bridge, full of lovely things. Pollock's Toy Museum in London has a tremendous range of toys on show and one of the most recent additions to the scene, the London Toy and Model Museum, has one of the best collections of mechanical toys you will ever see. The latter does, however, tend to prove the old theory that it is father, not mother, daughter or even son who is besotted with the toy train. I must confess to standing with the besotted. I particularly liked the reconstruction of an old model shop, and the earliest model engines, the 'dribblers' and 'piddlers', so called because of their unsociable practice of spouting water all over the living-room Axminster. Here there is also a more active side, with a working railway in the garden. But it remains, essentially, a place to go to look and admire rather than to do. A few, a very few, museums encourage more active participation.

The Museum of Childhood in Edinburgh has just acquired new premises amid the splendours of the Royal Mile. Perhaps 'new' is not quite the word, since the building itself has a long and interesting history, having been a theatre in the eighteenth century. Today the pomp of the royal exterior is soon lost, just as the visitor too becomes lost, in a world of childhood. All aspects are represented, but the greatest emphasis is on fun and games. There is a superb collection of dolls and dolls' houses, board-games and rocking horses, pedal cars and mechanical toys of all kinds. Most of the exhibits, alas, are rare and have become somewhat fragile in old age so that they have to stay put inside their cases, but film has been used to help show the magic of the mechanical marvels. It is a museum about children and largely for children – which explains its proud boast of being the world's noisiest museum.

One place which really can claim to have something for everyone is Sudbury Hall in Derbyshire. Here you will find a splendid country house of the reign of Charles II, its interior notable for magnificently carved woodwork and elaborate plasterwork by such well-known craftsmen as Bradbury and Grinling Gibbons. Outside there are walks on the lawn beside the lake. The whole estate covers 170 acres of land so there is plenty to explore and much to fascinate the adult visitor. Children, however, should head for what was once the servants' wing and their own museum. This is not to say that what they find will not also interest adults, but when this museum was set up it was decided that the primary aim should be to appeal to the children. Here there are toys to play with, objects that can be handled and examined and a whole range of special activities. Children can dress up in old costumes, and for those who want to know just what it was like to be a working child in the last century, there is a special chimney for them to climb. It really does manage that difficult combination of instruction and amusement in a most satisfactory way.

For many families in the past, both parents and children, home was a place of work not of play. It is easy to look at an old cottage and exclaim over its quaintness, whilst forgetting that the quaintness might have covered a life of real hardship. Look at a building such as the National Trust for Scotland's cottage at Kilbarchan in Renfrewshire. Thanks to the care quite rightly lavished on it by the Trust it appears, in estate agentese, a most desirable residence. So it is indeed, and there is little outward sign to give any hint of the life that was led here in the eighteenth century. It is only when you go

(overleaf) *Children being introduced to a fairground galloper at the Museum of Childhood, Edinburgh* (Museum of Childhood, Edinburgh)

(above) *The weaver's cottage at Kilbarchan* (National Trust for Scotland); (opposite) *Clog-making the traditional way at the Colne Valley Museum, Golcar* (Robert A. Carter)

inside and see the handlooms that you realise that this was a weaver's cottage where wool was turned into cloth. It is easy to romanticise the work. The popularity of craft movements has given the impression that weaving is a fun activity, little more than a hobby, but most weavers worked extraordinarily long hours at what was essentially a dull, monotonous and repetitive task. It might have seemed preferable to the new industrial life of factory and mill that was eventually to make the handloom weaver redundant, but few of us would care to cope with the hard work, uncertainty and poverty of the handloom weaver. We can, however, still admire the work and the craftsmanship.

The north of England is another great centre for handloom weaving and here the cottages display the unmistakable signs of the trade in the long 'weavers' windows' on the upper storeys of cottages. These ensured plenty of light for the loom shops at the top of the building. At Golcar, in the Colne Valley to the west of Huddersfield, a pair of cottages has been knocked together. Here

you can watch demonstrations of hand spinning and weaving and even clog making. They make proper clogs here, not just the fashionable variety but sturdy lace-up affairs – the best form of footwear you will ever find for keeping feet warm if you stand around in snow and slush. The wooden soles provide splendid insulation.

This is a little museum that I have been coming back to for many years – indeed, the first time I appeared in front of a television camera was to demonstrate the flying shuttle on a Golcar loom. But it is not just personal memories, nor the friends who live in the valley, that bring me back. This is a place which epitomises that northern character I wrote about in Chapter 4, a place where town and country, industry and agriculture, exist in extraordinary unity. And this is not the only worker's cottage on show in the valley. Go on to Marsden at the valley head, join the towpath of the Huddersfield Narrow Canal and you will come to Tunnel End Cottages, located not surprisingly at the point where the canal disappears under Standedge Fell in the longest canal tunnel in Britain, 3 miles 135yd of it. It is not in use at present, but in its working day, as it was not wide enough to allow boats to pass, the tunnel-keeper had to take charge of all traffic. This was his home and his office, and now houses an attractive little museum and information centre. Alongside the canal tunnel is the railway tunnel, or more precisely the railway tunnels, and there is a pleasant oddity to observe if you walk up on to the fell. High on the hillside you will see circular brick structures which occasionally emit clouds of smoke. These are the ventilation shafts, and the smoke is a sign that somewhere far beneath you a train is making its way between Huddersfield and Manchester.

Other industries had their own particular form of house or outhouse. At Chapel Street, Ruddington (just south of Nottingham), there is a little complex of cottages and workshops built in 1829 for framework knitters. It was a Nottinghamshire clergyman, the Reverend William Lee, who first invented a machine for knitting stockings, as early as the sixteenth century. He almost got royal approval and a royal patent, which would have made his fortune. The machine was demonstrated to Queen Elizabeth I who was most impressed – until she was told it could only make woollen stockings, not silk. She lost interest and Lee lost his patent and his fortune. In time the machines did spread throughout Nottingham and the surrounding area, and this is a reminder of a once huge trade. It is very much a living museum, where things actually work – a splendid example of local efforts saving a vital part of the local past.

There have been workers' houses, in the sense of houses in which people worked, for centuries. A more recent phenomenon is the house built for workers in a local industry. When Isambard Kingdom Brunel and Daniel Gooch looked out over green fields between London and Bristol and decided on the site of the Great Western Railway Works they were also deciding on the site of houses for the workers. It was to be Swindon New Town. By the 1850s over 150 houses had been built and there was still not enough accommodation. A large building was erected which became known as the Barracks. It was not very popular and was converted first into a Wesleyan Chapel and then into the Great Western Railway Museum. Where railmen once slept, the giants of the steam age now slumber. The village remains, a series of very attractive houses built of rich Cotswold stone, and there is now a Railway Village Museum in what was once a foreman's house. I first visited the village when it was in the process of refurbishment by the local authority, and some interesting features came to light. The architects found that in an earlier modernisation, old rails had been cut up for use as door lintels; and gas supply then arrived on an

*A knitting frame for making stockings at Ruddington* (Ruddington Framework Knitters)

outside main that could be seen halfway up the walls of the houses. It is an intriguing place, not least because it shows what a very fine effort a great Victorian company could make to provide decent living conditions for the employees. The sadness is that so few did.

The world of big industry has been with us for a comparatively short period of time: the world of farming and agriculture has a history that stretches back over millennia rather than mere centuries. The Butser Ancient Farm in the Queen Elizabeth Country Park at Horndean, Hampshire, is a re-creation of an Iron Age Farm of about 400BC. The most obvious feature is the great round-house, but the visitor soon realises that everything here is different from the familiar farm surroundings of today. The ground is ploughed by teams of oxen; the crops grown are all ancient varieties; and even the browsing sheep are of an old and now rare breed. This is far more than a museum; it is a controlled scientific experiment to advance understanding of farming methods of the past. The seriousness of the experiment in no way detracts from the enjoyment of the place – rather the contrary.

After this, the Acton family seem comparative newcomers, as they only began farming at Church Stretton in Shropshire in the thirteenth century. The old Home Farm and a small parcel of farmland now make up the Acton Scott Working Farm Museum. The accent is very much on the word 'working', for the aim of the museum is to show farming methods as they were practised at the turn of the century, when heavy work called for horses not the internal combustion engine. There are many reasons for visiting the museum, but high on most agendas will be the appeal of the heavy horses, those great patient, placid friends of man who did his bidding for so many centuries. It may even be that one day, if cheap fuel runs out, their day will come again. Whether it does or not, here at least one can enjoy the sublime sight of a shire horse hauling a plough, the rich, red earth turning behind it as the scavenging birds swoop and dip for the newly revealed insects and worms.

The old farm was not merely a home from which workers went out to tend the beasts and till the land. It was a centre of activity. Milk was churned into butter and cheese was made, proper cheese, full of flavour. This is one of those points in the narrative where an author is sorely tempted to gallop off on a favourite hobby-horse, for one could write pages on the great and good cheeses of Britain as once

*A reaper-binder at work at the Acton Scott Working Farm Museum* (Acton Scott Working Farm Museum: P. G. Bartlett)

made throughout the land. I shall resist temptation in favour of recommending one place where old skills, such as butter- and cheesemaking, are still demonstrated.

The Manor Farm at Cogges, on the outskirts of Witney in Oxfordshire, is an old farm that has been taken over by the local authorities and revived as a museum. And a very excellent and attractive museum it is too. At the centre stands the Manor House itself, restored to reflect the last days of its true glory, in the Edwardian age. But if there was no more than this, it would be just another furnished country house. What distinguishes it from others is the working end of the place. Perhaps the best of the outbuildings is the dairy, where regular demonstrations are given, while on some open days the kitchen is pressed back into service for visitors to see old country recipes resurrected into fragrant life. Beyond that is the farm, and beyond that is what archaeologists refer to as the deserted medieval village. Do not expect houses or even huts, for the village itself is now no more than a series of humps and bumps in the landscape. It is quite hard to envisage the former scene from such scant evidence, but those with a detective instinct will relish the task of discerning houses and streets among the grassy mounds. This is only one of many such villages in the region: some vanished after the terrors of the Black Death, but a great many more were destroyed as a deliberate policy, when landowners realised that the old arable land could be profitably turned over to raising sheep.

Within the bounds of the Cogges museum there is a complete story of centuries of change in rural England to be read. The Elvaston Castle Museum in Derbyshire, on the other hand, has set out, rather like Acton Scott, to re-create estate life at the turn of the century; not merely the farm life, but all the ancillary trades as well, from sawyer to blacksmith and wheelwright. It is a real, active working museum where visitors are positively encouraged to take their share of the work.

Farming in the Celtic lands has followed a very different pattern from that of England. There has, until quite recently, been a tradition of smallholding; and in some parts of the British Isles this tradition continues into the present day. Within the last few years I have stayed on Irish farms where mechanisation was all but unknown, where I have gone out to dig the peat with a spade and cut hay with a scythe and where the principal mode of transport was horse and cart. It is a way of life that can be seen to be steadily receding, and if it is not entirely to vanish, then we must look to the conservationists to keep it alive, so that future generations will be able to understand their nation's history.

The Scots have been especially good at realising that history lies as much with the ordinary life of ordinary people as it does with tales of war and mighty exploits. Not surprisingly perhaps, preservation has been strongest in those regions where change has been slowest to arrive, among the Highlands and Islands of the West. There are croft and farm museums on Skye, Shetland and Orkney and in the Outer Hebrides. In selecting one from them all I have no wish to denigrate the rest. I am simply putting forward one which seems best to convey the story of struggle against the hard world that typified so much of the crofting life. The Black House at Arnol on Lewis is as basic as a house can be. The walls are constructed without benefit of mortar, and above them a simple wooden frame supports a roof of thatch. The kitchen fire is a pile of peat on the stone-flagged floor with a hole above for the smoke, while a pot suspended over the fire on a long chain is the cooker. The furnishings are scarcely more elaborate than the cooking arrangements; everything here tells of life reduced to its most basic elements. It was in such a house that Prince Charles Edward Stuart hid out after the collapse of the Jacobite uprising and from which it is said he emerged some weeks later beneath a layer of soot. Yet in terms of space, the crofters fared better than some members of the community – those who earned their living on the water.

Even today, the sailor accepts the need for a certain lack of creature comforts. Perhaps the best-known group in Britain for making do with a bare minimum of space were the boat families of the inland waterways. Mother, father and children all crowded into the back cabins of the narrow boats that plied the Midland canals of England, living, eating and sleeping in a space roughly 8ft by 7ft (2.4m by 2.1m). It was a miracle of organisation that would defeat most of us utterly. Yet it was part of a way of life cherished by those who knew it well. If you go to the Boat Museum at Ellesmere Port, on the south bank of the Mersey, make a special point of looking at the narrow boat *Friendship*. The last owners were the Skinners, and when Mr Skinner died the boat was moored up at Sutton Stop, the junction of the Coventry and Oxford Canals. His widow had a home 'on the land' but came back to her old boat every day. She would lean over the cabin doors, happy to talk to anyone who chose to listen to her reminiscences of the working days, the hard but rich life she and Joe had enjoyed as 'Number Ones', owning their own boat and

*The Black House, Lewis* (Crown copyright, reproduced by permission of the Scottish Development Department)

taking cargoes as and when available.

The canal boat-people were unique in that the whole family spent their lives on the water, unlike others who went to sea as working men but returned to a base on land. Many of the latter might have envied the canal boatmen, for conditions for the seagoing sailor could be hard indeed. You can get some idea of this if you go up to Dundee and see the frigate *Unicorn*, launched at Chatham in 1824. She is the oldest British naval ship afloat, though she never saw action nor indeed was ever completed. In fact, thanks to the work of her present owners, the vessel is in a more complete form than at any time since the launch. And you certainly get a very clear notion of the claustrophobic conditions on board. The ordinary seamen had to make do with hammocks slung between the beams of the gun deck. Officers fared little better. Their cabins were minute, and the call to clear the decks for action meant just that. The wooden partitions of which the cabins were built were taken down and all belongings removed. There was not much permanency about any seaman's 'home from home'. Even the captain had guns in his cabin at the stern. There are stories told of peacetime missions when the captain used to cover the cannon with chintz to provide a touch of domesticity.

Coming nearer to our own time, there are still some whose jobs are accompanied by the most spartan of living conditions. This is true, for example, of those who man the offshore lightships. The old North Carr lightship now permanently moored at Anstruther in Fife had a working life that lasted from 1938 to 1975 and you can get a remarkably good impression of what life must have been like on board – except, of course, that the visitor walks round a ship safely tied to the quay, not riding out a long, heaving swell off Fife Ness. Yet even that must seem luxury compared to the way of life enjoyed, if that is the word, by the submariner. The A class submarine *Alliance* can be found preserved beside the submarine museum at Gosport, Hampshire. The vessel is 285ft (87m) long with a 25ft (7.5m) beam and into that space were crammed ballast tanks, engines, weaponry, instruments and a crew of seventy-four. The men slept in minute mess areas with three tiers of bunks, and as one watch reported for duty, the previous watch would take over their bunks. That was what they called the 'hot-bunk system', and most of us who come to look round the submarine can just be thankful that we do not have to live under such conditions.

Looking at the lives and homes of other ordinary people does at

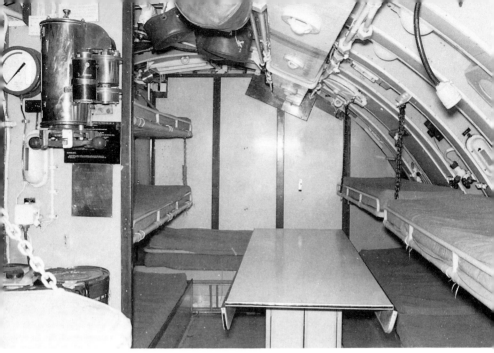

*Sleeping accommodation for a dozen men on the submarine* Alliance (Royal Navy Submarine Museum)

*The village shop at Morwellham (Anthony Burton)*

least go some way towards helping us understand the everyday life of the past – it also, in many cases, makes us appreciate our own comparative good fortune. It is good to know that so many examples of different kinds of home are laid out for us to visit, enjoy and possibly learn from. The selection described so far is no more than a sample, to which I should like to add one more – an example of a place where many of the themes already discussed all come together. It is a museum site, but one built around existing features, in no way relying on items brought in from outside. It is the popular village and open-air museum at Morwellham, on the Devon bank of the Tamar. It is a complex place, because a whole complex of things went on here, but at its simplest it depends on mines where minerals were dug from the ground and the transport routes required to take those minerals away for treatment. The transport route provides the first complexity: the Tavistock Canal high up the hillside was linked to the river bank by an inclined plane which, in turn, joined into a railway on raised wooden trestles that ran out to the quay. Here sailing barges and larger vessels called to load up with manganese, copper and arsenic from the mines. A complex operation requires a lot of people, and people need homes and facilities. These too have been restored alongside the industrial system, and they cover the whole social spectrum from the house of the assayer who controlled the movement of goods at the port to the tiny cottage of a miner. You can see pub and shop, tradesmen's workshops, and even the farm up the hill. Everything a community needed was found here. But for many visitors, the principal attraction is the visit to the mine. A narrow-gauge railway takes you deep into the old workings. This is one of many places where you can discover that other, dark world that exists beneath our familiar light world of the open air.

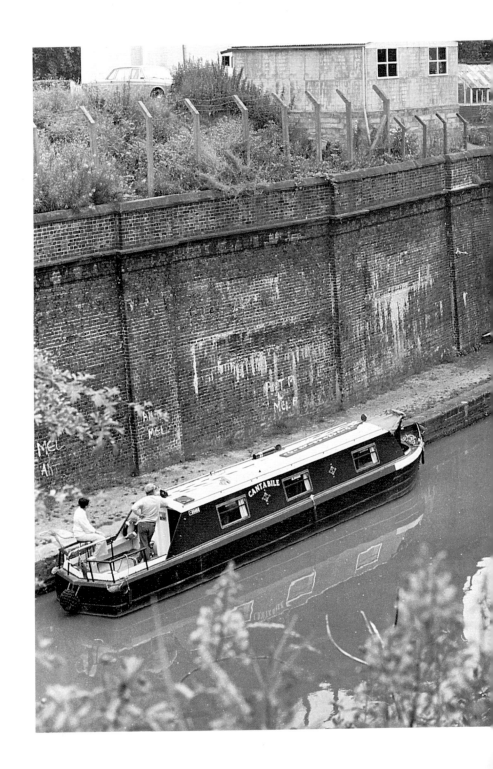

# 7
# Underground

*Pleasure boat emerging from the long journey through Harecastle tunnel on the Trent & Mersey Canal* (Derek Pratt)

This is not perhaps a chapter for claustrophobics, but those who feel just slightly apprehensive over creeping around through dark holes in the ground may be reassured – although there are places described here whose chief appeal is to the adventurous, rather more are about as daunting as a trip on the London Underground. Indeed, one of the recommended visits is a trip on the London Underground, though a very special part of it. I do not expect everyone to share my personal taste for wriggling down dark corridors of exploration, but I am sure that even those who believe that the entire notion of going to see what normally lies beneath our feet is rather repellent will be surprised at the tremendous variety of underground explorations that are possible even to the casual visitor. Nothing described here involves special caving equipment nor any specialised knowledge.

Perhaps the most obviously appealing of underground trips are those which take us into the great natural caverns. The best known are those around the Cheddar area in Somerset, though the largest cave complex, not just in Britain but in the whole of Western Europe, is that of Dan-Yr-Ogof, north of Abercraf, Powys. You can even find show caves in the unlikely surroundings of Torquay. Kent's Cavern can be found at Wellswood, a district of Torbay, where visitors are given a guided tour of the labyrinthine passages and illuminated grottoes. People come to such caves to admire the stalactites and stalagmites, which can achieve fantastic forms. They seem the stuff of fantasy and legend, and if we see trolls and petrified witches then so much the better. It is probably a more interesting explanation than an unvarnished account of accumulations of calcium carbonate built up over the aeons by water dripping through limestone. Those who have trouble remembering which name applies to which formation should note that a stalaCtite Comes down and a stalaGmite Grows up.

Such caves as these are undoubtedly very beautiful and are certainly very popular, though for me the appeal is limited. One grotto seems much like another, so that having seen one lovely show cave I feel no great urge to dash off to another – unless it has something to set it apart, and that something usually turns out to be human involvement. In fact, many caves were once inhabited, even if not very recently. Kent's Cavern, for example, was occupied tens of thousands of years ago, a span of time that all but defies understanding. Man lived here in the Ice Age and you can see some of the finds of the area at the Torquay Museum – remains from the time when the land was occupied by the bear and the sabre-toothed tiger. The museum also has a crude hand axe of stone, probably about 300,000 years old and one of the oldest man-made implements ever found in Britain. Little of this, however, is reflected in Kent's Cavern today, which is rather more concerned with the attractions of strange formations.

Those who prefer rather more adventurous excursions could visit the St Clement's Caves on the slopes of West Hill, Hastings, a tremendous system covering 4 acres and allegedly the haunt of smugglers. Everyone, I suppose, imagines a big cave near the sea to be a smugglers' hideout, and if there is any cave anywhere where reality and romantic fiction are likely to meet then it is in this corner of England. Rudyard Kipling knew the area well, for he lived just a few miles north of here at Batemans, near Burwash – a house, by the way, well worth visiting – and he wrote perhaps the best-known lines ever penned on the subject of smugglers. The ominous note sounded in the last line was no more than an accurate comment on the dangers of seeing too much in those violent days:

> Five and twenty ponies,
> Trotting through the dark –
> Brandy for the Parson,
> 'Baccy for the Clerk:
> Laces for a lady, letters for a spy,
> Watch the wall, my darling, while the Gentlemen go by!

Whether smugglers, in fact, ever trusted valuable contraband to anything as open as a cave seems somewhat unlikely, but the thought adds a piquancy to a visit – though the hopes of finding an abandoned brandy barrel are, to say the least, remote.

Other caves have more mundane associations, but are not necessarily any the less interesting. The limestone hills of Derbyshire are a great hunting ground for would-be underground explorers. There are natural caves galore and those who want a gentle introduction should visit Buxton Country Park, where they can combine a pleasant stroll through the woodland with a visit to Poole's Cavern. This is known as the 'first wonder of the Peak' and is certainly a fine natural cave, typical of the district. It was inhabited in Neolithic times, and the results of archaeological excavations are on show. But the great centre for cave exploration is Castleton.

*The stalactite cascade at Kent's Cavern, Torquay* (Kent's Cavern, Wellswood, Torquay)

*St Clement's Caves, Hastings, once the haunt of smugglers* (Hastings Tourism & Leisure Department)

Caves here have always been something more than just holes in the ground, for within their depths man has found minerals that he could exploit for profit. Each of the great caverns open to the public in this area has been put to use in some way or another.

One mineral in particular is found in profusion in the area – Blue John, a fluorspar which has been used for ornaments since at least Roman times. The obvious starting point for following this local story is the Blue John Cavern, on the A625 west of Castleton, opposite the shapely hill of Mam Tor; and with a name such as that the actual shape of the hill should require no further description. The cavern itself was formed by water erosion, and the cave system extends for over ¼ mile, the largest chambers rising some 200ft (60m) above the old stream bed. From here a series of Blue John veins, more than half of those discovered in the whole region, extend outwards. At some time or other all have been worked during previous centuries. Another equally rich, if not richer, source of Blue John was found at the nearby Treak Cliff Cavern. Why should such caves seem more interesting than others where the natural order has remained undisturbed? I can only give an entirely subjective answer. The Treak Cliff Cavern and Dan-Yr-Ogof have much in common, in that they boast similar, and equally attractive, features in their caves and pinnacles; yet I find the fact that man has worked so extensively in the one, hacking away through the long hours of a lightless day, provides a special fascination. I identify in imagination with those troglodytic workers fumbling through the dark.

The Speedwell Cavern, in the same area, was exploited for a different mineral, lead. A visit down this mine, however, is quite unlike any other, for as it is permanently waterlogged access is by boat down a mile-long underground canal. Originally, boats were hauled along by fixed chains, but nowadays an outboard motor provides an easier, if noisier, means of transport. The end of the line is a vast cavern with a 'bottomless' lake, and a complex of old workings. The story of these workings is explained in an exhibition, which includes photographs of mining days. In a way, one almost feels that it is now too easy to get down there, with an engine doing all the work, but once there the special atmosphere of the subterranean lake, deep and mysterious, exerts its influence. You do feel that you are indeed at the heart of a mountain and have entered another world. It is very easy to see this as a place inhabited by creatures out of Tolkien: dwarfs digging for mineral wealth, or more sinister orcs and even the wretched Gollum might be glimpsed emerging from the dark depths.

Nearby Peak Cavern is nothing like as creepy, though not a jot less spectacular. This is the largest natural cave in a district of big caves, and it was the space it offered rather than mineral wealth that provided the lure for entrepreneurs. This was the workplace of the Marrison family for more than 200 years, and for others who came to the caves before them. There was nothing especially romantic about their efforts, but they were undeniably useful. They made ropes: everything from thick haulage ropes to sash cords for windows. The manufacture of ropes involves the twisting of twine together, traditionally by a man walking backwards down a rope-walk adding the necessary twist as he went. It was an activity that required space, and the cavern supplied it. The end product may not have been as beautiful as a Blue John rose, but it was in great demand, and it was only the rapid spread of synthetic fibres that brought the business to a close. Work has ended, but the cave itself is as splendid as ever, and visitors can explore walkways that lead half a mile into the hill.

All this might seem a little tame to some, so here is something for those in search of a little excitement and a sense of adventure. The Bagshawe Caves are at Bradwell, in much the same area as Treak Cave, Speedwell and Blue John – you could easily spend a long weekend in the district and never see daylight. The cavern offers the same delights as the others – stalactites, fossils and underground passages – though the visitor has to work for them as there are a hundred steps down and, inevitably, a hundred steps up again. There is also an extra element. Those who contact the owners in advance (at The Caverns, Bradwell Head Road, Bradwell, near Sheffield) can opt for an introduction to caving proper, the really adventurous end of underground exploration. Caving is rather like mountaineering, in that it is almost impossible to define its appeal. But where the climber goes up the cliff in the open air, the caver scrambles down into the often watery dark. Both are admittedly dangerous sports, and those who can see no sense in risking life and limb in the pursuit of pleasure will never be convinced of their appeal. And the appeal of caving is certainly hard to understand even for those who, like myself, have enjoyed the perils of rock climbing. The charm of sloshing about waist-deep in icy water or even disappearing altogether in order to re-emerge in some new cave, is not immediately apparent. Not that this sort of experience is for beginners, and is certainly not expected of those who take their first lessons here in Bagshawe, but it is a commonplace among the experts. Those who go caving, rather like those who go climbing, discover very rapidly indeed whether their first excursion is the beginning or the end of a love affair. Those who find it is the beginning can look forward to exploring a whole new world that the rest of humanity will never see, and that is at least a part of the attraction.

I, perhaps somewhat perversely, have always baulked at the dirt, cold and dark of caving, but quite cheerfully accept the same conditions when exploring old mine-workings. Fortunately, for those who wish to be neither soaked nor begrimed, it is possible to see something of this latter world, just as it is of the natural caves, with a minimum of discomfort. The exploitation of the wealth below the ground dates right back into prehistory, to the Neolithic or Stone Age. Cartoon characters show Stone Age man as a hairy beast, holding a weapon made out of a hunk of rock strapped to a tree branch. He was a little more sophisticated than that. The most important material he used was flint, which can be 'knapped' – broken into large or small flakes which can be given a sharp edge and even polished smooth. The small flakes were used for arrow-heads and knives; the large pieces were shaped by craftsmen into efficient axes that could fell great trees. But first the flint had to be dug from the ground. You can see flint in plenty wherever you walk in East Anglia, but the very best flint was found underground. At Grimes Graves near Weeting in Norfolk is an area that looks like a World War I battleground, covered with shell holes. Those shell holes are in fact collapsed pits from which Neolithic man dug out his flint. Some pits have now been excavated, and one has been opened up to the general public. You clamber down a vertical ladder, to the bottom of a wide pit cut through the chalk, from the foot of which a series of long, low passageways lead off. The flint itself appears as a dark band at floor level, and it was a comparatively easy matter to remove the soft chalk using a pickaxe fashioned from a deer antler and then lever out big pieces of flint.

It is perhaps unfair to whet the reader's appetite when that appetite cannot be satisfied, but where now you can only peer down the lit galleries, once you could crawl. It is not hard to see why the practice was stopped. There was an element of danger and more than an element of dirt, for there are places where you can only wriggle on your belly through the wet chalk. But when you do visit

*Not a World War I battleground but the surface signs of the Neolithic flint mines of Grimes Graves* (Crown copyright, reproduced by permission of the Controller of HMSO)

one of the 'unimproved' pits, you feel that much closer to the miners of 4,000 years ago – and you can peer through into old workings that have remained undisturbed since work finished. You can see the heaps of broken chalk and flint, and even the remains of abandoned antler picks. It is a somewhat eerie sensation to stare into this world of thousands of years ago; eerier still if, as happened to me, your light goes out and you are plunged into total darkness. But if visitors can no longer explore that particular, undisturbed world there is compensation in the shape of the excellent small museum at the surface, where the workings of the old mine system are explained.

Stone Age gave way to Bronze Age, Bronze Age to Iron Age. They have been digging iron from the ground in the Forest of Dean for well over 3,000 years. The Phoenicians brought their boats up the Severn and traded for iron bars with the men of the forest. These are the men who began a long tradition, the tradition of the Free Miners of the Forest, which continues to this day. They decide their own affairs, meeting at the Speech Place in the forest centre. A hunting lodge was built on the spot in the seventeenth century, and later became a hotel but carries the name Speech House; and the foresters still meet there. The ancient mines also remain and one group, the Clearwell Caves, has been opened up. This is a series of inter-connected chambers some of great antiquity, some comparatively modern. You can see the Bat Passage, winter home to a variety of snoozing bats, and Chain Ladder Cave, where an old metal ladder can be seen heading down into an apparently impenetrable void. You can also see something of the work of the old mines. A black-ened roof tells of fire setting, a technique used in the days before the invention of explosives. A fire was lit against the rock and when the rock was red-hot water was dashed against it. The sudden cooling cracked the stone – it also filled the whole cavern with smoke and steam, and must have made life less than pleasant for the miners. The smoke has gone, but the blackened roof remains. The caves can be explored along lit passages, but there is also another form of exploration for special parties, who are taken down into the lower depths of the mine. I went with a party of young children who loved every minute of it – and who found it considerably easier to get through some of the narrower gaps than I did. It was most definitely not a route for the overweight, but I ranked it as a quite outstanding underground visit, and I was fascinated by the thought that each level we traversed represented a different level in a history that stretched back over so many centuries.

Moving forwards in time and sideways across the country, we come to the Romans and Wales, more especially to the little town of Pumsaint in Dyfed and the gold mines of Dolaucothi. Britain is not perhaps the first country to come to mind when thinking about gold, but it was once an important part of the national economy. And gold has a great advantage over, say, tin or iron, in that you only need a little of it to create a good deal of wealth. The importance laid on the local reserves by the Romans is apparent from the huge expenditure of effort and cash that went into the enterprise. The first step in a Roman gold-mining operation was known as 'hushing' – torrents of water were sent pouring down the hillside, washing away the soil to reveal the ore in the rocks beneath. The water came from the Rivers Cothi and Annel. The trouble was that the gold was high up the hillside and the rivers were down in the valley. Aqueducts up to 7 miles long had to be built to carry the water to the mine. You can still trace the watercourses today. Once the vein of ore was revealed, the miners followed it into the hillside, and you can explore the narrow passageways they cut. Much of what we now see, however, is of more recent date, representing a reworking of the old veins that

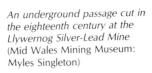

*Entrance to the Roman gold mine at Dolaucothi* (National Trust: Alan North)

*An underground passage cut in the eighteenth century at the Llywernog Silver-Lead Mine* (Mid Wales Mining Museum: Myles Singleton)

began in Victorian times. The exploration of these workings may not have the obvious glamour of following in the footsteps of the Roman miners – or to be more exact their Celtic underlings – but these do reach far deeper into the mountain. Once inside, it becomes like a three-dimensional maze: ladders lead up and down, passageways point off in all directions. Visitors are guided by experts, which is just as well, for without their help one might walk this subterranean world for ever. Here, one feels, is an introduction to a real world of mining: no pre-set lighting, no laid-out pedestrian walks, just this complex of routes formed by men who followed the gold wherever it led them. If you find the idea of this mine unappealing, then skip the next few pages, for you will not find what follows much to your liking either.

Gold is the most exotic mineral mined in Wales, but silver runs it a close second. The Llywernog Silver-Lead Mine was, to be honest, thought of as a lead mine first and silver mine second. At the peak of the Mid Wales equivalent of the Klondike gold rush, the mines around Aberystwyth produced in one year, 1856, over 8,500 tons of lead and just 1 ton of silver. This actual mine was begun in the middle of the eighteenth century, had its heyday a century later and closed at the beginning of the nineteenth century, not because the ore ran out but because huge new sources had been found in America and Australia. Today the old mine has been brought back to life. You can walk into the hillside to the workings, where you can still see streaks of ore in the tunnel roof, and the Blue Pool – not a fairy grotto but a prospecting pit sunk nearly 200 years ago. But the underground exploration is only a small part of the story; the main emphasis is really on the surface remains – the offices, the giant water-wheels that powered pumps to keep the mine dry, machinery for crushing and processing the ore, and a whole collection of exhibits that tell the story of mining. The total effect is to make it clear that mines were more than just holes in the ground. You do not just dig a hole, climb into it, hack out a lump of silver and go home a rich man. The different processes are all laid out as a miners' trail: over twenty places to pause along the way, either to see things work or to be told how they worked a century ago. There is one odd little building, looking like an outsize beehive built of stone. This is the gunpowder magazine set, not unreasonably, a long way from the rest of the buildings. To add to the appeal, there is the setting itself, high in the Plynlimon Hills.

The other great lead-mining region was Derbyshire, and those

*The Magpie lead mine in Derbyshire* (Peak District Mining Museum)

who want to get a complete picture of a very ancient industry could do no better than to combine a visit to Llywernog with one to the Goodluck Lead Mine at Via Gellia near Cromford. Where the former offers a splendid selection of reconstructed surface features and a brief excursion underground, the latter has left the bits and pieces that have survived on the surface more or less in the condition in which they were found, but has opened up extensive sections of the underground workings. The visitor who wants to get the best out of this museum should come ready for a little rough scrambling, which mostly means wearing good solid shoes, as dust-coats, helmets and cap-lamps are all provided. From the start, you are left in no doubt about what you are in for, as the first passageway is low and narrow, giving just the right feeling of setting off on an adventure. And adventure it proves to be, as you are taken along the narrow galleries and steep inclines and introduced to the simple tools of the

miners and the often crude devices used to break the ore out of the rock and move it to the surface.

The underground workings of the Goodluck Lead Mine might, possibly, give a misleading impression of the nature of Derbyshire mining. It seems here to be a very personal affair – look at the initials carved in the rock by miners celebrating the opening of a new section in 1831. It is true that much of the success of these mines rested on the age-old skills of the individual miners, but later development depended absolutely on the vast steam engines which were used to pump water from the mines and provide power for the cages running up and down the deep shaft. Memories of those days are preserved in the remains of the old Magpie Mine at Sheldon. This is a site I have known for many years, and I have never failed to experience a touch of excitement as the buildings of the old mine appear over the horizon. The engine-houses stand stark and bleak in the purity of limestone, quite sufficient in themselves to stir memories of the times when they lorded it over the shafts that led deep below the Derbyshire hills. It is perhaps unfortunate that the mine itself can only be investigated by the intrepid few prepared to descend on narrow, potholers' ladders into the depths; there is a whole world down there which can only be explored by the specialists. Even those who have to be content with looking at the surface features must be impressed by the sheer scale of the enterprise – and they might even get a bonus if they come here when the light is fading with a glimpse of the shifting shape of the mine ghost.

Enthusiasts of old mines are often quite startled when they visit Magpie, for the old engine-houses look very much as though they belong a few hundred miles away in Cornwall. This is not so surprising for it was Cornish engineers who came to Derbyshire to install the great engines. It is rather a shame that more is not being done to bring visitors to an understanding of the crucial role played by the mining engineers of Cornwall in bringing the age of steam into being. At East Pool, Camborne, there are two engine-houses, both containing their original engines. One, the smaller of the two, can be seen right beside the A3047 and the other, containing a truly massive engine, is on the opposite side of the road. You can go further back in time to older techniques of winning tin from the ground at Tolgus Tin at Redruth. Those intent on underground explorations should go to the Poldark Mine at Wendron near Helston. I find it somewhat sad that a story which is as genuinely dramatic as this should be thought to require the addition of a name from fiction to make it palatable to the great British public. Something of the attitude that the use of the name suggests carries over to the mine area. The aim has clearly been to provide a day out for the family, so that those who are bored by technicalities can find other amusements. Plenty of people seem to get a lot of pleasure from this mixture, but I prefer the attitudes displayed in my next two mining museums.

' The Chatterley Whitfield Colliery at Tunstall, Stoke-on-Trent, was until recently a working coal mine. I first visited the place in 1979 when work had stopped but the museum had not yet been formed. I went, in fact, with Jonathan Bryant, the curator who was to be responsible for the new museum. It was his first excursion into his new underground domain. Togged up in our best National Coal Board gear we entered the cage and hurtled down 750ft (223m) to the workings. Our guides were the men who had until recently been in charge of those same workings and they kept explaining how

*Until recently this was a working colliery, but is now the Chatterley Whitfield Mining Museum* (Chatterley Whitfield Mining Museum)

everything would be cleared up and lights brought down for the visitors, and Jonathan kept saying: 'No, no, don't change it, I want to keep the reality of the mine.' Changes have, of course, been made but only to help make the colliery comprehensible, to show the different techniques of mining. The essentials, however, remain the same: today's visitors still have to change into mine clothing, draw safety equipment and lights and follow the rules that would apply to a working miner. They still ride down in the cage, and the end result is that they get a glimpse of the reality of mining and the miner's life. I believe Jonathan's first instinctive reactions were absolutely right, and visitors really do appreciate that sense of realism. True, they are not getting the entire mining story – nor, in all probability would they want it. I have vivid memories of coal-faces where it seemed to rain dust, and that dust stayed with you for days and even weeks after a visit. Without experiencing the actual working conditions, you can perhaps never truly understand the life of the miner – but Chatterley Whitfield brings you very close to that understanding. The interest is not all below ground, though that is obviously the highlight – or should one say the lowlight – of any trip. The surface buildings are monumental and the preserved steam winding-engine is a joy to behold.

Chatterley Whitfield has now been joined by an equally splendid colliery museum at Blaenafon in South Wales (see pages 140–2). Everything that has been said about Chatterley Whitfield could be repeated for Big Pit. But just as no two towns are ever the same, so no collieries are ever identical. There are features here that you will not find in Staffordshire, such as the steam railway running from the pithead to the washery. But, on the other hand, there are Staffordshire attractions that are absent here. I have no intention of trying to construct an order of merit for two such magnificent enterprises. There is one factor however which, as a visiting Englishman, makes a trip to Big Pit a pure delight – the wonderful commentary provided by the former Welsh miners who act as guides to the underground workings. It was here at Big Pit that a moment occurred which for me said more about mining than a thousand displays could ever do. I was talking to one of the guides about the dangers of mining and asked him if there were any places in the mine which held special memories, scenes of accidents perhaps which still touched a nerve. There was no hesitation over the reply. Yes, he replied, there would always be that sense of awareness whenever he passed the place where his brother died. You cannot build moments like that into a museum; no statistics, no photographs, no reconstructions can ever carry the same emotion. Those moments live with the people, and the people remain a vital part of this museum. It is not a monument to technology, it is a monument to those who made the technology work.

Coal is the great mineral of South Wales, but in North Wales the slate industry dominated. It has been called the most Welsh of all Welsh industries. There are slate mines and quarries in other parts of Britain, but nothing on a scale that can match those of the principality. One of the great appeals of the slate industry lies in the setting of the mines and quarries, such as that of our first call, Chwarel Wynne in the lovely valley of the Ceiriog, south of Llangollen. The slate museum and quarry at Glyn Ceiriog offer, as a first sight a vision of a splendid verdant hillside, yet much of the hill is nothing more than one vast quarry heap. The next surprise might be a confrontation with the local bird-life, for strutting around the mine are resplendent peacocks – birds which manage to combine beauty of plumage with a cry as ugly and raucous as that of a laryngitic crow. These birds have not been brought in as a tourist attraction, for there have been peacocks here for almost a century. The mine itself has a history that goes back well beyond that, for there were quarries here as long ago as the ninth century. The present mine, however, is a creature of the Industrial Revolution, for it was transport that provided the key to getting the slate from the hills to the customers in the towns.

The Llangollen Canal runs through Chirk, crossing the end of the Ceiriog valley on a fine stone aqueduct – not perhaps as well known as the mighty Pontcysyllte across the Dee a few miles away, but a grand memorial to the engineer responsible, William Jessop (not as local guides still tell you, Thomas Telford). The mine was connected to the canal by railway, first using horses, then steam locomotives. The works reached a peak of prosperity in the early years of this century, but the scale of those works is not really apparent until you go underground. What seems at first a tiny hole opens up into great caverns and a complex of workings at different levels. Visitors are given a half-hour tour of the first two levels. Part of the appeal for me lies in the contrast between the wooded hillside above, with its nature trail and air of unspoilt beauty (though spoiled is what the hill literally is), and this other complex world where over seventy men once worked to remove thousands of tons of slate for the roofs of Britain.

This is typical of a number of small, remote mines where little now remains at the surface to tell of the once busy scene beneath. But turn to Blaenau Ffestiniog, the slate capital of Wales, and you cannot escape the stuff. It is everywhere: mountains of spoil on every hand, buildings of slate, roofs of slate, mines and quarries in profusion. Transport again has its part to play, but where at Glyn Ceiriog the railway is a memory, here it survives as one of the most famous steam lines in Britain. The Ffestiniog was built to carry slate to the harbour at Porthmadog, but today provides one of the most spectacular passenger railways you can find. There are two major groups of workings here, and if you are worrying about which to choose, do not bother: just go to both, for each offers a quite different experience from the other.

(overleaf left) *One of the huge caverns excavated for slate at Chwarel Wynne, Glyn Ceiriog* (British Tourist Authority); (right) *Visitors travelling in style at the Llechwedd Slate Caverns, Blaenau Ffestiniog* (Llechwedd Slate Caverns, Dave Williams)

217

DANGER
NO THOROUGHFARE

The Llechwedd Slate Caverns are in some ways like those already described, vast caverns carved out by man, but the approach is very different. Here you travel in style, in cars hauled by electric locomotives, and you go down to the depths on a rope-hauled incline of the type which was once so common in the area. It is rather like travelling a mountain railway, but inside the mountain instead of on the outside. The old mill has been reconstructed and you can see demonstrations of slate splitting, one of those crafts which looks deceptively simple but which requires great accuracy and a keen eye. The other complex is Gloddfa Ganol, in its working days the greatest slate mine in the world. The old tips dominate the whole town, mountains of slate scored by a complex of levels and inclines. This is more than just a mine, for up there on the hillside there was a whole community, a village where families lived as well as worked. More than anything else it is the sheer scale of the enterprise that astonishes. You can go on a short visit, but to get the best out of the place take the special Land-Rover tour to the very top of the hill, where the whole quarry system is spread out below.

It would be tedious to repeat descriptions for every slate mine, but I would like to put in a word for two other favourites: one in Wales, the Llanfair Quarry near Harlech and one in England, Carnglaze near St Neot in Cornwall. But for those who get really involved with the story of slate then an absolute must is a visit to the Welsh Slate Museum at Llanberis in Gwynedd. This is based on the Dinorwic Quarry Workshops and includes a tremendous array of old machinery, from a 50ft (15m) diameter water-wheel to a complete foundry where all the metalwork for the quarries was produced. And if you really want to take it one stage further, to get away from the formal world of museums and guided tours, let me commend a visit to Cwmystradllyn in the hills above Dolbenmaen, also in Gwynedd. It is not an easy place to find but it is worth the trouble. Here, in a splendid setting, is the old slate-cutting mill, which may sound as if it is scarcely worth the bother. Perhaps the popular name for the building might make it seem more enticing – the Slate Cathedral. The building, even in its ruined old age, is as dignified and majestic as any great ecclesiastical monument, while the very remoteness of the setting adds a romance to an otherwise ordinary tale of men working to provide material for roofs.

Not all holes in the ground are either natural or made for the uses of industry – nor are they necessarily to be found far out in the country. It comes as no surprise to be invited to go on a conducted

*Carnglaze Slate Caverns in Cornwall* (J. L. Rapson)

tour of the caves of the Derbyshire Peak, but a suggestion to go and view the caves not of Nottinghamshire but of Nottingham itself is quite a different matter: not 'cave', note, but 'caves' – a whole series of holes under this apparently solid city. The city authorities organise special cave tours and claim that there are more man-made caves in Nottingham than anywhere else in the land. Looking through the list, it is impossible to disagree. The whole place seems riddled with them, and they certainly afford a novel view of the city. Broadmarsh on the surface is shopping centre and bus station; underneath is a cave complex excavated in the eighteenth century for use by tanners – which must have been good news for the citizens, as tanning was a notoriously aromatic activity. The Oxfam shop in Bridlesmith stands next to the entrance to another group of caves which includes an ice-house. In pre-refrigerator days, cool holes in the ground were the only places where ice could be stored. Yet another set of caves can be found at Brewhouse Yard, where they form part of a museum complex. All these different caves were carved out for some special purpose – as stores and workplaces – and over the centuries their use has changed many times. A cave that

221

began as a medieval fish store might have gone on to become a Georgian wine cellar and could have done duty in more recent times as an air-raid shelter.

The caves, however, are only part of the story of underground Nottingham. Down below the castle, in the depths of the castle rock, is a secret passage, known as Mortimer's Hole. It gained its name from an event in 1330 when the Regent, Roger Mortimer, was holding his own parliament in what he believed to be the safety of Nottingham Castle. But someone knew of the secret entry and Mortimer was taken. There is still more to come. Wollaton Hall, the rather grand Elizabethan house on the edge of the city, home to an excellent museum, also has its underground passages. And not merely passages, for it can also boast its own subterranean reservoir, known as the Admiral's Bath. If you fancy a guided tour under instead of through Nottingham, then you can get details from the local information centres.

Exeter cannot boast such an array of underworld activity as Nottingham, but it does have a unique system of passages which are in fact a medieval water-supply. You can see them from an entrance in Princesshay. We tend to think of water mains running under a town as a very recent phenomenon, yet here we have a complex of aqueducts dating back hundreds of years. Perhaps we should not be too surprised, since wells are after all a very ancient way of obtaining fresh water from deep below the surface. This need to ensure water-supplies may lie behind one very strange and mysterious little passage. Carreg Cennen Castle in Dyfed is everything a castle should be, perched high on a precipice above the River Cennen. It seems impregnable, but that proves something of a delusion, for in the wars of the thirteenth century it changed hands several times and was captured by the Yorkists during the Wars of the Roses. They ordered it to be pulled down but, luckily for posterity, the demolition gang were less than conscientious. So we have a fortress that proved more vulnerable than appearances suggest and more vulnerable than its builders anticipated, for they expected to have to withstand lengthy sieges. They cut a passage through the rock to reach a spring that could supply fresh water for the castle. That, at any rate, is the most popular theory explaining the passage. Whatever its purpose, the old tunnel now provides an entertaining addition to the castle's list of attractions – especially if, as our family did, you arrive not knowing of the tunnel's existence and not armed with lights. We all stumbled around in the dark, while the offspring tried to terrify us, each other and anyone else who happened to be around at the time.

Coming closer to our own age and rather more sinister burrowings, the island of Guernsey was honeycombed with tunnels and excavations during the German occupation of World War II. The work was performed by slave labourers brought across from Europe (see page 82), and the largest of these caverns, the Underground Hospital at St Andrew's, has been opened up to the general public. Many of the other caves were used as shelters, bunkers and ammunition stores, and have either been filled in or used for more peaceful purposes. The story told at the museum is an uncomfortable reminder to those of us who lived in mainland Britain of just how close the evils of that time came to our shores.

We can now turn back to more cheerful topics to look at our last group of holes – transport tunnels, ways designed to get us under things which we cannot get round or over. The transport tunnel is actually a surprisingly modern phenomenon, dating back in Britain no further than the beginning of the canal age in the late eighteenth century. The first major effort was the Harecastle tunnel, carrying the Trent & Mersey Canal through Harecastle Hill to the north of Stoke. Work began with fine optimistic speeches in 1766, but eleven years dragged by before it was completed, and even then it was found to be inadequate. So a second tunnel was built alongside the first, and pleasure boats still chug over 1½ miles through the darkness. In building the tunnel, the workmen cut through ochre which still dissolves, turning the water into a remarkable resemblance to tomato soup. The Harecastle tunnel is not exactly a tourist attraction, and there is certainly not a lot to see along the way. The same cannot be said of Dudley tunnel in the West Midlands. This was more than just a means of getting from one side of Dudley Hill to the other, it was also a way of getting into a complex of limestone quarries beneath the hill. So a passage down the tunnel is a mixture of squeezing the boat down the narrowest of narrow openings and drifting through great caverns. The Black Country Museum runs a special, electrically powered boat into the tunnel; just one of the many attractions of this museum.

Dudley tunnel may be the only true underground experience on this site, but there is a tremendous amount to see here. It is comparable in many ways to Beamish and Ironbridge, in that old industries are being brought back to life and old buildings restored to re-create the environment of a century ago. Typical Black

Country trades are still practised, such as chain-making – and chain-makers can slake their thirsts in equally traditional and equally local manner at the restored pub. The tunnel is not strictly a part of the museum at all, but part of the far greater outside network of canals. This world too is reflected within the museum complex. I am particularly fond of the reconstructed boat-yard. Just take a close look at the workshop and see if it reminds you of anything. Note the height, and then look at the familiar narrow-boats outside. The shed is indeed made out of an old working boat turned on its side, part of the never-chuck-anything-away philo-sophy of the region.

The canals knew their finest hour in the eighteenth century. In the nineteenth century, it was the railways that caught the public imagination. No railway tunnel, however, can offer such exotic excursions as those along the old Dudley canal tunnel. But there is one other transport tunnel of great historic importance, that now holds a railway though it was not built to carry one, and which you can travel for the modest expenditure of the price of a journey from one stop on the London Underground to the next. It runs from Wapping on the north bank of the Thames under the river to Rotherhithe, and was the first tunnel under the Thames and, indeed, the first tunnel under any river. The engineer responsible was Brunel, not Isambard of railway and bridge fame, but his father Marc. Not that young Isambard was absent from the work, for, in fact, it nearly marked the end of his career. When the workings flooded during construction, he came very close to drowning. It was a long and costly undertaking, but proved a triumph for Marc Brunel's revolutionary techniques – even if it was not so successful as a roadway. Originally, it had been intended to have a long spiral ramp that would have allowed carriages down to the tunnel, but the money men baulked and the tunnel satisfied the more modest needs of pedestrians until the rails came. But, if you go down the spiral staircase at Wapping Underground, you can see the tunnel with its double-mouthed portals much as it was a hundred years ago, and London Transport have provided excellent explanatory panels. At the far end, the Brunel Exhibition Project has found a home in the building that stands over the old access shaft and inside this they are busy at work restoring the steam engine. It is good to see the memory of Marc Brunel being honoured, for he was, if not quite the genius that his son proved to be, an engineer of exceptional ingenuity and skill.

*Not perhaps a very exotic building, but it was here that work began on the first tunnel under the Thames. The Brunel Exhibition Project, Rotherhithe* (Brunel Exhibition Project: R. J. Barnes)

I visited the tunnel in the early hours of the morning, when the last train had gone, and was taken down to the empty platform and waved off for a walk under the Thames. It was quite an eerie experience, for one tended to remember the great inundation that flooded the whole area. But then I recalled the confidence of the Brunels who, after the flood, held a party down here complete with music by the Guards – military not railway. I could picture the scene in my imagination, even if I could not see it in reality. It set me thinking about the achievements of the Brunels, father and son. You could make a very interesting excursion, travelling around the country looking at their work, from the magnificently successful Clifton suspension bridge to the dismally unsuccessful Atmospheric Railway. It would be travelling with a purpose: the theme of our next chapter.

# 8
# Along the Trail

*Thomas Hardy's cottage at Higher Bockhampton* (Derek G. Widdicombe/Noel Habgood)

One of the problems of travelling somewhat aimlessly is that having everything, as it were, to look at, you end up seeing nothing. On the other hand, if I set out on my Brunel trail, which I have somehow never got round to doing, I should be looking out for things all the time – and would see not only the Brunel bits that were the excuse for the journey in the first place, but lots of other things as well. To this you could add the extra piquancy provided by the excitement of the hunt. I may not have done my Brunel journey – though I will – but I have followed other trails and found a great deal to enjoy.

There will always be many who ask no more from a route than that it will present them with fine scenery and perhaps also something of a challenge. For the very hardiest there are the long-distance paths, walks varying from a comparatively modest 70-mile stroll along the Dorset coast – no more than a week's outing for the experienced – to the gruelling Pennine Way, a high-level route of some 250 miles. Those who set out on such routes need to be well prepared and well equipped. They are emphatically not for the inexperienced, but they can be immensely rewarding. Mostly they have no 'theme' as such, unless you count following a coastline or a ridge of hills as a theme. One or two of these walks, however, do qualify as trails in the sense that you actually follow a route dictated by more than mere geographical associations. The Ridgeway Path, for example, is a walk through ancient history, for the route followed is that of the ancient Icknield Way and the Wessex Ridgeway. Not surprisingly, such paths come close to ancient settlements, with the grand climax arriving at Avebury and its stone circle, a monument as impressive as Stonehenge. Somewhat less venerable but not a jot less interesting is the Offa's Dyke path, part of which is described in Chapter 4, or you may prefer to follow the Sli Cuallan, one of the great roads radiating out from Tara, the ancient home of Irish kings (see page 125). This forms part of the Wicklow Way, still known in Gaelic as the Sli Cuallan Nua – an 80 mile walk through the Dublin and Wicklow mountains. You can continue on again for another 25 miles on the South Leinster Way. It is not, of course, necessary to walk the whole length of such paths to gain enjoyment from them, nor is it necessary in all cases to go on foot. Parts of many walks are designated as bridleways, which means they can be used by visitors on either bicycle or horse, though only the South Downs Way is open as a bridleway throughout. I regard bridleways as a mixed blessing, for they can too easily be churned up into a morass in bad weather, and use by bicycles too often includes use by motor cycles, which do little to add to the peace of the countryside. Most of us are, in any case, quite content to turn from the demanding long-distance paths to more modest walks, and even here the choice can be quite bewildering.

Theoretically, all you need for a countryside walk is a good map, with rights of way marked, and equipment suitable for the length of the walk and the nature of the terrain. In practice, the footpath shown with such clarity on the map does not always appear with equal distinctiveness on the ground, where it can be entirely obscured by the cloying mud of a ploughed field. There are definite advantages to following a carefully described route and there are literally hundreds of such routes available. I have in front of me a pile of literature on walks in the Isle of Wight. There are town trails of Newport, Cowes and Yarmouth specially produced for children, pointing out all kinds of interesting details and asking lots of questions. There is actually quite a lot that was new to this particular adult. A building close to Yarmouth pier has black squares painted on the walls, and they have been there since the 1700s. They are there because from a distance they look like gunports, and were intended to mislead the French about the strength of fortifications. Apart from these town walks, there are several country walks to choose from. There are seven long-distance trails: the coastal path is about 60 miles, but others all provide a good day's walking, and all are waymarked so that there is never any problem over access and routes. That is just one advantage of such established walks. The other major appeal is the information provided about what to look for along the way: buildings of interest as well as natural features.

Many people have no desire to walk anywhere much at all, and prefer seeing things by car or bicycle, using minor roads rather than footpath and bridleway. I find motoring a tedious occupation, but I tried out a local motor trail and was surprised how interesting it was. Having a whole series of things to look out for and lots of stopping places reduced the motoring part to a minimum. This route was a motor trail along the Cherwell Valley in Oxfordshire. It is only 46 miles long, but it manages to incorporate no fewer than fifty-five places of interest, ending with a great favourite of mine, Hampton Gay. There is not a great deal to Hampton Gay, although there was once very much more. The most obvious feature is the

Manor House, in ruins since a fire of 1887. The outer walls stand, though trees now grow in the hall, and odd details have somehow survived, like the little casement window drooping from its scorched hinges. In the fields outside are a series of ridges and lumps which mark what were once houses and streets, the medieval village. Like so many villages in this part of the world it was destroyed when the land was given over to grazing sheep: we often found fragments of old pottery when walking through the fields. The church is still there, though the village has gone, and in the graveyard you can see the monuments to those who died in a Christmas Eve accident in 1874 when a train was derailed and crashed into the Oxford Canal. Add to all that the remains of the old water-powered paper mill and you have a spot which combines pleasant country scenery with reminders of other times.

The Cherwell Valley should be visited now by those who wish to enjoy its peaceful charms, for plans are already advanced for the construction of a motorway along it – and then it will be goodbye to peace for ever. Or so one supposes. I am comforted by a somewhat gloomy thought expressed over 100 years ago by John Ruskin, deploring the arrival of the railway at Monsal Dale. He wrote of the desecration of the vale, of the intrusion of an industrial world into a region where once the gods would not have been ashamed to stroll. He could never have guessed that a century later the railway would be dead and the route handed over to walkers. Perhaps even motorways will not last for ever. This, however, is not a prospect which most of us can expect to live to experience, so go to the Cherwell while there is still time. The river runs into the Thames at Oxford, and the mightier river is not at the moment under any great threat, though it is not so very long ago that there was actually a serious proposal to build an Oxford relief road across Christ Church Meadows. There is another trail in the same general area which offers views of Oxford that do not stop at the more familiar colleges of the city centre. The council has produced a pamphlet suggesting a circular walk along the banks of the Oxford Canal and the river. It brings you to interesting little areas such as Jericho, introduces you to the delights of Port Meadow and Iffley and gives a reminder that even ancient university cities have a living to earn. Lucys ironworks has been established by the canal for over 150 years. This is quite a long walk and all walks tend to become a compromise between the competing demands of good, hearty exercise and a desire to contemplate the details of the landscape. Another series of

trails, 'On Foot in Oxford' are very much concerned with details –
and without time to wander would you ever notice what an
extraordinary variety of footscrapers are on show outside the houses
in St John's Street?

Not everyone can walk, so all credit to those authorities who lay
out trails especially suited to the needs of the disabled. Llyn Brenig,
the reservoir on the head-waters of the River Dee in North Wales
forms the focus of a series of trails including an archaeological trail
stretching for 10 miles around the lake's perimeter. Along the way
you can see whole layers of history exposed. There are Stone Age
settlements dating back nearly 8,000 years, Bronze Age burial
mounds and, coming rather more up to date, shepherds' temporary
houses of four centuries ago. For those more interested in the non-
human aspects, there is also a nature reserve. And there is a centre
where all aspects of the region are explained: archaeology, geology,
human history and natural history. And how good it is to note that
those limited to wheelchairs can also appreciate the area, for special
concrete paths have been laid out for them.

Betws-y-Coed is a far more popular, far better-known beauty
spot on the edge of Snowdonia. The river rushes down the valley in a
series of cascades, and all around are walks through the forest and
up into the hills. It is too easy for those of us who are blessed with all
our faculties to think we have a monopoly on the appreciation of
natural beauty. It is not so, and to its great credit the Forestry
Commission has taken the point. It has not just laid out wheelchair
paths but has also provided hand-rails to guide the blind. Those who
wonder why the blind should want to visit a beauty spot should think
of the pleasures of smelling a pine forest, and of hearing the songs of
birds or the rush of water over rocks. Another walk for the blind in
an especially popular tourist area is the Whitestone Trail near
Tintern in the Wye Valley. Again there is easy walking, hand-rails
for guidance and an additional benefit, cassette recordings that
explain the significance of the sounds heard on the forest walk. This
seems to be an area where the Welsh have taken the lead in showing
what can be done to make the countryside accessible to all – and
three hearty cheers they deserve for their efforts.

One form of walk which could be made far more available to the
handicapped is walks along disused railways, since whatever
convulsions might afflict the surrounding countryside, the railway
must, by its very nature, follow a level track. There is no shortage of
routes to choose from, as almost a hundred old lines have already

*Walkers now use the old railway viaduct across the Derwent Valley* (Anthony Burton)

been officially opened as walkways. In recent years, I have walked over many of these routes, and among my favourites is that which once ran from Consett to Newcastle, following the Derwent valley. The river dominates the line, which has to cross and re-cross it on tall viaducts, which afford the walker wide views of the surrounding country. This is a splendid introduction to railway walking for those who fancy giving it a go, but for those who suspect that a railway walk might get a little tedious there is a new walk incorporating the railway into a circular tour. The other area covered is that of the Gibside Estate, and this really is a walk with something for everyone. There may not be much railway in this walk, but what there is could scarcely be bettered, for there are two high viaducts. For non-rail enthusiasts there are woodland walks, hill walks and some quite remarkably fine architectural remains. There are distant views of noble, if ruined, Gibside Hall, and the statue of British Liberty can hardly be missed since it stands on the top of a

140ft (42m) high column. The major attraction, however, is the Gibside Chapel, a Palladian building designed for Sir George Bowes as a family mausoleum.

It seems rather odd that the handsomest building for miles around should have been intended for the dead rather than the living, and it is approached by an equally impressive avenue, ensuring that the arrival of the family dead would never be less than triumphal. Nowadays, avenue and mausoleum are in the guardianship of the National Trust. This is a walk of remarkable contrasts. On the one side are stately homes, on the other industrial remains, both threaded together by the line of the disused railway. In fact, I chose this particular route instead of many other railway walks I have tried precisely because it demonstrates so well how, once you set yourself on one trail – in this case the pursuit of long-dead railway lines – you are likely to find far more than you bargained for, in this case the long-dead members of the Bowes family.

The railway walk is just one way of investigating a fragment of the historic past. But the pursuit of history can prove one of the most attractive and fruitful ways of gaining an introduction to the country as a whole. Not that the starting point for an exploration makes that much difference. Visitors to Llanfairfechan, on the north coast of Wales, might go and visit the Aber Falls, and then be lured away into the hills to look for the Roman road, the hut circles and the standing stones; while those who set off on the History Trail are as liable to be seduced by natural beauties. The great thing to remember about all trails is that you are following them to suit yourself and your own interests, and there are no penalties for straying from the preordained path.

There are, however, some trails laid out with a very definite, well-defined purpose. Bwlchgwyn, near Wrexham, is home to Milestone, the Geological Museum of North Wales. The trouble that many people seem to find with geological museums, and indeed with many kinds of museum, is the inability to relate the objects seen inside with the world seen outside. There is, for example, a rock garden at Bwlchgwyn, but somehow in nature rocks refuse to arrange themselves into neat, docketed order. But from here you can set out to walk the surrounding country armed with museum leaflets, and when you follow the recommended routes you find, miraculously, that museum world and natural world do actually meet. There are two walks, neither very arduous. The one takes you on a tour of

233

inspection of the Nant-y-Ffrith stream as it gurgles and plunges down the hillside; the second takes you round a disused quarry. The latter is, in some ways, the more interesting, for once you have grasped what you should be looking for, you find yourself discovering fossils of shells and plants and a rich variety of rock formations. This is an open-air lecture, where the script is written in stone and earth, in the changing patterns of the landscape itself. With just a minimum of help, you find a simple walk has been turned into an engrossing lesson. Museums are becoming increasingly aware that what they contain within their walls only represents a part of the story. There is a tremendous gain in both interest and understanding when the story within the walls can be related to the world outside. The trail is one way of achieving that end.

A museum trail of quite a different nature can be found threading its way out from the city of Leeds. It follows the towpath of the Leeds & Liverpool Canal out from the heart of the city, along the valley of the Aire to the village of Rodley in what is a quite surprisingly rural atmosphere. This is not just a trail set by a museum, but a trail to museums. There are three museums to be met along the way, each housed in buildings of considerable, if very different, historical interest. The first to be met is Armley Mills, one of the earliest of the woollen mills on which the city's prosperity was built and, in its day, one of the biggest mills in the world. Next to appear on the walk is Kirkstall Abbey. These are magnificent ruins which would be major tourist attractions if they were found in different surroundings. Fine though they are, they lack the romantic setting of Fountains or Tintern. One happy result is that they are never so crowded as their more popular monastic brethren. The twelfth-century gatehouse is now home to another major museum, a folk museum with reconstructed streets and houses. These are the main attractions of the walk, but they are by no means the only pleasures. The canalside walk is itself a delight, with a steady procession of locks, lifting the canal up the valley, and there are some forty sites of interest listed along the way. You might even, if you come this way on a summer weekend, receive an unexpected bonus as a distant whistle announces the imminent arrival of a steam excursion special, doing a railway round-trip from York through Leeds and Harrogate. The route crosses the canal, and then runs beside it to Kirkstall.

*The geological garden at Bwlchgwyn* (Anthony Burton)

The Leeds trail is a very clearly defined route, following the canal all the way, a restriction which some might find irksome. Indeed there are those who dislike the whole notion of following someone else's preordained route. Well, you are not obliged to wait for others to construct a trail. In fact, the first 'trail' I ever followed was decided on on the spur of the moment by myself and a couple of friends during my undergraduate days. I was at Leeds University at the time, virtually unaware of the canal's existence, but an ardent admirer of the scenery of the Lake District. We went to Windermere and, instead of walking and climbing, decided to go boating, not in random fashion but to pick up the landmarks made famous in the books of Arthur Ransome, for the adventures of the Swallows and Amazons took place against a background largely based on Windermere. It was here that they sailed, on these islands that they camped, and it was on the shore that the ever-patient parents waited for their sea-rover children to return to reality from their fantasy voyages. This was the first time I became aware of the delights of this kind of trailing – the pure pleasure of finding and recognising a feature on the land which had previously been no more than words on the page. Here were Rio Bay, Cormorant Island and even Octopus Lagoon: what I did not know then was that there

*Captain Flint's houseboat* – Esperance *on Lake Windermere* (Windermere Steamboat Museum)

was another splendid relic of those fictional times waiting to be discovered.

Those who have read the books will certainly remember Captain Flint's houseboat – and what a pleasure to find that it too was based on reality, on a twin-screw steam yacht built for a local industrialist in 1869, the *Esperance*. You can see her still, a sleek vessel with steeply raked clipper bows, just as Ransome described her, at the Windermere Steamboat Museum. There may be larger collections of old boats elsewhere, there may be collections with more impressive exhibits, but you will never see such pure elegance as is on show here. And they work: to see these old launches out on the water, or better still to travel in them, is to be taken right back to an earlier age. This is a world of gleaming mahogany and brass, decorative canopies, plush upholstery – and steam, the beauty and the romance of the peaceful days of the steam engine.

The special appeal of the literary trail comes in adding a new reality to an old fictional friend: Ransome's invented world suddenly becomes solid fact. It depends, of course, on knowing the book in the first place: there is little point in knowing that you are looking at the Swallows' campsite if you have no idea who the Swallows were. The next few trails are chosen to try and give as wide a literary sample as possible, but are in no way intended to be comprehensive. I still think that the very best trails are those where you start with the author's work and then do the detective work for yourself, for there is nothing quite like the excitement of being able to say: 'Yes, this is it. I've found it, and it's just as I've always imagined it.' Some authors are easier to follow than others. James Joyce's *Ulysses* should be among the simplest, for Joyce was very exact about the movement of his characters in their one day of meandering through the real streets of the real city of Dublin. He is precise, but also complex. Everything does fit together with remarkable accuracy; characters meet and part and meet again, running to an exact timetable. But that complexity can be bewildering, even if the start at least presents no problem. It is a testimony to the power of literature over reality that the place most commonly associated with James Joyce, the building we think of as his home and which is indeed now home to the Joyce museum, is one he went to as a lodger and where he stayed just six nights. It is the martello tower at Sandycove, Dún Laoghaire. Its fame derives less from Joyce's brief stay as much as from his making it the starting point of the epic novel. It is here that 'Stately, plump Buck Mulligan' comes out to

*The martello tower where James Joyce briefly lived, Sandycove, Dublin* (Irish Tourist Board: Bord Failte)

greet the morning. It was a short episode in the book and a short episode in Joyce's life, yet somehow the place seems to hold the essence of both. I know of no literary museum so imbued with the spirit of an author.

To move on from here in an attempt to follow the movement of the characters is more difficult. It is all there in the book and many of the places do survive, and not just the public buildings either. You can still visit the Ormond Bar, where the barmaid sirens sang and Eccles Street, home of Leopold and Molly Bloom. Indeed, as you walk the streets it is hard to believe that *Ulysses* is a work of fiction at all, so clearly does Joyce's world emerge. It is a pleasure to walk the streets of Dublin under any circumstances, for this is surely one of the great cities of Europe, but to walk in the steps of Dedalus and Bloom is to see the city with a special awareness. Those who wish to make the pilgrimage without the labour of deciphering the route from the novel itself can do no better than to read Frank Delaney's book *James Joyce's Odyssey*, and if you lose your way, it is no great matter, for Dublin itself will always be there to enchant you.

Getting lost is the best way of becoming acquainted with any city.

For those who want to widen their literary horizons rather than concentrate on the minutiae of a particular book, the Thames and Chilterns Tourist Board have a Literary Heritage Trail which offers a choice of tours, and provides ample opportunity for homage to a very catholic selection of authors. The Thames Valley, not surprisingly, has several aquatic themes on offer. The river was the setting for *The Wind in the Willows*: Kenneth Grahame spent much of his childhood at Cookham Dean, while the reaches of the river at Pangbourne were the inspiration for E. H. Shepard's famous illustrations. Jerome K. Jerome stayed at the Barley Mow at Clifton Hampden, where he wrote a good deal of *Three Men in a Boat* and repaid the hospitality by singing its praises: 'It is, without exception, I should say, the quaintest, most old-world inn up the river . . . Its low-pitched gables and thatched roof and latticed windows give it quite a story-book appearance, while inside it is even more once-upon-a-timeyfied.' In spite of a serious fire in recent years, the pub is still very much as Jerome described it – and it would still be, as Jerome commented, undesirable for a young lady with heroic pretensions to draw herself up to her full height, for 'she would bump her head against the ceiling each time she did this'.

Other literary notables in the Thames Valley include H. G. Wells who worked in Rodgers & Denyers, the Windsor drapery store, and used the experience to amuse his readers in *The History of Mr Polly* and *Kipps*, and Oscar Wilde whose time in Reading gaol is more sombrely portrayed. Moving further afield into Oxfordshire, there seems no end to literary associations. Here is Kelmscott, where William Morris's achievements are celebrated at the Manor House which was his home; while at the opposite end of the social scale stand Cottisford and Juniper Hill, so movingly evoked in Flora Thompson's work where they reappear as Lark Rise and Candleford. Surprisingly perhaps, given the recent popularity of the books, the villages and the surrounding country remain unspoilt. Or perhaps that is not quite the way to put it, for it suggests a sort of fossilised environment. The country is unchanged only in the sense that there is no great *Lark Rise to Candleford* industry sprung up. It is still working, farming land, reflecting the changes that time has brought to the whole area. It remains, as it was in Flora Thompson's day, a region with a living to earn. The Flora Thompson connection is quite unlike others met on these trails, for here you feel is the place where her whole career and her entire literary output had their origins and their life. Most of the other stops on the trail are staging-posts on well-known literary careers. Pope wrote much of his translation of *The Iliad* in the gatehouse at the manor house in Stanton Harcourt – a house with a splendidly preserved medieval kitchen. Thomas Hughes, author of *Tom Brown's Schooldays*, spent his own early years at Uffington in the Vale of the White Horse. And so the list goes on, and not even the published trail manages to encompass all the possibilities. Robert Graves, for example, lived at World's End Cottage in the attractive village of Islip and wrote much of *Goodbye to All That* there – and occupied himself in the local community, becoming the founding chairman of Islip Labour Party.

In between the two extremes of following a specific route to cover the events of just one book and visiting every spot in a specific area with literary associations, come those trails which deal with one author but a multitude of works. How successful such trails turn out to be depends very much on how tied the writer is to the locale. I can see little point in going, for example, to a village in Kent to view the house in which an author penned a history of New Zealand. There

*Souter Johnnie's cottage at Kirkoswald* (National Trust for Scotland: Stewart Guthrie)

is, however, a great deal to be said in favour of seeing the Scotland known by Robert Burns. It is certainly difficult to think of any poet who has found such a place in the hearts of his fellow-countrymen. There are others with special affinities with particular regions, Wordsworth and the Lakes for example, but none to match Robert Burns. There are, in fact, two areas particularly associated with the poet: the region around Ayr and that around Dumfries. Of the two areas it is the former which has the stronger connections.

> Auld Ayr, wham ne'er a town surpasses
> For honest men and bonnie lasses

He was born nearby in Alloway, so that it is no surprise to find the town making the most of the connection, producing a thriving Burns industry to rival the Shakespeare industry of Stratford-upon-Avon. But if Burns is to be remembered for only one work, then it would surely have to be 'Tam o' Shanter'. In Kirkoswald you will find the grave of the real-life Tam, Douglas Graham, and just across the road is the cottage of cobbler John Davidson, better known as Souter Johnnie. If Scots have a Mecca of their own to which they should go on pilgrimage, this is it. But I really cannot resist putting two extra dots on the Burns map. First is Dalswinton near Dumfries where he was taken for a ride on an experimental paddle-steamer in 1788, making him the first poet to be moved, literally if not metaphorically, by the power of steam. The second dot comes on a far less likely place: Greenwich on the Thames. The famous clipper the *Cutty Sark* derives its name from the garment worn by the witches who tried to tempt Tam. Those who know the poem will remember that they also tried to prevent Tam's escape by grabbing his horse, but were left holding the tail. A horse's tail can be seen clutched in the hand on the figurehead.

Running Burns a close rival as an author with special local associations is Thomas Hardy, to such an extent in fact that the phrase 'Hardy country' has become something of a cliché. But the associations are so direct and the evocation of town and country scenes in the book so vivid that no Hardy enthusiast will object if occasionally the obvious is pointed out. The starting place has to be Dorchester, a graceful town which has acknowledged its famous son by erecting a statue to his memory. Hardy himself had already done far more for the town by making it known to generations of readers. Everywhere there are memories. Some are reminders of the realities of Hardy's life, such as 39 South Street, home of the

*The Johnson Birthplace Museum in Lichfield* (Johnson Birthplace Museum)

architect John Hicks for whom Hardy worked; others recall scenes from the novels, especially *Far from the Madding Crowd* and *The Mayor of Casterbridge*. You can still find the coaching inns and pubs, the Kings Arms and the White Hart, featured in the novels, and see the churches in which he worked as an architect and which he reworked into his fiction.

Hardy is not essentially, however, an urban writer but a man of the countryside – not some fanciful pastoral idyll of a countryside but a real landscape where lives were often bitter and hard. His is a landscape which carries the weight of history so that, uniquely in English writing, you feel that when an event is described in the lives of the characters, you are hearing just one instalment in a story that stretches back for centuries. It is possible to follow a Hardy trail in which specific places relating to specific events are pointed out. You can visit Hardy's own cottage at Higher Bockhampton, where he was born and where he worked. But there is only one real way to explore and appreciate Hardy country and that is to leave the road and the car and set out on foot. Walk the heathland near his home, explore the country and get to know the feel of the soil. Hardy knew this land intimately and described it not as a general landscape but specifically, as a place which had a character built up layer upon layer through the ages. It really matters very little where you go in the area. Head for the empty spaces on the map and there you will find Hardy country.

Everyone has favourite authors, and in the case of the more famous there are published trails to follow. You can visit places associated with Samuel Johnson in the Midlands, starting with his birthplace at Lichfield. Or, starting in the same place, you can desert Doctor Johnson to follow a route through George Eliot country. It was this trail that finally answered the question posed at the beginning of this book. What is there to say about Nuneaton? Well, George Eliot was born here as Mary Ann Evans in a farmhouse on the estate of Arbury Hall. The farmhouse, alas, is not available for homage by Eliot devotees, but the Hall itself is open, an Elizabethan manor that was Gothicised in the eighteenth century. Nearby is Griff House, now a hotel on the Coventry Road, where the family moved and George Eliot spent much of her childhood. The house and its surroundings were to feature in many of her books, notably *The Mill on the Floss*. Nuneaton itself has a George Eliot collection in the local museum and George Eliot memorial gardens off Church Street, where the faithful lay a wreath every June. So I hope I have made some amends to the good citizens of Nuneaton by publicly admitting that their town is far more interesting than I had ever believed.

Having mentioned authors from England, Scotland and Ireland, I cannot end without saying something of Wales. Perhaps you might care to visit number 5 Cwmdonkin Drive, Swansea, where Dylan Thomas was born in 1914. This is the Uplands district of Swansea and a local trail takes you on the round of places associated with the young poet. But those who set out to trace Thomas connections are more likely to head further round the coast to Laugharne, south of Carmarthen. Here he had his cottage and this was the village that was translated into Llaregyb in his most popular work, *Under Milk Wood*. I must confess I could feel little of the atmosphere of the imaginary town in the real town. The flat sands of the bay seemed to have little to do with the soaring verse and prose of the play. The village of Milk Wood remains a place created of vivid images not of bricks and mortar. What has it to do with reality? Thomas provided his own answer in the name itself, and you can find that answer by reading Llaregyb backwards. In any case, I believe that those who really want to pursue Thomas to his own favourite haunts might be as well to leave Wales altogether and go to London for a Soho pub crawl.

The arts provide a fine excuse for stomping the country, and the visual arts have a special advantage. You can look at a painting of a landscape, find the subject and then go and see how it looks today, how your vision compares with the artist's. Sometimes you can go to tremendous trouble to track down a particular view only to discover that the vista of fields and woods is now a housing estate. But, in the case of two of Britain's greatest artists, you can see their country-side and find that much of it is still as they saw it. *The Painters' Way* is a booklet by Hugh R. P. Turner describing a route designed to show the walker the world of John Constable and Thomas Gains-borough. It is 24 miles long, but can easily be split into sections, which is really the more sensible way to take it as the whole point of the exercise is to take time to stop and look. Mr Turner provides detailed notes on the route and points out those special places connected with the works. I find it a great advantage to take a pocket-sized illustrated book of the paintings along for direct comparison – though there are certainly places where no aide-mémoire is necessary. When you follow the lane down to the river at Flatford, you scarcely need to be an art expert to recognise the scene of one of the most famous paintings of all time, 'The Hay Wain'. The entire route runs from Sudbury to Manningtree and follows the valley of the Stour. There is more here than just the specific views to enjoy – Constable's Dedham Vale, Gainsborough's house in Sudbury – for the whole countryside was one that the artists knew in detail as much as in the wider view. It is in trying to see it through their eyes that those who come after can get a new understanding of the beauty of the area. No one who has seen Constable cloud paintings will ever walk under an East Anglian summer sky and not carry something of the painted image with him (or her). Trees and plants, rivers and meadows, all take on a special significance, just because two great men have gone before us and shared with us their vision.

There are those artists such as Constable and Gainsborough who bring us a new vision of the countryside, and others who produce

*Flatford Mill today, still very recognisable as the building Constable painted* (Derek G. Widdicombe)

what one might call more domestic images, though domesticity may be on a somewhat grand scale. In 1685 the Edict of Nantes was revoked, one of those facts we dimly remember from history lessons without being quite sure what, if anything, it signified. For French Protestants it signified the end of tolerance of their religion, and thousands came to settle in England. These were the Huguenots and they brought with them their own crafts and skills, their own ideas of style in furniture, painting and the decorative arts. As far as the wealthy of the land were concerned, what they chiefly brought was new ideas, and they rushed to employ the Huguenot craftsmen to decorate their houses. A Huguenot trail was produced in 1985 to celebrate the 300th anniversary of their arrival in Britain. The trail centres on the East Midlands and shows how Huguenot influence spread to some quite surprising places, which one thought of as essentially English, such as Chatsworth House and Lincoln Cathedral. But if one were to pluck just one name from the list it would be Boughton House, near Kettering in Northamptonshire. It began life as a monastic foundation, expanded over the years and was suddenly assaulted by the French influence in the 1690s. An army of craftsmen descended on the old house to add murals and

decorative ceilings, to hang paintings, bring in new furniture and even change the structure of the building. The Tudor monastery was transformed into a miniature, if somewhat anglicised, Versailles.

If the visual arts seem an obvious starting point for looking at things, then a musical trail has no such obvious appeal. Music remains fundamentally an abstract, a series of noises – though it can evoke a sense of place. In some cases the connection is especially strong, Benjamin Britten and the coast of East Anglia being an obvious example. Elgar has equally strong connections with Worcester, Malvern and the countryside of the Malvern Hills. He certainly felt that the music should belong to the country and reflect the spirit of a place. English music he said should have 'something broad, noble, chivalrous, healthy, and above all an out-of-doors sort of spirit'. But it is when you turn to song that connections often come out at their strongest, and modern times have seen the emergence of a group of singers and song-writers whose associations with one place could scarcely be clearer. The Magical History Tour has to be a Beatles trail and it has to be in Liverpool. You can of course go to Beatle City for what is described in the brochure as a 'multimedia experience' but the trail is really more fun. Did you ever wonder what Penny Lane really looks like? Or Strawberry Fields? The city has a squad of 'Beatle Guides' to lead you on your way. This also provides a chance to discover the whole city and find what a place of surprises it is.

Once you start looking for subjects for trails there seems to be no end to the possibilities. For a complete contrast, we could turn from the arts of peace to the arts of war. There are various ways to approach the subject. You can set off to trace the career of famous warriors. Horatio Nelson is probably thought of in terms of his most famous ship, *The Victory*, where his life ended: but his life began in East Anglia, and the Nelson trail looks at the domestic life of the man rather than his better-known public appearances. There are points of interest in the King's Lynn area but the main focus is on the Burnhams, splendid places with resonant names: Burnham Ulph, Burnham Thorpe, Burnham Market, Burnham Overy and Burnham Overy Staithe. This is the area where Nelson was born and where his father, the local vicar, preached. Here young Horatio first saw the sea, here he married and here his own children lived. The district seems full of his memories, memories that take their

*The Huguenot influence at Boughton House, Kettering* (Country Life)

most tangible form at the Lord Nelson Inn at Burnham Thorpe, which houses a fine collection of memorabilia. The appeal of such a trail seems to lie in part in the pleasant and attractive nature of the places visited and also in the reminder that the heroic public figure began life as a mundane private person.

If the warrior himself does not appeal, then the battlefield might. There were many battles fought on native soil but one which had as profound an effect on English history as any was that which brought the Wars of the Roses to an end in 1485, the Battle of Bosworth Field. It is a battle probably best known for the impassioned cry of the leader of the defeated forces, King Richard III: 'A horse! a horse! My kingdom for a horse!' The king never said anything of the sort but Shakespeare gave him the lines and they have stuck. In fact, what we think about the battle depends in large measure on the bard. He wrote Richard as one of the blackest, and most fascinating, villains of all time, whilst turning Henry Tudor into a paragon of all the virtues. That neither character bore much resemblance to his dramatic counterpart is immaterial, for it is Shakespeare that we remember, not history. The battlefield, 2 miles south of Market Bosworth in Leicestershire, has its own centre, where the significance and pattern of the struggle are explained. After visiting the centre you can wander off along the pathways where the different phases of the battle are described on signposts.

Bosworth was the last battle of a prolonged, stop-and-start war. It was a civil war between the rival houses of York and Lancaster, and was essentially a battle between the nobility, fought out by armies of retainers and mercenaries. The Civil War of the seventeenth century was a very different matter: Parliament against the king, people against the crown. It was never quite that simple, however: some areas sided with the king, others with Cromwell; families divided over who was in the right. War raged for three years, until the royalists were defeated at Naseby in 1645. The battles were waged up and down the land, but the Civil War trail I want to recommend centres around the king's stronghold of Oxford. Paradoxically, however, it begins at Huntingdon where Cromwell was born, and the more easterly parts of the region are certainly much associated with the Puritan faction. At Chalfont St Giles, for example, you can visit the cottage of Cromwell's greatest propagandist (and has any man ever had a better?) John Milton. But then,

*Inspiration for a famous song: a stopping-off place on the Beatles' trail* (Merseyside County Council)

249

just down the road at Forty Green, Beaconsfield, you come across a very ancient pub, the Royal Standard of England, given that name because it was one of the places where Charles II hid out. Those who have little taste for history might be tempted by the knowledge that the pub gratifies other tastes as well, with good ale and some two dozen different cheeses on offer.

Other stops along the way, which runs round in a circle through Oxford, include other pubs – notably the King's Head and Bell in Abingdon – where Charles held councils of war, and numerous stately homes whose occupants sided with one faction or the other. Broughton Castle, for example, was home to a Cromwellian leader, while Rousham House just down the road was a Royalist stronghold. One of the fascinating features of the tour is the way in which Royalist and Puritan centres seem to sit side by side, a reminder of the bitterness of the conflict which quite literally turned neighbour against neighbour. Battles were fought all around Oxford, and some are refought regularly today as the volunteers of organisations such as the Sealed Knot dress up in costumes of the period to struggle again with alarming realism for possession of Cropredy Bridge or Brill Hill. The trail lists twenty-six sites of interest, and if you want to do them all justice then you will need to set aside a few days for the tour.

The Civil War was not limited to one area, but the Pitchfork Rebellion was limited to the West Country and mainly to Somerset. It began in 1685 when the Duke of Monmouth, one of Charles II's numerous illegitimate progeny, decided to lead a rebellion against James II. You can follow the entire course of his movements with little difficulty, and take in some lovely spots along the way. The start is at Lyme Regis, where the duke landed, rallied a somewhat motley army and set off for London. They got as far as Keynsham, near Bristol, but were turned back in a somewhat indecisive battle. The final encounter came at Sedgemoor near Westonzoyland (near Bridgwater in Somerset) where the duke's forces of farmers and workers were defeated and massacred. The superb church at Westonzoyland dominates the surrounding low-lying land and here some 500 rebels were held prisoner. Five died within the church and twenty-two were hanged. Today you could scarcely imagine a more peaceful spot, and it takes a real effort to envisage the time when this beautiful building was filled with the dead and dying.

*Westonzoyland church where prisoners were held after the Monmouth rebellion* (Anthony Burton)

The name Pitchfork Rebellion suggests a great popular army on the march, but it was really just another movement headed by an aristocratic leader. If you want to follow in the steps of a very different sort of people's army, then try following the path of General Ludd and the Luddites. There is probably no more maligned, nor misunderstood, group in industrial history than these, generally portrayed as mindless idiots standing in the way of progress. They were the machine-breakers whose leaders hid under the pseudonym of Ned Ludd.

The Pennine Heritage Network has produced a booklet giving the background to the Luddite movement and tracing a particular uprising of 1812, when a new form of machine, the shearing frame, was systematically attacked and destroyed. It was a time of great violence when a few mill-owners were actually murdered and rather more workers were hanged. The Luddite trail takes you down the Colne Valley between Marsden and Huddersfield. This is an area in the heart of the old woollen industry and it was here that the worst of the violence was seen. That history gives new perspective to a walk by the Huddersfield Canal, past the mills which were attacked by rioters and past the cottages where the men who joined Ludd's army lived. Were Luddites moronic vandals? Or were they simply desperate men who recognised that the machines that promised long-term prosperity meant for them short-term starvation? Outside Marsden church is the tomb of Enoch Taylor, the man who made the new machines. The Luddites named the means of destruction after him – Enoch's Hammer. Enoch, they declared, made the machines and Enoch would break them. I stood there the other day and wondered what I would have thought in 1812 if my family had been literally starving to death. Follow the trail for the scenery if for nothing else, but ask yourself the question as well.

We have now moved on to the industrial world where there seems to be a plethora of trails, to the numbers of which I have added one or two myself. My most recent effort is 'The Cotton Kingdom', concentrated, not surprisingly, on the north-west of England, and is designed to help tourists find the best of the museums in the region. I took the idea of museums to include mills where machinery has been put back to work for the benefit of visitors: Queen Street Mill in Burnley is a steam-driven weaving mill where visitors really do get a glimpse into the working parts; not just the sight of a loom shop, but the noise and the smell of it as well. Included too is magnificent Trencherfield Mill at Wigan with its mighty mill

*The restored steam engine at Queen Street Mill, Burnley* (Queen Street Mill, Burnley)

engine restored to all its former glory. This is a motorist's trail, but those who would like to visit just a few of the places and perhaps get closer acquaintance with the countryside at the same time can take to feet or to boat.

The Leeds & Liverpool Canal between Wigan and Burnley takes you through the heart of the cotton country, including a journey around the hillside above the chimneys of Blackburn. The great advantage of this route to boaters is that it is comparatively unfrequented – the popular section of this canal lies further to the east – and the towpath provides a good route for walkers. This is quite a long route, 38 miles in all, not exactly a day's outing, but for those who do not know the region it can be a revelation. The mill towns are there all right and are full of interest. Walk the canal at Burnley and you will find the old mill buildings have all been identified with descriptive plaques, and a great deal of restoration work in the canal area known as the Weavers' Triangle has been done. The surprise comes in between the towns. You leave the buildings behind and at once you are in the heart of Pennine hill country. It gives a whole new perspective to the notion of an industrial area.

Canals provide a good introduction to old industries, even when the canal is not in use. The Moira Trail in Leicestershire incorporates a large part of the disused section of the Ashby Canal, alongside which is the most impressive feature of the walk, the massive blast furnace where iron was once made. It is one of the finest and best preserved of its kind. It is not, however, necessary to follow canals to find the industrial past. The Wales Tourist Board has been particularly good at setting out trails, producing a whole book of them called *A Glimpse of the Past*. I have followed several and, as with the canal trail, it is surprising how often you can forget the original objective, being seduced away by the enticing scenery of the valleys. The last of these tracks which I followed was the Torfaen Trail which took me on a route from Pontypool to Blaenafon. On this route it was the sad loneliness of a deserted colliery village high on the mountainside above Abersychan which caught my imagination – rows of deserted cottages, their once tended gardens now overgrown and abandoned. There was little sign left of what had once given life to the community. Even the spoil-heaps were rapidly vanishing beneath grass and scrub. Soon, one felt, it would be as if it had all never been, as the deserted village fell into decay. A melancholy site, but a beautiful spot where I spent so long and explored with such pleasure that I must confess I never completed the trail that day. But then that is one of the great advantages of such trails: they are there to introduce you to new experiences, and those experiences are not always what you expect.

You can follow another coal trail in Scotland, the Heritage Trail, wandering through the Lothian coalfield from Prestonpans to Newtongrange. It provides a splendid climax at the end of the journey, the Lady Victoria Colliery, a giant among mines. It was closed in 1981 after nearly a century of work: now it is being renovated, to be reopened as a major mining museum, complete with what cognoscenti will recognise as a paragon of its kind, a horizontal duplex winder of 1890 – and which others will be happy to know is a huge steam engine, due to steam again.

All this talk of industry and coal may not be everyone's taste and

Scotland is famous for a taste of another kind. The Malt Whisky Trail is based on the great distilleries around the valley of the Spey. The scenery is Highland and so is the malt, and surely never did drink and scenery fit better together. A day in the hills with a dram to keep out the cold is one of the finest recipes I know for contentment. The object of the trail is to take you to those distilleries where visitors are welcomed and where they can see the golden liquor being produced. All the great glen names are here, Glen Livet, Glen Farclas, Glen Fiddich, and these are real glens not just names on a bottle. And if you feel that there is a limit to the number of distilleries you wish to visit, then there is the scenery there to be enjoyed, distant glens to be explored. And at the end of the day you can return to a little inn and perhaps follow the example of Mr Robert Burns and his friends.

> Oh! Willie brew'd a peck o' maut,
> An Rob a' Allan cam' to pree;
> Three blyther hearts, that lee long night,
> Ye wad na find in Christendie.
> We are na fou, we're nae that fou,
> But just a drappie in our e'e;
> The cock may craw, the day may daw,
> And aye we'll taste the Whasky O.

Burns and his friends were no doubt as guilty as Sir John Falstaff in imbibing copious quantities of liquid with little concern for more solid fare. The young Prince Hal on seeing Falstaff's bill cried out, 'O monstrous! but one half-pennyworth of bread to this intolerable deal of sack.' Well, we travellers through Britain will be more abstemious in our ways, and will not neglect to feed ourselves well and properly – and by properly I mean with good traditional food. The hunt for real food could be thought of as another trail, but as it is a trail that will take us to all parts of Britain – where there are also discoveries beyond the gastronomic to be made – it deserves a chapter all to itself. In any case, what better way to end a book than with a feast, and I shall ignore the ghostly voices of Burns and Falstaff who might well have other ideas on that point.

# 9
# Traditional Fare

*A traditional interior for a very old building: Frugal Food, Abingdon* (John May)

As I mentioned at the beginning of Chapter 4, I visited the Tamar valley while writing this book; during the visit I went off on a shopping expedition to Tavistock. There are many excellent reasons for visiting the town. Industrial historians know it as one of the stannary towns, where tin has been assayed and given the official stamp of approval since the thirteenth century. Hunters after transport relics potter around the old canal basin and warehouses behind the carpark. The general sightseer is happy to wander past the municipal buildings, rather grand and baronial, but built of an odd, green volcanic stone, and then to stroll round the back to the cosy market. But I was there to shop, and that was how I discovered Creber's. In an age of mass marketing one can easily forget the delights of the decent, old-fashioned grocer. Chesterton despised the gentleman:

> God made the wicked Grocer
> For a mystery and a sign,
> That man might shun the awful shop
> And go to inns to dine.

But Chesterton had never faced scampi and chips in a basket. Nor, indeed, had he ever shopped in a supermarket, let alone its gargantuan relation, the hypermarket. Had he done so he might well have sung a different song; and surely the sight of Creber's would have won him over. Hams wrapped in brown paper hang from the ceiling. They choose their own teas and pack them themselves – they even pack up *your* shopping, wrapping up items in paper, a rare treat. Old signs have been refurbished as decoration: offers of 'Pink Pills for Pale People' are still on show here. The place looks inviting; you feel as if enormous care has gone into the shop, and in the right way. Above all you can buy real food, traditional food full of flavour. It is, happily, not unique.

Throughout Britain there are similar shops offering similar quality; some general shops, others specialised. Here in my own town of Abingdon, I can buy wholefoods – grains, rices, pulses – scooped fresh from the sack on the floor and weighed out in just the quantity I want and not in the amount a manufacturer feels I ought to want. And thinking of these two shops, Creber's in Tavistock, Frugal Food in Abingdon, it occurred to me that they had something else in common as well. The buildings themselves are full of character, the sort of places that positively invite inspection. But this is not to be a survey of shops and restaurants but rather of the things they sell. There are a few strange and even quite exotic foods; but mostly I want to remind readers of qualities that still exist, regional qualities in particular that have survived the bland approaches of the mass-marketeers. I set out from Creber's with the desire to hunt down traditional food, and found that my search revealed other delights as well. So please join me in a somewhat hectic day's eating, starting quite naturally with breakfast.

Breakfast is the quintessential British meal: an alternative claim could be entered in favour of afternoon tea, but that is rather more of a stopping-off point, a refuelling stop between meals, than a full meal in its own right. Where does one go for the traditional British breakfast? Once, the railways provided an answer, for breakfasts on trains were masterpieces of traditional cooking; but, alas, they are no longer quite what they were. The full breakfast – the kedgerees, the devilled kidneys – would now seem to be the preserve of the London clubs, and even there it seems things are not quite what they were. Still, I do have a happy memory of standing in line at the Athenaeum, between the Lords Spiritual and Temporal, waiting for my tray full of very traditional fare. Yet the true breakfast, the hearty meal of bangers, bacon and eggs, and whatever else is available – succulent field mushrooms or tasty bubble-and-squeak – is still with us. You can find it in the transport café, though even the old caffs are an endangered species, as the heavy traffic heads off to the motorway and the dull and drab motorway service areas. Those who are still offered a good, filling breakfast should count themselves lucky – though only a few days before penning these lines I was given just such a breakfast in the pub where I was staying. But, for those of us who breakfast at home, all is not lost. The good breakfast is still available and the traditional ingredients are still there to be enjoyed.

A good rule in cooking, and indeed in many things, is to start with the plain and only then move on to the fancy. And of all the plain fare on offer in these islands, porridge carries the prize for the combination of taste and simplicity. As with all good food, there are endless arguments over the correct method of preparation. In the matter of porridge, however, I am a complete traditionalist, one of those who believe it is best prepared by cooking oatmeal and water and eating the resultant mixture with salt. Others have different views, but however the porridge is prepared its quality ultimately depends on the oats that go into its making. The hunter after the perfect porridge must, necessarily, also be in search of the best oatmeal. One could draw an analogy between oats for porridge and flour for bread: the less intervention there is between the natural produce grown in the field and the milled grain the better. A good porridge hunt has to begin with the meal mill, and there can be few better places to start any search for porridge and oatmeal than Scotland.

Preston Mill, East Linton (in Lothian) is a superb example of the old style of water-powered mill. Its main attraction to a modern visitor probably lies in its picturesque appearance, the rough grey stone of the main building contrasting with the rich red of the pantiled roof; the elegant cone of the drying kiln, rising high above the low walls of the grinding mill. It is, by any standards, a rich, sumptuous building, a structure of contrasting materials and contrasting colours. Ever since I first saw it, I have felt that it added to my enjoyment of porridge, for the lovely building and the oatmeal are for ever joined in imagination. The illusion could, however, be destroyed if the porridge fell below the high standards set by

*Preston Mill, East Linton where oats were prepared for the porridge makers* (National Trust for Scotland)

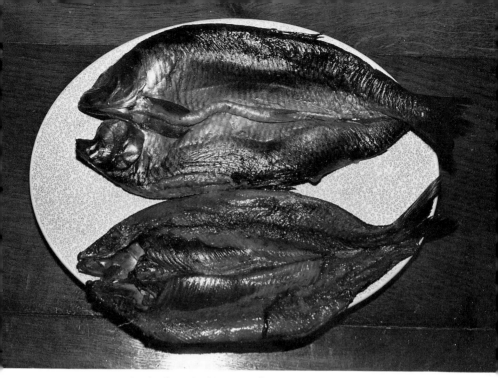

*A pair of genuine kippers* (Anthony Burton)

Preston Mill. It need never do so, for the dish is simplicity itself: heat together oats, water and salt, but not too violently. Keep the mixture stirred (in a clockwise direction only according to purists) using a porridge stick or spurtle. I bought my spurtle in the Highlands some years ago, but it was only when I came to consider the matter more closely in order to write about it that I realised how much the association with places added to the appreciation of the food.

Keeping with the Scottish theme, that country shares with East Anglia the distinction of offering superb smoked fish – though the latter occasionally goes one better, for a Suffolk hotel where I stayed recently had grilled plaice on the breakfast menu. But most of us, if we think of fish and breakfast think of the mighty kipper. It is properly produced by splitting herrings open, soaking them in brine and then smoking them over smouldering oak chips. The kippery is a great sight: the glowing ashes, and the row upon row of herrings turning gently golden in the smoke. It is also one of the world's great smells. As a young boy I wandered off from the holiday beach at Whitby and found a smoke-house. I was entranced, but my parents were less amused at being in charge of this singularly aromatic child. Of the many places with rival claims to producing the best kipper, few would dispute the right of the smokers of Loch Fyne to appear high on any list. And those who set off to hunt the kipper will have an excuse to visit this lovely region. The loch itself is a thin finger of water pointing up from the Sound of Bute, right into the mountains, almost joining in with the end of Loch Lomond. The northern end of the loch is the more mountainous but my favourite port is Tarbert at the other end. This is still a working harbour, bringing in the fish, the town little more than a thin line between water and hills. At summer weekends, you will see the old Clyde puffer *VIC 32* (see pages 37–8) at the quay, waiting for a fresh load of holiday passengers. And if you become dissatisfied with the place you can hop on a ferry for the energetic, healthy delights of Arran or the more 'spiritual' delights of Islay and Jura. All this and kipper too!

The east coast of Scotland has alternative smoked delights to offer. Aberdeen is home to the finnan haddock, the smoked haddock. Many places these days offer a strange, violently yellow-coloured fish which they claim to be finnan haddock. It is no such thing, and when once you have tried the real thing, delicate in colour as well as in flavour, you will never accept the substitute. Better still, in my view, and almost unknown outside Scotland is the Arbroath smokie, haddock again, but smaller than the finnan and smoked whole, not split. The smokies first appeared not at Arbroath itself, but a little to the north at Auchmithie. It is a tiny but delightful village set high on the red sandstone cliffs. There is not a great deal to it: two rows of restored fishermen's cottages in the town centre and a track down to the tiny harbour. Those who feel that they must also pay their respects to Arbroath itself will not be disappointed, and there are one or two odd little features to look out for. Go, for example, to the Arbroath Museum at Ladyloan. This is housed in the old signal station, so look out for the circular tower and what appears to be a flagpole with a ball hung on it. This is in fact a signal aimed at the distant Bellrock Lighthouse, the ball being raised and lowered on the pole. Odder still is the building on Keptie Hill: at first sight some grand, ancient castle. On closer inspection it looks like a folly but is, in reality, a heavily disguised water-tower.

In Scotland, I can think of no better start to the day than a bowl of porridge and a smokie, but further south, in England, other delights can seem as appealing. The Traditional English Breakfast appears on practically every menu in every boarding house, pub and hotel in the land, but in the event turns out, too often, to be neither traditional nor English. Battery-farm eggs, thinly sliced Danish bacon and watery, tinned Italian tomatoes all float on a pond of indeterminate oil. So let us put that to one side and look for a proper sausage, decent bacon and allow ourselves a little extra luxury with genuine ham. The problem is: where do you start?

I have in front of me a very fine book on sausages, complete with an A to Z of sausages from the Aberdeen to one which I hope is more easily digested than it is pronounced – the Zwyczajna from Poland. Even ignoring the more startling foreign versions, there are still fifty-six listed for England alone, though some, such as oyster sausage, are, to say the least, rare creatures. But as this is a brief summary aimed as much at travel as at gastronomy, let us take just one, but one of the best, of the English sausages: the Cumberland. This is unique in that it is not twisted into links, but comes from one great spiral from which a length is cut. The quality depends very much on the skills of the individual butcher and the ingredients used, for though Cumberland sausage is a pork sausage it is one which should always be well seasoned with herbs, preferably fresh, and pepper. Often the best examples can be found on market stalls, so why not try Penrith, which has two markets a week? This is a robust, rather than an obviously charming town, not surprising in a spot close to the border and once inevitably prey to the border raiders. It is a frontier town, a defended town – and a very ancient town. It is still mercifully free of the holiday crowds that swarm round the Lakeland towns to the south, and it is yet another of those places which more than repay time spent on exploration.

There are many places one could commend for sausages, but mention bacon and first thoughts are inevitably of Wiltshire. Long before railways had ever been dreamed of, there was an important town of Swindon, or Swine down as it started out in life. This is a wonderful county to explore, if only because it features so rarely on tourist itineraries. I first came to know it through the old woollen towns that thread the Avon – Malmesbury, Chippenham, Trow-bridge and Bradford – towns that still carry the badges of old prosperity in the grand houses built by the successful merchants. Down the A4, the old Great West Road from Bath to London, sits the town of Calne, a place that would for ever have remained just another market town on a busy road if it had not also been a stopping-off point for the drovers, bringing Irish pigs from the port at Bristol to London. There, in Butcher's Row, was a firm of family butchers who bought up pigs from the drovers and cured them for bacon, a process which involved keeping the meat cool and rubbing in salt, saltpetre and the other ingredients which give the bacon its particular flavour. The Butcher's Row family business prospered, and when one member of the family learned the secret of using ice to keep his curing house permanently cool for year-round use, the business began to increase. Smoke-houses were added and the enterprise grew until it became a factory industry. The family name was Harris and the works are still there beside the disused arm of the old Wilts & Berks Canal. But Harris bacon is no longer produced in Calne. It has spread throughout the country. There are, however, still places where you can buy the home-cured variety. Happily, we are still a long way from the time when only a standardised product can be obtained. Some prefer home-cured bacon, some favour factory-cured, but when we turn to ham can there be any argument?

I suppose as a native of the county I should put in a word for York ham, which at its best is quite superb, but no one needs my advice to visit that great city. So I would like to recommend one little village and the unlikely setting of a village store. The village is Peasenhall in Suffolk and there is very little about the shop to indicate that there is anything special on offer – until you see the proud announcement that they are purveyors of hams to the Royal Family. And there they are inside, among the conventional packets of biscuits and tins of soup – pink, juicy hams, sold whole. No doubt there are other hams as good, but again Peasenhall is a splendid place to visit. Call in and see the local carpenter turning out – literally – fine hand-made furniture, or if your interests lean towards the macabre, go and view the scene of the famous Peasenhall murder. And do look out for the village hall, an extraordinary place that looks as if it belongs on the Steppes of Russia.

Bread is an essential ingredient in any breakfast and there has been, thank heavens, a steady movement away from the cottonwool texture and bland-to-the-point-of-nullity flavour of the white, sliced loaf. Think of bread at its best and you think of stone-ground flour, and having made an excursion to visit a Scottish water-powered meal mill, why not turn off the road for a wind-powered grain mill? There are a number of preserved mills which still produce flour; one of the grandest and indeed one of the largest mills in the whole country is Skidby Mill near Beverley (Humberside). This is a tower mill, that is to say the main structure is built of brick and the sails are attached to a rotating cap which can be turned to bring them into the wind. It stands six storeys high, dominating the landscape, and works on summer Sundays, though it is open throughout the summer and also has a museum of milling.

Different areas have different forms of bread. Soda bread is available throughout Ireland, and very good it is too. It differs from other bread in that baking soda is used instead of yeast for leavening. In Wales you can get laver bread, which is not bread at all, but seaweed, which you buy washed and dried and mashed up into a most unappetising-looking sticky mess. Do not be deterred. Fry it rolled in oatmeal or fry it plain with bacon and it makes a delicious breakfast. But those who prefer more conventional breakfasts will be heading for the toast and marmalade. There has been a good deal of controversy surrounding the origins of marmalade but most experts now seem to agree that the honour of its invention lies with James Keiller of Dundee. In the eighteenth century, Mr Keiller received a cargo of oranges from Seville which were so bitter that no one would buy them. So he handed them over to his wife who chopped them up, peel and all, and made an orange jam. But why should it be called marmalade? The answer seems to be that the flavour was not unlike that of another popular preserve of the period, which was called marmalade because it was made from quince or 'marmelo'. Whatever its origins it remains as popular as ever, and suitably fortified we can continue on the travels that will take us up to lunch.

Not everyone can manage the long haul from breakfast to the midday meal without a little fortification along the way. Sugar may rot your teeth, but it is an excellent source of instant energy. Toffee – 'origin obscure' says the dictionary, so we need not worry about that – is at its best a good, old-fashioned sweet, one that goes with bull's-eyes and humbugs and all the other things that most of us give up, however reluctantly, as we leave childhood behind. There was a great charm about the old-style sweetshop, where sweets were kept in tall jars and weighed out into paper bags, for grubby childish hands. Less grubby but equally traditional, is toffee in a tin, and Farrah have been making and selling their Harrogate toffee in the town since 1840. We need not linger in their shop too long, for we shall be popping back to the town for tea a little later on. Harrogate and Harrogate toffee are holiday posh; seaside rock is holiday loud, cheery and brash. And Blackpool rock-makers are kings of the

*Kendal Mint Cake, the explorer's friend* (Anthony Burton)

trade. It is the way they make the stuff that is so fascinating: the way in which the great strings of gooey sugar are twined together to make patterns, and even, by what seems a minor miracle, to produce a name running through the middle. As long as Blackpool thrives, then surely Blackpool rock will thrive alongside it – and so too will the profession of dentistry. Seaside rock is eaten for fun, or brought home as a sticky souvenir, but one similarly constituted confection has earned a reputation as the mountaineer's friend. Kendal Mint Cake has been carted around the Lakeland fells by generations of walkers and climbers: it has been taken across the Alps and munched on mountain-tops from Kilimanjaro to Everest. This is a real energy-pack and has given thousands of climbers an excuse to indulge a sweet tooth without a pang of conscience. It can also give you an excuse to visit Kendal, a town that sits on the edge of Lakeland without quite becoming a part of it, a town with many characteristics in common with Penrith. It is well worth a visit, and if you stock up with the Mint Cake which is everywhere on sale you can be sure of keeping going until lunch.

Everyone has his (or her) own notion of what constitutes a proper lunch. At one extreme is the business lunch, which in my experience is 90 per cent lunch and 10 per cent business, and at the opposite end of the scale is the hasty sandwich at the desk. When I was growing up in Yorkshire lunch was often enough a visit to the fish and chip shop. Fish and chips are among that long list of things that people are always telling you are not what they used to be; and for once they are often right. It is all a question of having the right, fresh food: fresh fish not frozen, a light, newly prepared batter, good firm potatoes peeled on the spot and the right material for frying. It is essential to fry at a high enough temperature to crisp up the batter immediately so that the fat will not soak in and turn it soggy. Fish and chips have also never been quite the same since the authorities – that strange, unapproachable body – decided that eating chips out of newspaper was bad for us. No one ever produced any evidence, no horrific tales of young lads clutching their throats gasping out, 'It was the paper killed me,' before expiring in agony. No, it was decreed to be bad for us and there was an end of the matter. The joy of reading stale news through the grease has been lost for ever. Other countries still think of it as an English tradition, however. While researching at the University of North Carolina, I found a side street with an 'English Fish and Chip Shop'. They had almost got it right: they put the newspaper on the table and served the fish and chips on a plate on top of that. The high quality chippie is still to be found. My favourite is in Golcar in Yorkshire, the old weaving village above the Colne Valley (see pages 188–9). No plates here, no tables and chairs, just fish and chips wrapped up to take away – after you have joined the inevitable queue of connoisseurs.

The only real rival in the North of England to fish and chips is pie and peas. The pie can be meat pie, potato pie – in fact almost any kind of pie you fancy, but the peas must be mushy peas. The correct way to serve this delicacy – or to many southerners, atrocity – is to have your hot pie in a bowl surrounded by the peas which should be liberally doused with mint sauce and pepper and the whole lot eaten with a spoon. This is perhaps rather more of a Lancashire than a Yorkshire dish, though it is known in both counties. The meat and potato pie appears in the West Country transformed into the Cornish pasty, a much maligned creation, though too often the criticism is all too richly deserved. Minced-up something is added to

*As good a place as any to eat Cornish pasties and contemplate the life of the miner: St Agnes Head* (National Trust: Mike Williams)

a great deal of potato and encased in pastry as leaden as the hearts of those who manufacture the confection. The true pasty is a much tastier object derived from the 'oggie' taken down the tin and copper mines to be eaten in the darkness of the underground lunch-break. The true pasty should have meat in chunks and turnip mixed in with the potato for extra flavour and moisture. Where can you find the real thing? That is a difficult question to answer. A Cornish friend is constantly approaching fresh sources of pasty with high optimism only to retreat in gloom when the object is tasted. The best thing I can suggest is to make your own, take it to some spot such as St Day or Gwennap Down among the gaunt ruins of the Cornish engine-houses and eat it there while contemplating the remains of the mining past. My own favourite spot is in the valley that leads away from the sea at Porthtowan: a wild valley with engine-houses up in the hills and even down by the beach itself. If your pasty has not worked, at least you will have a marvellous scene to enjoy.

The fishermen of Cornwall once had their own pasty, known as stargazy pie, which consisted of pilchards placed whole in the pie crust, their heads left out to stare at the sky. Pilchard fishing has, alas, died out and stargazy pie with it. Other fish snacks do survive in traditional form, however, especially in London. Eels are a bit like mushy peas – you love them or hate them. The London eel-seller has been around a very long time. There are jellied eels available from street stalls or from special shops such as Cooke's Eel Shop in Dalston, which has been on the go for more than 100 years. There are eel motifs everywhere you look: mosaic eels at the door, glass eels at the window and, of course, live eels waiting for the slaughter. Here you can purchase eel and mash, a decidedly substantial meal. There used to be dozens of such places in the East End but walk down the Old Kent Road today and you will find only one genuine survivor. What you will find though are a great many pubs and for me the pub is the ideal spot for a midday break. I am not going to write on the virtues of real ale and the merits of different beers or this chapter would never end, but I want to look instead at traditional pub food.

It has to be said that for every pub offering a decent snack lunch there are many more which provide something which is a disgrace to the name. The ubiquitous ploughman's lunch would all too often leave a hard-working farmhand fainting from starvation, but the real thing does still exist. The North Star at Steventon in Oxfordshire does a gargantuan version, with masses of good bread, a variety of cheeses, pickles, and ham and cold meat for good measure – such a special offering that you have to order in advance. The trouble with celebrating such dishes in book form is that, too often, by the time the reader gets there everything has changed. Well, provided not too much else has altered, the North Star will always be worth a visit: high-backed wooden settles, real ale from the local brewery and a good story to go with the pub. The name is only indirectly connected with astronomy. It derives from one of the more famous locomotives that ran on the nearby Great Western Railway. In the days before the tracks reached Oxford, this was the alighting point for travelling dons who, sensible men, repaired to the North Star to wait for the Oxford coach – hoping, I dare say, that it would not arrive too soon.

The other familiar bar food which is too often a pale imitation of its grander relation is the pork pie. Now we must travel across country to the famous centre of pie manufacture, Melton Mowbray in Leicestershire. This is the headquarters both of pie-making and fox-hunting, and an almost embarrassingly picturesque spot: the magnificent church stands by the village green; there are narrow streets, and ancient houses and inns. They have been making pies here for over a century and a half, proper pork pies, hand raised – literally, for no baking tins are used in the genuine Melton Mowbray pie. You can see exhibits in the museum, or better still find the real thing at Dickinson & Morris, a comparative newcomer who can claim little more than 130 years in the trade. They have another claim to fame here, for this is also a great centre for Stilton cheese, but we shall be looking at the cheese story a little later.

Some will find the notion of a cold lunch not to their taste and will expect to be inwardly warmed as well as fed. The pub can often meet that need as well. Just the other day I found myself in Faversham in Kent, a town as lovely as any in the South East, but one which balances its fine preserved houses, many dating back to the Tudor age, with a real working life that exists visibly and prominently in the town beside the old docks and warehouses. Lunch-time was passed at the Sun, where the menu promised and the cook produced a genuine home-made steak and kidney pudding. There are few delights more to be savoured than that of cutting into a good steak pudding. As the suet crust opens, the gravy flows and the aromas that have been locked in with the cooking are released. I cannot guarantee the pub menu here any more than that of the North Star but I can guarantee that a visit to Faversham will be a pleasure. Do look in at the chemist's shop below its gilded sign of pestle and mortar, and you will find the fixtures and fittings of a century ago. The contents, however, are modern – and can help with any digestive problem incurred by an overindulgence in lunch.

If the ploughman has a lunch that is traditionally cold, the shepherd has his hot. Shepherd's pie is such a familiar item that we take it for granted, a simple mixture of beef, onion and potato. But it can be greatly improved by the addition of one extra ingredient, a good dash of Lea and Perrins Worcestershire sauce. Every day, it seems, one reads in the press of secrets leaked from the cabinet office, of military plans passing to foreign agents and industrial

*Melton Mowbray – home of the pork pie* (Melton Studios)

271

espionage discovering the designs of competitors. No one has ever extracted the secret of the sauce in Lea and Perrins. The ingredients are there on the label, but the art lies in finding the right mixture and the right length of time for the sauce to mature in the casks stored down in the factory cellar. It might also be worth noting that if the visit to the chemist's seems unappealing, then the sauce mixed with tomato juice is a well-tried antidote to the excesses of ale.

Refreshed and spiced up with sauce, we can travel on until tea. This essentially British repast comes in a variety of forms. There are afternoon teas in England – a phrase redolent of palm courts and string trios – and high teas in Scotland, where as unwary travellers have often discovered too late, the high tea is not just the main meal of the afternoon but also the last. If England is the spot for true afternoon tea, then the most English of all English teas are those of the spa towns. Go to Bath, Leamington Spa or Harrogate and you can find the real thing – even on occasions, the string trio as well. Fancy cakes – a lovely phrase – toasted teacakes oozing butter, scones, sandwiches and tea made using loose tea-leaves and not, emphatically not, the tea-bag. The publishers of this book, David & Charles, need do no more than walk a little way from their office to visit Madge Mellor's of Newton Abbot where the food is as traditional as the waitresses' uniforms.

There are still regional variations to be made on the theme of teas. The clotted cream tea of the West Country needs no special introduction but there are other local delicacies to hunt out and enjoy as well. Staying with the West Country, there is saffron cake. The real thing is hard to find – though imitations abound – and is expensive. Saffron itself, made from the stigma of the saffron crocus, is a decidedly expensive product. If you despair of finding the cake, you can at least find the town whose prosperity was built on its special ingredient: Saffron Walden in Essex. Saffron is no longer grown there but it has, quite literally, left its mark on the town. Many of the buildings boast excellent pargeting (ornate plaster-work) incorporating illustrations of the plant. None is finer than the old Sun Inn, now, alas, no longer offering saffron cake nor indeed cakes of any variety for it has been turned into an antique shop. The town also boasts one of the finest, if not the finest, earth mazes in Britain on its common. Unlike the familiar mazes such as Hampton Court, designed to puzzle and deceive, by leaving visitors shut away between high hedges, the earth maze is a mysterious convolution formed on the ground. Why was it made? No one seems to know.

Banbury cakes are still made in Banbury in Oxfordshire, even though the 'Original Cake Shop' in Parsons Street has gone, demolished to make way for new shops – an all too sadly familiar tale. The cakes are flat pastry cases of mixed fruit with, in the best of them, a good nip of rum. Banbury itself is one of those towns that is desperately in need of a bypass, clogged with traffic edging past the famous cross to which one is encouraged to ride a cockhorse, though even if you did you would get stuck at the traffic lights like everyone else. Get away from the main road however, and there is still much to enjoy, including the splendid muddle of a boat-yard where working canal boats have been built and repaired for 200 years, and where working methods have changed little throughout that time. And look in at the museum, where the story of Banbury cakes is told in displays. A close relation to the Banbury cake is the Eccles cake, but Eccles itself has lost much of its old identity. Joining up with neighbouring Salford as part of Greater Manchester and squeezed between motorways, it can still at least boast one great attraction. Eccles like Banbury has a canal connection – two canal connections to be precise. Just to the east of the town, the eighteenth-century Bridgewater Canal is carried across the nineteenth-century Manchester Ship Canal on a remarkable aqueduct. Because the latter waterway has to be kept clear for large, tall vessels, the original aqueduct was replaced by one that pivoted on a central tower. The whole trough full of water is swung across without, it seems, a drop ever being spilt. This is the Barton Swing Aqueduct, one of the most remarkable structures on the whole canal system.

Other regions have their own specialities. Those who take the advice offered in Chapter 2 and visit Portland in Dorset should certainly look out for Portland dough-cake. Lardy-cake is native to neighbouring Wiltshire, and is another form of dough-cake. Other cakes travel further afield. Think of oatcakes and you think of Scotland – yet there is a traditional Potteries oatcake to be found in Staffordshire. As with so many matters culinary the secret lies in hunting down the local speciality.

Local specialities can often seem hard to come by in the evenings, when dinner in the popular imagination seems divided between British food, by definition dull, and foreign varieties, exotic and exciting. Yet are there any meats more flavourful than Welsh lamb or prime Scottish beef? And has man invented anything better than a real Yorkshire pudding, the one cooked with the juices from the meat dripping down into the pudding, so good a dish that it can be eaten on its own? But we are rather rushing ahead of ourselves. Fish might perhaps start our meal and what a splendid array of native offerings we can look forward to, including, of course, the native oyster. It is odd to think in this day and age, when oysters are an expensive rarity that they were once so common as to be considered as food fit only for the peasants and the poor. There are still places where they can be enjoyed in all their glory without taking out a second mortgage, notably at the Butley Orford Oysterage in Orford, Suffolk. It is a plain, unassuming sort of place with nothing in its décor to differentiate it from any ordinary fish restaurant. But here you get not just the local oysters but a whole range of fishy delicacies. I have had a quite splendid meal of oysters followed by smoked eel eaten with a view across Orford Market Square, snuggled under the shadow of the castle. And this really is local food. The owner has his own oyster beds, and if you go out into the marshland of Suffolk you may still see men setting their eel traps. It is a place where food and surroundings exist in harmony.

Other native shellfish often seem neglected. The shrimp is often ignored in favour of its allegedly grander – but frequently frozen – relation, the prawn. Morecambe Bay is a great centre for shrimping and the local potted shrimps are a worthy companion to any meal, or even a meal in themselves. You can still buy them up and down the Lancashire coast, and just before writing these lines I was enjoying them in a Lancaster pub. It was down at St George's Quay, surely one of the best traditional waterfronts in the country. Old warehouses line the river and in the middle of the row sits the handsome classically porticoed Customs House – a dignified reminder of former glories. Those who look down on the shrimp as too small for consideration can always turn their eyes westward to Dublin and the Dublin Bay prawn; the most Irish of fish for it does not come from Dublin nor is it a prawn. It is in fact a small Scandinavian lobster which used to be sold in the Dublin market. You will not see many these days – at least not under the old name – though the search for them will give you one more excuse to make the pilgrimage to that fair city.

Scotland is home to the salmon. You get it elsewhere but it is to Scotland that the sporting fisherman will inevitably turn his eye.

*The river front at Lancaster where you can purchase fine smoked food and Morecambe Bay shrimps* (Anthony Burton)

The valley of the Tay is as good a place as any either to try and catch the beast or simply to enjoy the success of others. To follow the river inland from the port of Dundee is to discover Scottish scenery in every mood. It takes you through the handsome city of Perth. At Aberfeldy you cross the water on the elegant bridge built by General Wade as part of a road-construction programme designed to keep the rebellious Highlanders under control. If you go this way, pause to look at the inscription in Latin which declares, rather vain-gloriously, that this represents the finest achievement in road-building since the Romans. Finally you reach the waters of Loch Tay and the very heart of the Highlands, with Ben Lawers just a little short of 4,000ft (1,215m) rising above its waters. To walk the hills and then return for a meal of local salmon, smoked as a starter or poached as a main course, is one of life's great treats. When I did just that in the spring of 1985, I followed it up with another local speciality, venison, for deer are still stalked on the local estates.

There is, it seems, an almost endless number of local variations on food, and in among them you will find some surprises. What could be more Gallic and less English than a dish of snails? Well, the Romans ate English snails as a regular part of their diet, and in the Mendips you can still follow their excellent example. The Romans also came to the Mendip Hills to mine and smelt lead, and remains of those old workings can still be seen. Later generations of miners came after the Romans and they too left their marks on the land. One obvious sign is that of the Miners Arms at Priddy, where Roman taste and industrial history meet. It might be a long time since any miner worked round here let alone popped in for a pint, but once they did. And now it is a place where you can eat big, delicious local snails.

After such a day of feasting, one course might be as much as anyone could be expected to manage. For those prepared to carry on, a traditional roast might follow, or if you are looking for something different, try doing a little shopping around the markets of Lancashire. The market at Bury lays claim to having the oldest-established tripe stall in Britain, though I have no doubt there are others who will dispute the claim, just as there is no end to the arguments over how it should be eaten. All tripe comes to the customer cleaned and partly cooked. I was brought up to eat tripe and onions, simmered in milk, but I do have to confess to equal delight in the French method of frying tripe with garlic and cooking

*(previous page) General Wade's bridge at Aberfeldy (John May)*

it in cider, whilst I have never really taken to the true tripe enthusiast's favourite of cold tripe deluged in vinegar. But of all the regional dishes that have achieved fame perhaps none is better known than the haggis. Piped in for a Burns Night supper, it is at once the most ceremonial and yet most humble of objects. The ingredients are certainly simple enough – a sheep's belly stuffed with oatmeal, liver, heart and other assorted sheep's innards and a good deal of seasoning. It is perhaps an impertinence for a mere Sassenach to comment on the merits of the dish, but there is a shop in Inverness which claims to sell the prize haggis, and if there is a better then I do not know it. The other great attraction of Inverness is the remarkable Caledonian Canal. In order to get ships from the sea into the canal, a high artificial embankment had to be built out from the shore, a finger of rock plunging into the deep water. The canal was then cut in this artificial peninsula. It was a mighty work and a tribute to the engineer Thomas Telford. There is another tribute here as well. The engineer's friend, the poet Robert Southey, wrote verses praising Telford and you will find them inscribed in stone here at the very end of the canal at Clachnaharry.

To end our meal and our tour, what could be better than a good cheese? It is sad that so much poor cheese is on offer in shops and supermarkets, when the real thing is so splendid. If you want to see the full range, then you can do no better than visit Patrick Rance's shop at Streatley on the Thames in Berkshire. Major Rance is a true, dedicated enthusiast who knows about cheese, writes about cheese and sells superb specimens. English cheesemakers have often had to fight a bureaucracy more concerned with standard-isation than encouragement of local variation. Anyone who loves cheese can scarcely read of the killing off of blue farmhouse Wensleydale in its native valley without coming close to tears. It is, however, still possible to find other genuine farmhouse cheeses made in real farmhouses by traditional methods. You can buy such delicacies in the best shops, but how much more rewarding it is to hunt the cheese down in its natural habitat. And, if an author might be allowed to let his prejudices show through, then where could one find better hunting than among the dales and moors of North Yorkshire? Follow the valley of the Swale westward out from the lovely town of Richmond, right on until the valley ends and the Pennine hills rear up all around you. It is here in the solid, stone farmhouses set among a web of grey stone walls that the old cheesemaking skills are still practised. You need to look hard, but patient search will be rewarded: doubly rewarded for besides discovering your cheese you will have enjoyed some of the north's finest scenery.

To sit in a good traditional inn after a good traditional meal and then to look out at the land that produced the fare is to come as close to heaven as any mortal has a right to expect. In many years of travelling around Britain, I have been lucky enough on just a few occasions to find that perfect combination. I have sat back and reflected that however much you may travel there are still discoveries to be made. My hope is that this book will encourage others not merely to share my enjoyment of a few out-of-the-ordinary places, but to go on to find new delights for themselves. For there is still your own undiscovered land waiting for you.

# Further Reading

The following list is not intended in any way to be comprehensive, for there are literally hundreds of guidebooks about Britain. Instead, I have tried to list those books which will help the reader to get more detailed information about the particular subject dealt with in each chapter.

## Beside the Seaside

Hallman, Robert and Davids, Stephen. *Coastal Britain*, 1984 Batsford

Robinson, Adrian and Millward, Roy. *The Shell Book of the British Coast*, 1983 David & Charles

Walton, J. *The English Seaside Resort*, 1983 Leicester

## Island Retreats

Booth, David and Perrott, David. *The Shell Book of the Islands of Britain*, 1981 Guideway Publishing Ltd.

Crookston, Peter (ed). *Island Britain*, 1981 Macdonald

McNally, Kenneth. *The Islands of Ireland*, 1978 Batsford

Shea, Michael. *The Country Life Book of Britain's Offshore Islands*, 1981 Country Life

## Country Pursuits

Burton, Anthony. *Walking the Line*, 1985 Blandford Press

—— and Pratt, Derek. *Canal*, 1976 David & Charles

Hoskins, W. G. *The Making of the English Landscape*, 1977 (second edition) Hodder & Stoughton

McKnight, Hugh. *The Shell Book of Inland Waterways*, 1975 David & Charles

Mossman, Keith. *The Shell Book of Rural Britain*, 1978 David & Charles

Muir, Richard. *Shell Guide to Reading the Landscape*, 1981 Michael Joseph

Newby, Eric and Petry, Diana. *Wonders of Ireland*, 1969 Hodder & Stoughton

Sandford, Ernest. *Discover Northern Ireland*, 1976 Northern Ireland Tourist Board

Wilson, Ken and Gilbert, Richard. *The Big Walks*, 1980 Diadem Books

## Provincial Pleasures
Aston, Michael and Bond, James. *The Landscape of Towns*, 1976 Dent
Clifton-Taylor, Alec. *Six English Towns*, 1978 BBC
—— *Six More English Towns*, 1981 BBC
—— *Another Six English Towns*, 1984 BBC
Lloyd, David. *The Making of English Towns*, 1984 Victor Gollancz

## How the Other Half Lives
Alcock, Sheila (ed). *Museums and Art Galleries in Great Britain and Ireland* (annual) British Leisure Publications
Automobile Association. *Stately Homes, Museums, Castles and Gardens* (annual)
Brunskill, R. W. *Illustrated Handbook of Vernacular Architecture*, 1978 (second edition) Faber & Faber
Reid, Richard. *The Shell Book of Cottages*, 1977 Michael Joseph

## Underground
Burton, Anthony. *The National Trust Guide to Our Industrial Past*, 1983 George Philip
Mason, Edmund J. *Caves and Caving in Britain*, 1977 Hale
Waltham, Antony. *Caves*, 1974 Macmillan

## Along the Trail
Most trails come in pamphlet form and are available locally.

Delaney, Frank. *James Joyce's Odyssey*, 1981 Hodder & Stoughton
Drabble, Margaret. *A Writer's Britain*, 1979 Thames & Hudson
Eagle, Dorothy and Carnell, Hilary. *The Oxford Literary Guide to the British Isles*, 1977 Oxford University Press
Kipling, Lesley and Hall, Nick. *On the Trail of the Luddites*, 1982 Pennine Heritage Network
Wales Tourist Board. *A Glimpse of the Past*, 1981
Trevor, William. *A Writer's Ireland*, 1984 Thames & Hudson

## Traditional Fare
Campbell, Susan (ed). *Guide to Good Food Shops*, 1981 Macmillan
Hartley, Dorothy. *Food in England*, 1954 Macdonald & Jane's
Mabey, David. *In Search of Food*, 1978 Macdonald & Jane's
Rance, Patrick. *The Great British Cheese Book*, 1982 Macmillan

# Index

Numbers in *italic* refer to illustrations

Abbotsbury, 25–6
Abercraf, 202, 205
Aberdaron, 80
Aberdeen, 65, 262, 263
Aber Falls, 233
Aberfeldy, 278, *276–7*
Abersychan, 254
Aberystwyth, 32, 211, 250
Abingdon, 140, 152, 250, 258, *256–7*
Alderney, 82, 83
Allihies, 52–3
Alloway, 241
Amlwch, 80
Anglesey, 79–80, 81
Anstruther, 42, 197
Antonine Wall, 109, *110*
Aran Islands, 62–3, *54–5, 62*
Arbroath, 262
Arbury Hall, 243
Armagh, 177, *178–9*
Arran, 78–9, 262
Ashton, 99
Auchmithie, 262
Avebury, 228
Avonmouth, 29
Ayr, 241

Badger Cross, 166–7
Ballycastle, 59
Bamburgh, 43
Banbury, 273
Bardsey Island, 80
Barnstaple, 184
Barry Island, 30–1
Barton, 273
Basildon New Town, 182–3
Bath, 133–4, 146, 177, 272, *134*
Beaconsfield, 250
Beadnell Bay, 43
Beamish, 145, 223, *146*
Beara Peninsula, 52, 59
Bearsden, 109
Beaumaris, 152
Beckley, 100

Belfast, 159, *126–7*
Bell Rock Lighthouse, 262
Ben Lawers, 278
Betws-y-Coed, 231
Biggar, 153–7, *153*
Bignor, 168
Birkenhead, 34
Blackburn, 253
Black Mountains, 118
Blackpool, 18, 35, 265–6
Blaenafon, 140–2, 216, 254, *141*
Blaenau Ffestiniog, 211–12, 217, 220, *210, 219*
Blarney Castle, 120
Bloody Foreland, 59
Blythburgh, 46
Boa Island, 123, *121*
Bodmin Moor, 92
Bosworth Field, 101, 249
Botallack, 27
Boughton House, 245–7, *246*
Bowmore, 77–8
Bradbury, 185
Bradford on Avon, 263
Bradwell, 206–7
Breckland, 97–9
Brecon Beacons, 101, 118
Breidden Hill, 117
Brewood, 128–31, *129*
Brighton, 23
Brill, 250
Bristol, 177, 191, 225
Brodick, 78
Bromsgrove, 164, 165
Broughton Castle, 250
Brownsea Island, 84
Brugh Na Boinne, 123–5, *124*
Buckie, 42
Bullers of Buchan, 40, 42, *41*
Burnham Thorpe, 247, 249
Burnley, 252–4, *253*
Burrow Bridge, 94–5, *94*
Burrow Head, 36
Burton on Trent, 158

Burwash, 203
Bury, 278
Bute, 79
Buxton, 203
Bwlchgwyn, 233–5, *234*

Cader Idris, *14*
Caerleon, 30, *30*
Caerwent, 29
Caldicott Levels, 29
Callanish, 73
Calne, 263–4
Calstock, 89–90, *89*
Camborne, 214
Canals: Ashby, 101, 254; Barrow
    Navigation, 120; Brecon &
    Abergavenny, 101; Bridgewater,
    273; Caldon, 101; Caledonian,
    279; Chesterfield, 101; Coventry,
    101, 195; Cromford, 104; Grand
    Union, 13; Huddersfield Narrow,
    190, 252; Kennet & Avon, *86–7*;
    Leeds & Liverpool, 35, 235, 253–4;
    Leicester, *12*; Llangollen, 99, 217;
    Manchester Ship, 273; Middle
    Level, 99; Oxford, 195, 230; Ripon,
    101; Shropshire Union, 34, 128;
    Tavistock, 199; Trent & Mersey,
    223; Wilts & Berks, 264
Canglass Point, 52
Canvey Island, 170
Cape Wrath, 40
Carbost, 75
Cardiff, 30
Cardigan Bay, 32, 80
Carew, 31–2
Carlisle, 107
Carmarthen Bay, 31
Carn Glooze, 27
Carreg Cennen, 222
Carrick, Donegal, 52
Carrick, Strathclyde, 38, *39*
Carrick-a-Rede, 59, *58*
Castleton, 203–6
Cauldon Low, 102
Cauldron Snout, 106
Chalfont St Giles, 249
Charterhouse, 95
Chatham, 197
Chathill, 169, *171*
Chatsworth, 245
Cheddar, 95, 202
Cheddleton, 101
Chedworth, 167
Cheesewring, 92

Chepstow, 117
Chesil Beach, 25, 95
Cheviots, 107, *108*
Chippenham, 263
Chirk, 217
Church Stretton, 192, *193*
Chysauster, 166–7, 168, *166*
Clachnaharry, 279
Clare Island, 60, 62, *61*
Clear Island, 65
Clearwell, 209
Clevedon, 29
Clew Bay, 60
Clifton Hampden, 239
Cobbler mountain, 38
Cockley Cley, 167, *167*
Cogges, 194
Consett, 232
Cookham Dean, 239
Corrieshalloch Gorge, 115, *116*
Cotehele, 90–1
Cottisford, 239
Cowes, 229
Crich, 145
Cromford, 212
Cropredy, 250
Cross Fell, 107
Cumbraes, the 79
Cwmystraddlyn, 220

Dalswinton, 241
Danescombe, 89, 90
Dartmoor, 92, *93*
Dedham Vale, 244
Deerham, 138
Delabole, 27
Dervaig, 77
Devenish, 123
Didcot, 150
Din Lligwy, 80
Dinorwic, 220
Dolbenmaen, 220
Dorchester, 95, 241–2
Dorusdain, 115
Dounby, 71
Dover, 19–21, 167
Downhill, 47, 52
Doyden Castle, 27
Drogheda, 123
Dublin, 120, 158, 228, 237–8, 274
Dudley, 223–4
Dun Aengus fortress, 63, *62*
Duncansby, 40
Dundee, 197, 265, 278
Dungeness, 22, 23

Dun Laoghaire, 237–8, *238*
Dunloe, *124*
Dunnottar, 42
Dunstanburgh, 43, 169
Dunton Plotlands, 182–3, *183*
Dunwich, 46
Durness, 40
Dursey island, 40

East Linton, 260–1, *260*
Easton, 25
Eccles, 273
Eden Valley, 107
Edinburgh, 143, 157, 173–4, 176–7,
   179, 184, *156, 174–5, 176, 186–7*
Eigg, 78
Elgol, 75
Ellesmere Port, 34, 195, *34*
Elsdon, 107–8
Elvaston, 194
Ely, 99
Embleton Bay, 43
Etruria, 101
Exeter, 222
Exmoor, 92

Fair Isle, 67
Falkirk, 109
Falls of Glomach, 115, *114*
Falls of Measach, 115
Farne Islands, 84–5
Faversham, 271
Felixstowe, 47
Fishbourne, 168
Five Sisters of Kintail, 115, *113*
Flatford Mill, 244, *245*
Forest of Dean, 208–9
Fort William, 39
Fountains Abbey, 235
Froghall, 101

Galloway, 35, 112
Galway Bay, 52
Gatehouse of Fleet, 36
Giant's Causeway, 47, 56
Gibside, 232–3
Glasgow, 37, 39, 78, 112, 180, 182,
   *181*
Gloucester, 157, *158*
Glyn Ceiriog, 216–7, *218*
Goathland, 105–6, *106*
Golcar, 188–90, 267, *189*
Goldcliff, 20
Golden Cap Hill, 11, *9*
Gop Cairn, 32

Gosport, 197, *198*
Gower, 31
Grimspound, 165–6, 167
Guernsey, 82, 84, 223
Gwennap Down, 268

Hadrian's Wall, 107, 109, 146–7
Hameldown Tor, 165
Hampton Court, 272
Hampton Gay, 229–30
Harecastle, 223, *200–1*
Harrogate, 235, 265, 272
Harrowhill Wick, 42
Hastings, 203, *204*
Haytor, 92, *93*
Hebden Bridge, 105
Helensburgh, 180–2, *160–1*
Helston, 214
Heptonstall, 105
Hereford, 149–50
Herm, 82, 84
Higher Bockhampton, 243, *226–7*
High Force, 106
Hodbarrow, 35
Holyhead, 80
Holywood, 163–4, *164*
Horndean, 192
Hoy, 71–2, *71*
Huddersfield, 190, 252
Huntingdon, 249

Icknield Way, 228
Inishmurray, 60, *54–5*
Inverness, 279
Iona, 74
Ironbridge, 223
Islay, 77–8, 262
Islip, 240
Ivychurch, 21

Jarlshof, 68, *68*
Jedburgh, 152
Jersey, 82
Jethou, 84
John o' Groats, 40
Juniper Hill, 239
Jura, 78, 262

Kelmscott, 239
Kendal, 266–7, *266*
Kettering, 245
Keynsham, 250
Kidsdale, 36
Kilbarchan, 185, 188, *188*
Killaloe, *122*

285

King's Lynn, 247
Kinlochbervie, 40
Kintail, 115
Kirkoswald, 241, *240*
Kirkwall, 69, 72
Knocknagallaun Mountains, 52–3
Kyle of Durness, 40
Kyle of Lochalsh, 115

Lamb Holm, 72, *72*
Lancaster, 274, *275*
Land's End, 26, 27
Langton Herring, 26
Laugharne, 243–4
Lavenham, 97
Laxey, 79
Leadhills, 111
Leamington Spa, 272
Ledbury, 131, 165
Leeds, 235–6
Lerwick, 67
Lewis, 195, *196*
Lichfield, 243, *242*
Lincoln, 245
Lindisfarne, 85
Liverpool, 35, 247, *248*
Llanberis, 220
Llanfairfechan, 233
Llanfair Quarry, 220
Llangollen, 117, 216
Llyn Brenig, 231
Lochinver, 39
Lochs: Fyne, 262; Gaorsic, 115;
    Goil, 38; Holy, 38; Katrine, 112,
    *112*; Lomond, 112, 262; Long, 38;
    Tay, 278; Torridon, *37*
Logan, 36
London, 146, 149, 150 178, 184, 191,
    202, 224, 241, 269, *148, 149, 225*
Long Melford, 97
Looe, 26
Loughs: Erne, 120–3, *121*; Neagh,
    123
Lowther Hills, 109
Lundy, 81, *81*
Lyme Bay, 11, *8–9*
Lyme Regis, 250
Lynton, 29

Magho, Cliffs of, 123
Maiden Castle, 95
Mallaig, 39
Malmesbury, 263
Malvern Hills, 247
Man, Isle of, 79

Manchester, 179, 190, 273
Manningtree, 244
Manside Camp, 109
March, 46
Market Bosworth, 101, 249
Market Drayton, 131
Marsden, 190, 252
Maryport, 35
Meeting of the Waters, 120
Melton Mowbray, 271, *270*
Menai, 79, 184
Mendip Hills, 95, 278
Merthyr Tydfil, 118
Metherell, 91
Middlesbrough, 132–3, *132*
Mildenhall, 46
Millom, 35
Milton Keynes, 131–2
Moher, Cliffs of, 52, *50–1*
Monsale Dale, 230
Morecambe Bay, 35, 274, *275*
Moretonhampstead, 165
Morvich, 115
Morwellham, 199, *198*
Muck, 65
Muckleflugga, 65
Mull, 75–7, *76*
Mull of Galloway, 36

Nantwich, 131
Naseby, 249
Nelson, 105
Neston, 46
Newark on Trent, 138–40, *139*
New Bradwell, 132, *130*
Newcastle, 232
Newgrange (Brugh Na Boinne)
    123–5, *124*
New Lanark, 142
Newport, 29, 229
Newton Abbot, 272
Newtongrange, 154
North Harris, 73
North Leigh, 167
North Yorkshire Moors, 105–6
Norwich, 169–70
Nottingham, 190, 221–2
Nuneaton, 11, 243

Offa's Dyke, 117
Old Man of Hoy, The, 71–2, *71*
Old Romney, 21
Orford, 46–7, 274
Orkney, 67, 68–72, *195*
Otmoor, 100

Out Stack, 65
Oxford, 99, 100, 135, 230–1, 250, 269

Pangbourne, 239
Panperthog, 118–20, *119*
Parys Mountain, 80
Peasenhall, 264
Pembroke, 31
Pendle Hill, 105
Pennine Hills, 279
Penrith, 263, 266
Penzance, 166
Perth, 143, 278, *144*
Plymouth, 170
Plynlimon Hills, 211
Polzeath, 15
Pontcysyllte, 217
Ponterwyd, 211, 212, *210*
Pontypool, 254
Poole, 84
Pope's corner, 99
Portbraddan, 47
Porthmadog, 217
Porthtowan, 269
Port Isaac Bay, 27
Portland, 23–5, 273, *24*
Port Logan, 36
Portquin, 27
Portree, 75
Port William, 27
Prestatyn, 117
Prestonpans, 42, 254
Priddy, 278
Puffin Island, 81
Pumsaint, 209–11, *210*

Quaker's Yard, 118

Radnor Forest, 117
Rannoch Moor, 39
Rathlin, 56–7, 59, *57*
Reading, 239
Redruth, 214
Rhum, 78
Richmond, 279
Ripon, 150, 152
Robin Hood's Bay, *44*
Rochdale, 145, *147*
Romney marshes, 21, 23
Rothley, 109
Rough Castle, 109, *110*
Rousham, 250
Rowley, 145
Ruddington, 190–1, *191*

Rufus Castle, 25
Ryhope, 149

Saffron Walden, 272
St Agnes Head, 27, *268*
St Andrews, 143
St Day, 268
St Ives, 166
St Just, 27
St Martin's, 82
St Mary's, 82
St Neot, 220, *221*
St Ninian's Cave, 36
Samson, 82
Sanday, 71
Sandwood Bay, 40
Sark, 82–4, *83*
Scilly Isles, 81–2
Seahouses, 84
Sedbury, 117
Sedgemoor, 94, 250
Selkirk, 157, *154–5*
Shackerstone, 101
Sheffield, 206
Sheldon, 213–4, *212*
Shetland Isles, 65–8, 195
Silbury Hill, 32
Singleton, 162–3, *163*
Skara Brae, 70–1
Skelligs, 63–5, *64, 66*
Skidby, 264–5
Skye, 74–5, 77, 78, 195, *74*
Slane, 123
Sli Cuallan, 228
Slieve League, 52, *16–17*
Smoo Cave, 40
Snaefell, 79
Snailbeach, 117
Snarestone, 101
Solway Firth, 35
Somerset Levels, 94–5
Somerton Moor, 94
Sound of Bute, 262
Southend, 170
Southport, 35
South Voe, 67–8
Southwold, 45
Spey Valley, 255
Spurn Head, 44, 45
Stac Pollaidh, 39
Stamford, 157–8, *159*
Standedge Fell, 190
Stanton Harcourt, 240
Stanton St Gabriel, 10–11
Stein, 75

Steng Cross, 109
Steventon, 269, 271
Stoke Heath, 164–5
Stokenchurch, 13
Stoke on Trent, 223
Stokesay, 168
Stonehenge, 73, 228
Stornoway, *73*
Streatley, 279
Stromness, 69
Sudbury, Derbyshire, 185
Sudbury, Suffolk, 244
Suilven, 39, 117
Sullom Voe, 66
Sumburgh, 68
Swaffham Prior, 97, *96*
Swansea, 30, 243
Swindon, 191–2, 263

Tantallon, 43
Tara, 125, 228
Tarbert, 78, 262
Tavistock, 250, 258–9
Teesdale, 106
Tenby, 173, *172*
Thetford, 97, *98*
Thor's Cave, 104
Tingwall, 68
Tintern, 104, 231, 235
Tobermory, 77
Todmorden, 105
Tonbridge, 150
Toome, 123
Torquay, 202–3, *204*
Torridon, 115
Tory Island, 59–60
Trelawnyd, 32
Tresco, 82
Tretower, 168
Trowbridge, 263
Tunstall, 214–6, *215*
Tywyn, 32

Uffington, 240

Ullapool, 39, 115, 117

Vale of Crucis, 117
Valley of the Boyne, 123
Via Gellia, 212–3

Wadsworth Moor, 105
Walberswick, 45–6
Walsall, 152
Walsingham, 152, *151*
Wanlockhead, 111, *111*
Wapping, 224
Wash, The, 45
Waterhouses, 102
Watford Gap, 13, *12*
Weald, The, 96
Weardale, 106
Weeting, 207–8, *208*
Welshpool, 117
Welwyn, 147
Wendron, 214
Wensleydale, 279
Weobley, 131
Weston-super-Mare, 29, *28*
Westonzoyland, 250, *251*
West Stow, 97–8, 167, *98*
Wetton, 103
Whaligoe Steps, 42
Whitby, 43, 261–2
White Island, 123
Whitepark Bay, 47, *48–9*
Whithorn, 36
Wicken Fen, 99
Wigan, 35, 135, 252–3
Wight, Isle of, 84, 229
Windermere, 236–7, *236*
Wirral, 32–4
Woodchester, 167
Wye Valley, 29, 231
Wymondham, 136–8, 139

Yarmouth, 229
York, 235